Migrating Your SAP Data

 **PRESS**

SAP PRESS is a joint initiative of SAP and Galileo Press. The know-how offered by SAP specialists combined with the expertise of the publishing house Galileo Press offers the reader expert books in the field. SAP PRESS features first-hand information and expert advice, and provides useful skills for professional decision-making.

SAP PRESS offers a variety of books on technical and business related topics for the SAP user. For further information, please visit our website: *www.sap-press.com*.

LeBlanc, Andrew
Enterprise Data Management with SAP NetWeaver MDM
2008, 350 pp.
978-1-59229-115-1

Whealy, Chris
Inside Web Dynpro for Java (2nd Edition)
2007, 532 pp.
978-1-59229-038-3

Schloemer, Bernard
Mastering SAP NetWeaver Master Data Management
2008, 90 pp.
978-1-59229-176-2

Heilig, Loren; Karch, Steffen; Pfennig, Roland; Hofmann, Christine
SAP NetWeaver Master Data Management
2007, 332 pp.
978-1-59229-131-1

Michael Willinger, Johann Gradl

Migrating Your SAP Data

Galileo Press

Bonn • Boston

ISBN   978-1-59229-170-0

2nd revised and extended edition

Editor Stefan Proksch
Copy Editor Ruth Saavedra, Saratoga, CA
Cover Design Silke Braun
Layout Design Vera Brauner
Production Katrin Müller
Typesetting Typographie & Computer, Krefeld
Printed and bound in Germany

© 2008 by Galileo Press
SAP PRESS is an imprint of Galileo Press,
Boston, MA, USA
Bonn, Germany

Contents at a Glance

1   Introduction 13

2   Managerial Foundations for Migrating Data to
      SAP ERP 21

3   Technical Basics for Migrating Data to SAP ERP ... 41

4   Batch Input 51

5   Extended Computer Aided Test Tool (eCATT) 99

6   Computer Aided Test Tool (CATT) 147

7   Legacy System Migration Workbench 167

8   SAP Accelerated Data Migration 263

9   Techniques for Avoiding Programming 281

10   Assessment of Data Migration Techniques 303

11   Migrating Fixed Assets with Microsoft Excel 315

12   Outlook and Related Areas 341

A   SAP ERP Tables for Selected Master and
      Transaction Data 353

B   Glossary 357

C   The Authors 365

Contents

1 Introduction **13**

2 Managerial Foundations for Migrating Data to SAP ERP **21**

2.1   Data Migration as a Subproject 21
2.2   Preliminary Considerations 23
     2.2.1   Defining the Dataset for Migration 23
     2.2.2   Identifying Dormant Data 24
     2.2.3   Measures for Reducing the Data Volume 25
     2.2.4   Preparatory Measures for Extracting the Legacy Data 26
     2.2.5   Addendum: Accounting Considerations 26
2.3   The Data Migration Process from the Project Perspective 33
     2.3.1   Basic Customizing 33
     2.3.2   System Presentations in SAP ERP 33
     2.3.3   Business Reengineering 33
     2.3.4   Simulating the Data Migration 34
     2.3.5   Mapping (Field Matching) 34
     2.3.6   Data Extraction from the Legacy System 36
     2.3.7   Manual Postprocessing of the Extracted Data 36
     2.3.8   Selecting a Data Migration Technique 37
     2.3.9   Uploading the Data in SAP ERP 37
     2.3.10 Testing the Business Processes in SAP ERP 38

3 Technical Basics for Migrating Data to SAP ERP **41**

3.1   Basic Terminology 41
3.2   The Data Migration Process from a Technical Perspective 42
     3.2.1   Exporting the Data 42
     3.2.2   Reading the Data 43
     3.2.3   Converting the Data 43
     3.2.4   Importing the Data 46
     3.2.5   Verifying the Data 47

3.3   Overview of Technical Procedures for Data
        Migration 48
        3.3.1   Batch Input 48
        3.3.2   Extended Computer Aided Test Tool 48
        3.3.3   Legacy System Migration Workbench 49

4   Batch Input 51

4.1   What Is Batch Input Processing? 51
4.2   How Does Batch Input Work? 51
        4.2.1   What Is a Batch Input Session? 52
        4.2.2   How Do I Process a Batch Input Session? 55
        4.2.3   How Do I Create a Batch Input Session? 58
4.3   Standard Batch Input Programs 59
        4.3.1   RFBIDE00 – Customer Master 60
        4.3.2   RFBIKR00 – Vendor Master 61
        4.3.3   RFBISA00 – G/L Account Master 61
        4.3.4   RFBIBL00 – Financial Documents 61
        4.3.5   RCSBI010, RCSBI020, RCSBI030,
                 RCSBI040 – Material BOMs 62
        4.3.6   RM06BBI0 – Purchase Requisitions 62
        4.3.7   RM07MMBL – Material Documents 63
4.4   Batch Input Recording: General Approach 63
        4.4.1   Creating the Batch Input Recording 63
        4.4.2   Generating an ABAP Program from a
                 Batch Input Recording 67
        4.4.3   Modifying the Generated ABAP Program 72
        4.4.4   Creating and Processing the Batch Input
                 Session 80
        4.4.5   Call Transaction and Batch Input Session
                 in Case of Error 82
4.5   Batch Input Recording Combined with Microsoft
        Word Mail Merge Processing 84

5   Extended Computer Aided Test Tool (eCATT) 99

5.1   What Is the eCATT? 99
5.2   History of the eCATT 99
5.3   Availability and Functionality of eCATT and CATT 101
5.4   Preparing the System for Using the eCATT 102
5.5   How Does the eCATT Work? 105
        5.5.1   Recording a Test Script 106
        5.5.2   Executing a Test Script 113

5.6   How Can You Use the eCATT for Data Migration? 121

     5.6.1   Parameterizing Input Fields 121

     5.6.2   Generating the File Format 124

     5.6.3   Arranging the Data According to the
           File Format 129

     5.6.4   Loading Data 134

5.7   Tips and Tricks 138

     5.7.1   General Recommendations 138

     5.7.2   Modifying Test Scripts 139

     5.7.3   Initializing Field Contents 142

     5.7.4   Table Maintenance with the eCATT 145

6   Computer Aided Test Tool (CATT) 147

6.1   Basic Terminology 147

6.2   Preparing the System for Using the CATT 148

6.3   How Does the CATT Work? 148

     6.3.1   Recording a Test Case 149

     6.3.2   Parameterizing the Input Values 155

     6.3.3   Executing a Test Case 163

7   Legacy System Migration Workbench 167

7.1   Overview of the LSM Workbench 167

7.2   Data Migration with the LSM Workbench 170

     7.2.1   Getting Started with the LSM Workbench 171

     7.2.2   User Guidance: The Main Steps of
           Data Migration 175

     7.2.3   Maintaining Object Attributes 178

     7.2.4   Maintaining Source Structures 181

     7.2.5   Maintaining Source Fields 182

     7.2.6   Maintaining Structure Relations 187

     7.2.7   Maintaining Field Mapping and Conversion
           Rules 189

     7.2.8   Maintaining Fixed Values, Translations, and
           User-Defined Routines 202

     7.2.9   Addendum: Files 209

     7.2.10   Specifying Files 211

     7.2.11   Using Wildcards in File Names 215

     7.2.12   Assigning Files 216

     7.2.13   Reading Data 217

     7.2.14   Displaying Read Data 219

	7.2.15	Converting Data	221
	7.2.16	Displaying Converted Data	223
	7.2.17	Importing Data	224
	7.2.18	Object Overview	226
7.3		Recordings	228
	7.3.1	Creating and Editing Recordings	230
	7.3.2	Using a Recording	235
7.4		Long Texts	237
	7.4.1	Long Texts in the SAP ERP System	238
	7.4.2	Target Structures and Field Mapping	238
	7.4.3	Importing Long Texts	242
7.5		Periodic Data Transfer	243
7.6		Transporting Projects	247
	7.6.1	Creating a Change Request	247
	7.6.2	Exporting Projects	247
	7.6.3	Importing Projects	248
7.7		Preparations for Using IDoc Inbound Processing	249
7.8		Advanced LSM Workbench Features	252
	7.8.1	Display Variant and Processing Times	252
	7.8.2	Global Variables	253
	7.8.3	Global Functions	254
	7.8.4	Reusable Rules – Naming Conventions	255
7.9		Tips and Tricks	256
	7.9.1	Determining the Transaction Code at Runtime	257
	7.9.2	Skipping a Record	257
	7.9.3	Skipping All Records of a Transaction	258
	7.9.4	Duplicating a Record	258
	7.9.5	Assigning Multiple Source Structures to a Target Structure	259
	7.9.6	Error Messages in the Conversion Log	260
7.10		Summary	261

8	SAP Accelerated Data Migration	263
8.1	Availability	263
8.2	Overview of SAP ADM	264
8.3	Specific Features	265
8.4	Overview of the Typical Process	267
8.5	Typical Process in Detail: Process Cockpit	268
	8.5.1 Start	268
	8.5.2 Defining the Scope	269

8.5.3   Migration Customizing at Project Level 271
8.5.4   Work Steps per Migration Object 274
8.6   Development Cockpit 276
8.7   Checklist for SAP ADM 280
8.8   Additional Information on SAP ADM 280

9   Techniques for Avoiding Programming 281

9.1   Problem Area: Data Conversion 281
9.2   Techniques for Converting Data 282
9.2.1   Modifying Structures 282
9.2.2   Modifying Field Contents 286
9.2.3   Accessing Data in the SAP ERP System 297
9.3   Summary 301

10   Assessment of Data Migration Techniques 303

10.1   Advantages and Disadvantages of the Procedures 303
10.1.1   Batch Input 303
10.1.2   eCATT 306
10.1.3   LSM Workbench 307
10.2   Reasons for Favoring a Certain Procedure 308
10.2.1   Complexity of the Migration Task 309
10.2.2   Quality of the Legacy Data 309
10.2.3   Data Volume 309
10.2.4   The Importance of Data Security 310
10.2.5   Reusability 310
10.2.6   Restrictions 311
10.2.7   User-Friendliness 311
10.2.8   Summary 312

11   Migrating Fixed Assets with Microsoft Excel 315

11.1   Assessment of Procedures for Migrating Fixed Assets .. 315
11.2   Types of Legacy Data Transfer 319
11.2.1   Legacy Data Transfer at End of Fiscal Year 319
11.2.2   Legacy Data Transfer in Mid-Year 320
11.2.3   Other Options for Transferring Asset Data 321
11.3   Case Example: Migrating Fixed Assets with
Microsoft Excel 322
11.3.1   Which Data Should You Transfer? 323
11.3.2   Data Format for the Transfer to SAP ERP 324

	11.3.3	Formatting Data with Visual Basic	327
	11.3.4	Assigning the Data to ERP Fields (Mapping)	334
	11.3.5	Uploading the Data to SAP ERP and Log File	336
11.4	Preparing to Go Live		338
	11.4.1	Setting Reconciliation Accounts	338
	11.4.2	Transferring Balances	339
	11.4.3	Activating the Company Code	340

12 Outlook and Related Areas 341

12.1	Data Transfer Workbench		341
	12.1.1	Features	341
	12.1.2	Particular Strength: Data Import via BAPI	343
	12.1.3	Combination with the LSM Workbench	344
12.2	Data Migration Between SAP ERP Systems or within an SAP ERP System		345
12.3	Data Migration in SAP CRM		347

Appendix 351

A	SAP ERP Tables for Selected Master and Transaction Data		353
	A.1	Financial Accounting	353
	A.2	Controlling	354
	A.3	Logistics	354
B	Glossary		357
C	The Authors		365

| Index | 367 |

1 Introduction

Data migration is hardly new to IT professionals. It is a constant requirement that is integral to each software update. In most cases, however, a successful upgrade doesn't resolve all problems. Changing economic conditions and standard operating procedures within a corporation frequently leads to organizational restructuring, which, in turn, requires a reorganization of the datasets in existing IT systems. Furthermore, the major issues inherent in data migration aren't adequately covered in the current literature, which is precisely what motivated us to write this book.

In many cases, project managers underestimate the quantity of resources that data migration can tie up for the duration of a project. This frequently results in staffing bottlenecks and, therefore, financial ones as well.

Staffing bottleneck: data migration

Data migration projects are usually carried out by programmers (i.e., individuals with detailed technical knowledge). But, because programmers are responsible for all the applications in an installation, this merely contributes to and exacerbates the staffing problem.

Keeping this programmer staffing issue in mind, you would benefit from having data migration techniques in place that can be implemented not only by programmers, but by consultants as well (i.e., those individuals without highly technical skills). Ideally, the user departments — those departments that supply the data — should be able to trigger data transfers and migration projects, and model them in the IT systems. For this purpose, however, you need to have migration techniques that are easy to learn and require very little programming.

Programming-free data migration

Nonetheless, we're well aware that there will always be situations in which specific project requirements are so complex that a minimal amount of programming is still necessary. Still, we'd like to consider programming as a last resort, a recourse that should be used only when all other data migration techniques fail to achieve the required results. Therefore, this book will focus less on techniques for programming data migration and more on methods that enable you to avoid having to program.

Area of application When a legacy system is replaced with SAP Enterprise Resource Planning (SAP ERP),[1] these programming-free techniques are supplied by SAP. The procedures provided aren't limited to specific ERP applications, either; they can be used in a wide range of applications — Accounting, Logistics, and even Human Resources Management (HRM). Regardless of which application is used, the general procedure remains the same. Moreover, the type of data that has to be migrated is immaterial. For example, it is just as easy to migrate master data from Human Resources (HR) as it is to migrate transaction data from Financial Accounting (FI).

The reason why this method is so attractive is that it isn't limited merely to the traditional ERP applications, but also is available for some of the latest products that build on the SAP NetWeaver technology, such as SAP Customer Relationship Management (SAP CRM) and SAP Supply Chain Management (SAP SCM). Regardless of the specific application, the procedures themselves are so flexible that they permit the optional integration of any customer-specific ABAP coding required for the migration, which makes them almost universally applicable. The availability of these methods in the individual SAP applications is discussed in the upcoming chapters.

Intended audience Because custom programming should remain the exception, however, this book is primarily intended for individuals who don't necessarily require programming skills themselves, but who might have to use programming, directly or indirectly, in the course of their work. This includes *SAP consultants* hired to implement a data migration within their own organizations or for an external customer, as well as *project managers* who need an overview of the individual methods available in order to make qualified decisions. This subject is also relevant for *SAP developers* who want to learn about efficient migration techniques to save time and money. The methods described in this book could make the need to write and test custom programs for data migration, so-called "throwaway programs," a thing of the past.

---

1   SAP officially replaced the name "mySAP" with "SAP" in March 2007.

Experience also shows that the simplicity of the data migration procedures enables the *user departments* to migrate data themselves, rounding out our intended audience. Consequently, the role of user departments is no longer limited to that of data supplier. With their knowledge of the data migration methods on the one hand and their years of experience with the legacy IT system on the other hand, the user departments will most certainly play an active role in data migration projects going forward.

Because our intended broad audience cannot be expected to have an equivalent skill base, we have chosen the explanations and case examples in this book to be comprehensible and practical for readers both with and without detailed technical knowledge of the SAP system. We must assume, however, that readers have a basic understanding of SAP NetWeaver, Windows 2000/NT/XP, and common Microsoft Office products such as Word, Excel, and Access in order to define the scope of this book. Although readers will find that knowing the business context for certain issues is helpful, it is not a prerequisite for understanding the descriptions in this book.

Prerequisites

> **Note**
>
> The terms *data migration* and *data transfer* are used synonymously in this book. The data source can be any legacy IT system, assuming an initial data transfer is involved, in addition to a live SAP ERP system, if the dataset must be modified to meet organizational changes.

The data migration is frequently underestimated and not perceived as a fully qualified, independent subproject within the overall project. Therefore, **Chapter 2** addresses the preparatory measures for data migration, which are critical to the success of any project. These measures include the selection of the project team, definition of the project schedule, and issues involving which data will be transferred and how it will be translated into the SAP terminology. These processes should represent the starting point of any data migration project, regardless of which specific methods are used.

Data migration as a subproject

Chapter 3 deals with the basics of data migration. It introduces the basic terms that are used repeatedly throughout the rest of the book. It also describes the steps that are involved in every data migration, along with a brief overview of the data migration techniques provided by SAP.

Data migration basics

Batch input technique

Once Chapters 2 and 3 have familiarized you with the basics, **Chapter 4** introduces the conventional method for migrating data: the *batch input technique*. In addition to a general introduction, this chapter introduces both the standard batch input programs for data migration supplied by SAP and custom batch input programs that are relatively easy to write. Because the latter require programming, however, which we want to avoid wherever possible, the batch input technique is discussed here in combination with Microsoft Word mail merge processing, which makes programming-free data migration possible.

eCATT and CATT

This theme of avoiding programming continues throughout Chapters 5, 6, and 7. **Chapter 5** introduces the *Extended Computer Aided Test Tool* (eCATT), a tool that was originally developed to test business processes, but that also can be used for data migration. In addition to introducing the eCATT in general, this chapter discusses how this tool can be used for data migration, which is illustrated by using a detailed case example from the enterprise accounting area. In addition, **Chapter 6** briefly describes the "traditional" CATT because, as you will see, you can use eCATT for data migration purposes only from SAP Basis Release 6.40, that is, as of SAP R/3 Enterprise.

LSMW

For cases in which the requirements of a data migration prove to be too complex for the eCATT, the *Legacy System Migration Workbench* (LSM Workbench or LSMW) introduced in **Chapter 7** is a much more flexible tool than the eCATT, although the similarities between the two tools are unmistakable. The LSM Workbench lets you transfer data from non-SAP systems to an ERP system with minimal programming required. This tool is the right choice whenever the structure of the legacy data differs significantly from the structure of the data in the ERP system — making data conversion unavoidable — or when the legacy data has to be augmented with data already in the ERP system.

Accelerated Data Migration

Chapter 8 introduces a data migration solution developed by SAP, *Accelerated Data Migration* (ADM), which, for various reasons, is currently only available with consulting services. This solution focuses on handling very large data quantities within a relatively short period of time. However, the benefits of this solution are somewhat marred by the fact that it doesn't involve any profound data consistency checks, and therefore deviates from the methods described in Chapters 4 through 7, which are based on the principle of "security before speed." The risk in not adhering to this maxim should always be considered therefore when employing this data migration solution.

If you have read through to Chapter 8 and you still think you will have to resort to programming for your own data migration, we highly recommend that you read **Chapter 9**. This chapter utilizes numerous examples to show how the migration dataset can be prepared with Microsoft Excel or Microsoft Access, for example, using the described programming-free method instead of a custom-written program to migrate the data to the ERP system.

Avoiding programming

After the individual data migration methods have been introduced, **Chapter 10** looks at each of these methods with a critical eye. In particular, this chapter describes the advantages and disadvantages of each technique and attempts to pinpoint the best procedure for a given situation.

Rating migration techniques

Chapter 11 is a special case because the data migration method described here, in contrast to the procedures covered in the previous chapters, is not application-independent, but instead can be used only in Asset Accounting. In addition to the necessary Customizing settings for the migration, a case example in this chapter illustrates how you can use Microsoft Excel to transfer both asset master data and the corresponding transaction data to SAP ERP, provided this data has the required format.

Migrating fixed assets with Microsoft Excel

Chapter 12 informs you of recent developments and areas related to data migration, such as the Data Migration Workbench. In addition, this chapter takes a closer look at the subject of data extraction from live ERP systems.

Outlook and related areas

As mentioned above, datasets within existing IT systems must also be adapted to changing framework conditions over the course of time. The **Appendix** provides you with a module-specific overview of selected SAP ERP tables that typically must be processed during a restructuring. Familiarity with these tables will help you find the relevant data in the system, via accelerating the overall process. In addition, all the relevant terminology for this book is listed and defined in a glossary.

Appendix

This book is structured to allow you to jump directly to the specific chapter that interests you without having to read all the previous chapters (see Figure 1.1). Alternatively, this book is also intended as a comprehensive project manual for data migration that can be read sequentially. Once you have read it in its entirety, you will be able to plan, judge, and execute your own migration projects. Detailed case examples, illustrated with numerous screenshots, will help you to achieve this goal.

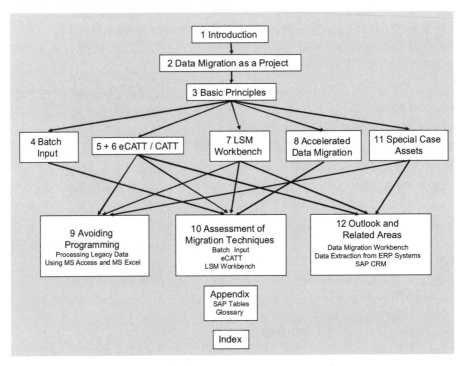

Figure 1.1 Book Structure and Dependencies Between Chapters

Changes and enhancements in the second edition

For the second edition, the entire material was profoundly revised and, wherever necessary, corrected or rendered more precisely. The texts, figures, and terminology have been adapted to the current Release SAP ERP 6.0. A chapter on the *Accelerated Data Migration* solution, which has been developed by SAP after the publication of the first edition, was added (see Chapter 8).

In addition, the eCATT was aligned more closely with our considerations so as to reflect the disadvantage of the CATT, which is no longer fully available since SAP ERP 2004. On the other hand, eCATT has unfolded its full functionality, which is required for data migration purposes, only from SAP ERP 2004 onwards. Knowing that many users have not yet implemented SAP ERP and won't do so in the near future, we also dedicate the traditional CATT its due place among the different migration methods. In doing this, we hope that we can meet the different requirements for information among our readers.

This book predominantly describes techniques and methods used in the current Release SAP ERP 6.0. Whenever there are substantial differences to the older Releases SAP R/3 4.6C, SAP R/3 Enterprise, and SAP ERP 2004, we will describe these differences in detail.

Focus on
SAP ERP 6.0

In the course of the transition from SAP R/3 to SAP ERP, SAP introduced a number of new concepts: SAP Business Suite, SAP ERP, SAP ECC, and SAP NetWeaver. The entire "solution family" is referred to as the SAP Business Suite. It comprises the five solutions, SAP ERP, SAP CRM, SAP SRM, SAP PLM, and SAP SCM. The SAP ERP solution consists of a large number of components. However, not all of these components must necessarily be installed. A "minimal" SAP ERP installation consists of the SAP NetWeaver Application Server as part of SAP NetWeaver — the technical platform — and the ERP Central Component (ECC), which represents the application layer. Consequently, SAP NetWeaver Application Server and ECC can be regarded as the successors to SAP R/3. Figure 1.2 illustrates the interrelationships.

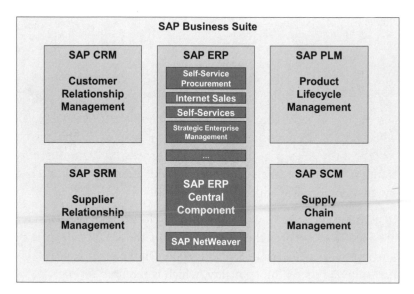

Figure 1.2 SAP Business Suites, SAP ERP, SAP ECC, and SAP NetWeaver

Table 1.1 shows an overview of the major parameters of the SAP R/3 and SAP ERP releases:

	R/3 4.6C	R/3 Enterprise	ERP 2004	ERP 6.0
Basis Release	4.6C	6.20	6.40	7.0
NetWeaver Release	–	–	NW 2004	NW 7.0
ECC Release	–	–	ECC 5.0	ECC 6.0

Table 1.1 Parameters of the Different Releases

We would like to thank Frank Densborn, Hans-Joachim Ölschläger, Jonathan Maidstone, and Werner Hillebrand for supporting us with their profound expertise.

We hope that you will enjoy reading this book and find it helpful in your data migration projects, endeavors, and responsibilities.

Michael Willinger and **Johann Gradl**

In order for a data migration to deliver the desired results, it should be discussed at an early stage. Furthermore, it has to qualify as a subproject within the overall implementation project. Lastly, sufficient project resources must be reserved for migration activities.

2 Managerial Foundations for Migrating Data to SAP ERP

2.1 Data Migration as a Subproject

Frequently, data migration doesn't get the attention it deserves. All too often, project managers fail to realize that, depending on the project scope, data migration can tie up staffing resources and financial resources as well. Staffing bottlenecks will occur whenever the data migration technique restricts the migration activities to a select group of individuals. Because custom data transfer programs are often used, it becomes readily apparent that a lack of resources among programmers is the primary cause of the bottlenecks. As mentioned in Chapter 1, the objective of this book is to introduce migration techniques that are easy to learn, ensure data security, and, ideally, don't require any custom programming. Consequently, data migration is no longer the sole responsibility of programmers. Because individuals who don't possess complex programming skills can be involved in the migration process as well, the likelihood of staffing bottlenecks occurring is significantly reduced.

Staffing bottleneck

The need to manage limited project resources is not the only factor that makes data migration an independent subproject within an overall implementation project. Another aspect that you should not underestimate is the information conveyed within the migrated data, that is, the data quality. For example, it is indisputable that the open items in the legacy system have to correspond to those in SAP ERP — both individually and cumulatively — in order to ensure data consistency between the systems. This alone is far from sufficient, how-

Foundation for business processes

ever. Because data migration is the foundation for all subsequent business processes in SAP ERP, you must also migrate information that may not appear to be relevant, but that may be the control data that ensures a smooth handling of downstream processes.

Therefore, it is not enough to simply ensure that the migrated data is quantitatively complete. You must also investigate whether the migrated data can handle the operative transactions in the new system, and whether it has the necessary information for the decision-making processes. In the open items example, this means that, in addition to verifying that the amounts are correct, you must also ensure that the due dates are calculated properly because they can have a direct impact on an enterprise's liquidity planning. Missing or incorrect information can steer decision-making processes in an entirely unintended direction.

Data migration as an iterative process

For this reason, we recommend that you design your data migration project as an iterative process. This means you can begin testing the data migration as soon as you have extracted the first data from the legacy system and Customizing in SAP ERP permits the data migration (later in this book, we'll address the latter in detail). Based on the initial results, you can then check in a subsequent step whether all the information required for smooth handling of the downstream processes is available. This involves comprehensive system testing and potential changes to the Customizing configuration. If information is missing, you must first determine where to obtain it, and repeat the data migration process until you achieve the results that you want. Note that you can never execute the *data migration* or *test the business processes* in isolation; these two tasks are inextricably woven together.

System comprehension

Again, this last aspect emphasizes the importance of data migration in an overall implementation process. In this context, the individuals who are responsible for the data migration are well advised to deal with the processes in the legacy system early on, and to examine how these processes can be mapped in SAP ERP, especially if a *business reengineering* is required when the new system is being implemented. Because no one knows the legacy IT system better than the user department staff, they should be involved in the processes from the start, in order to prevent staffing bottlenecks in this area as well. With this approach, the user department staff will become familiar with the philosophy of the SAP ERP system step by step, and will be better able to determine what data must be provided to ensure a smooth system migration.

2.2 Preliminary Considerations

At the start of the project, you can determine the preliminary considerations that will shape the subsequent migration project based on the legacy system, without requiring detailed knowledge of the SAP ERP system.

2.2.1 Defining the Dataset for Migration

The data to be migrated can be divided into the following categories:

▶ **Master data**

Master data is data that remains unchanged over a long period of time. It involves information that you always need for the same purpose. Of course, it makes sense to migrate only the master data that is actually used. Dormant data (see Section 2.2.2), data without any operative use, should be flagged as such in the legacy system to exclude it from the migration process.

Relevance

▶ **Transation data**

Transaction data has a short lifecycle and can be assigned to specific master data. It is sometimes also referred to as "posting documents." In this case, you must clarify just how detailed a history of the legacy system should be mapped in SAP ERP. Specifically, you must decide whether you want to migrate the individual posting documents, or line items, or only need the accumulated, updated values, namely, the balances. If you decide to migrate the line items, you must determine the number of items in the past fiscal years that you want to migrate, and which role the cleared items (for information purposes only) have to perform. If you decide to migrate the balances, the legacy system must remain available to provide detailed information, at least during the transition phase.

Line items or balances

Past experience shows that most migration projects use a combination of line items and balances. Many managers decide to migrate all the line items for customers and vendors and use them to continue the business processes in SAP ERP. Conversely, the line items are not integral to balance sheet accounts and income statement accounts. The specific situation is what determines which data has to be migrated.

2.2.2 Identifying Dormant Data

Analyzing the legacy dataset

You should always think of a change to a new IT system as an opportunity to examine your legacy data and eliminate data that, while still stored in the legacy system, has no operative use now or in the future. Your time investment in this task will more than pay off, as it will ensure a consistent, orderly data basis in the new system. In addition, this procedure can significantly reduce the data volume for migration and, therefore, lessen the overall time required for the data transfer.

The issue here is how to identify this dormant data. The following examples describe several methods.

Relevance of the legacy dataset

▶ **Master data**

If the legacy can analyze which master data has not been used actively for a longer period (two years, for example), this analysis can be the starting point for deciding whether the identified data will be needed in the future. If not, you can flag the data as being not relevant for migration, thereby excluding it from further migration steps.

Redundant legacy data

You will frequently encounter situations in which identical master data exists several times in a legacy system. While this data is saved under different identification numbers, its contents are identical or nearly so. In this case, an analysis can help you to discover whether this situation exists in your system. If it does, you can flag the redundant data as being not relevant in order to exclude it from further migration steps.

The situation becomes somewhat more complex when transactions are based on the redundant master data. In such situations, you will have to change the identified postings in the legacy system or auxiliary external system (such as Microsoft Excel) before you can eliminate the redundant master data. If you don't do this, migrating the transaction data will cause errors, because the transaction data will not have the corresponding master data in the new system.

Regardless of the issues that we just addressed, the affected user departments should always investigate whether the current operative master data will continue to be used in the same manner in the new system, or whether the history should start anew with the successor system. Classic examples include charts of accounts that have grown over time and yet consist of many individual accounts. In this case, you must ask yourself, "Is all the master data really needed, or would it be more expedient for information and control purposes to consolidate the master data and reduce it to a more manageable amount?" If you decide on the latter, posting changes will be required.

Grouping master data

► **Transaction data**

Zero values

You may discover that your legacy system contains transactions that the SAP ERP system cannot identify as such. Such cases involve postings with zero values. To avoid problems with the subsequent migration from the start, you should search your legacy dataset for such transactions and eliminate any such items found.

What do you want to do with transactions that can be allocated to the same master data record, but which balance to zero when added together? Is there a reason for this situation that justifies identifying the items separately, or has someone merely forgotten to clear the items in the legacy system? Analysis in the legacy system will help you to answer these questions. If the analysis indicates that balancing the items would be beneficial, you can do so directly in the legacy system, or in an auxiliary system. This step will have a direct impact on the migration data volume.

Balancing items

2.2.3 Measures for Reducing the Data Volume

The question as to how detailed duplication of the legacy system's history will be in the successor system has a major influence on the data volume. But even if you decide to migrate the line items, several measures can help you to reduce the numbers of these items prior to migration:

► If processes can be closed, they should not be set to a status such as "Open" or "Partially complete"; instead, set these processes to "Completed". Depending on the application, items with this status may be excluded from the data migration.

Close processes

Payment before
the due date

▶ If your economic situation and company policy permit it, you might consider paying outstanding vendor invoices before executing the data migration in order to take advantage of cash discounts. Not only will this shrink the volume of data to be migrated (assuming paid items aren't relevant for the migration), but it will also help to reduce your expenses.

▶ Another possible approach is to adjust your payment pattern to keep credit memos to a minimum.

2.2.4 Preparatory Measures for Extracting the Legacy Data

How do I extract
the data?

As long as the user departments or other individuals responsible for extracting the legacy data are not sufficiently familiar with the processes in the SAP ERP system, it makes little sense for them to provide an initial data extract for testing the legacy data transfer in this early project phase. Nonetheless, at the start of the project, you should check whether the legacy system can collect all the information contained in the master and transaction data and export it to one or more files. One significant question to ask yourself here is whether the legacy system has standard functions for creating such data extracts, or whether custom programming will be required. In the latter case, you must clarify whether in-house expertise is available, or whether you will have to bring in external consulting resources, which will have to be scheduled accordingly.

2.2.5 Addendum: Accounting Considerations

If you want to migrate transaction data, you must deal directly with accounting issues that have to be solved prior to the data migration. Hopefully, we will have presented this rather dry and sometimes irritating subject, and the extent to which it affects the data migration, in such a way that makes it easy to comprehend. The following information will help you to better understand Chapters 4 and 5, which are both dedicated to the migration of transaction data. Here, the main issue is *how* the transaction data, such as open credit items, will be migrated in SAP ERP.

Migration account

It is clear that the gross amounts from invoices and credit memos will have to be identified in the credit and debit columns of the corresponding vendor accounts. But what about the corresponding off-setting postings? One option in this case is to configure a *migration account* in the general ledger (G/L) that transfers only the open items and receives all the offsetting entries from the data migration. To document the special status of this account, the account number "9xxxxx" is usually selected. The following example illustrates this option:

Vendor 1 has two open invoices (I) in the amounts of $100.00 and $200.00, and a credit memo (C) in the amount of $50.00. Vendor 2 has an outstanding invoice in the amount of $150.00.

Example 1

From an accounting perspective, the vendor accounts look as follows:

Vendor 1		Vendor 2	
Debit	Credit	Debit	Credit
C $50	I $100	Balance $150	I $150
Balance $250	I $200		

The migration account looks as follows:

Migration Account	
Debit	Credit
I $100	C $50
I $200	Balance $400
I $150	

As this example shows, the balance of the migration account is the exact sum of the balances of the vendor accounts to be migrated. This means the migration account is ideal for an initial comparison of the totals between the legacy system and the SAP ERP system. If the totals are identical in both systems, you can simply check a random sampling of the vendor accounts to confirm their accuracy.

In most cases, the migration account is not assigned to a balance sheet item, which means it is identified as a non-assigned account under the bottom line. If you migrate your data at the start of a fiscal year and use only one migration account for the vendor data, open

Attributes of the migration account

sales items, and figures from the remaining balance sheet accounts, this account will balance to zero, assuming the data migration runs without errors. In this case, you can consider the migration account as an account that mirrors all the postings to be transferred from all accounts. You can draw parallels to an *opening balance sheet account*, which mirrors all the opening balances of the *opening balance sheet* and also balances to zero. In contrast to an opening balance sheet account, which contains only opening balances (one balance per account), the migration account can also explain the reason for these balances, as it lists the corresponding line items.

Reconciliation accounts

But, what does "transferring the remaining balance sheet accounts" mean? These are all the accounts listed in the financial statements, provided they don't represent *reconciliation accounts*. Here, a reconciliation account is a general ledger account that records the transactions from *subledger accounting*, such as accounts payable and accounts receivable. You cannot post directly to the reconciliation accounts. Instead, they receive all the values automatically as soon as a corresponding posting is created in the subledger. Generally, several accounts from subledger accounting — several vendor accounts, for example — point to a shared reconciliation account. This identifies the subledger transactions in general ledger accounting for the financial statements. Because the corresponding vendors and customers are posted to directly during the migration of the vendor/customer open items — that is, the posting takes place in the subledgers — the integration of the general ledger and the subledgers indicates that no further postings to the reconciliation account are needed, therefore, you can exclude the reconciliation accounts entirely from the data migration process.

Migrating assets

When *asset values* must be migrated, the situation differs. Here, integration of the general ledger and the asset subledger is not ensured for the duration of the legacy data transfer. Therefore, after the data migration, you must manually post to the reconciliation accounts in Asset Management. Because direct postings to reconciliation accounts aren't supported in the application menu for Financial Accounting, however, the corresponding functions are located in Customizing for Asset Management. The special features associated with the migration of asset values are described in detail in Chapter 11.

Like the migration of balance sheet accounts, the migration of the *Profit and Loss* (P&L) *accounts* must also be clarified. If you migrate the data at the *start of a fiscal year*, the decision is clear. Because all the P&L accounts transfer their balances to the *retained earnings account*, which you define in Customizing for Financial Accounting, at the end of the fiscal year, they all have a zero balance at the start of the new fiscal year. This, in turn, means they don't contain any transactions from the current year and therefore can be excluded from the data migration. If you migrate your data in *mid-year*, however, transactions may have taken place in the P&L accounts, and, therefore, will have to be migrated. In the latter case, note that the P&L accounts have not yet passed their postings on to the retained earnings accounts, which is identified in the financial statements. This means the assets and liabilities are not directly equal; the profit or loss currently in the P&L accounts still must be added. Thus, the migration account will have a balance after migration of the balance sheet accounts, which corresponds exactly to the amount of profit or loss. The following example illustrates this situation:

Fixed assets (FA) show a balance in the amount of $1,000 and current assets (CA) show a balance in the amount of $500. In addition, the opening balance of stockholders' equity (SE) was $500, which means the P&L account now shows a profit (PROF) of $500 that has not yet been transferred to the retained earnings account. Therefore, this amount is not allocated to SE yet in the financial statements. If you take into account the current payables (PAYB) in the amount of $500, you obtain the following results:

Financial Statement	
Assets	**Liabilities**
FA 1,000	SE 500
CA 500	PAYB 500

Profit and Loss Statement	
Debit	**Credit**
	PROF 500

Note that the value for the payables is made up of a large number of G/L accounts and line items, for example, and also contains the open credit items – represented by the vendor reconciliation account. As just described, all of these line items will result in an appropriate off-setting posting in the migration account. To present a simple, easy to follow financial statement, however, we have chosen to omit a breakdown of FA, CA, SE and PAYB into G/L accounts and their line items. We used the same strategy with the identification of the profit in the profit and loss statement.

Given these basic assumptions, and after migrating the balance sheet accounts (including subledgers), the migration account would look as follows:

Migration Account	
Debit	**Credit**
SE 500	FA 1,000
PAYB 500	CA 500
Balance 500	

Therefore, the balance in the migration account, after the migration of the balance sheet accounts, corresponds exactly to the amount of the profit or loss — the amount of revenues in the preceding example — that has to be migrated. Once the revenues have also been migrated to SAP ERP, the migration account looks as follows:

Migration Account	
Debit	**Credit**
SE 500	FA 1,000
PAYB 500	CA 500
PROF 500	

Summary: the balance of the migration account is always zero

To summarize, the following rule applies. After a successful data transfer, the migration account must always have a balance of zero, regardless of whether the data migration was performed at the start of a fiscal year or in mid-year. If the data is migrated at the start of a fiscal year, the migration account doesn't have any P&L components, and, therefore, shows only the transactions in the subledgers and other balance sheet accounts. If the data is migrated in mid-year, however, the migration account may also contain P&L components. It should also be apparent that the migration account always represents all the transactions to be migrated as a mirror image of the postings to the G/L accounts, or the postings in the subledgers.

Alternatively, you can work with multiple migration accounts. For example, you can have one migration account for vendors, another migration account for customers, and still another for fixed assets as well as other balance sheet and P&L accounts. In this constellation of accounts, the balances of the different migration accounts will add up to zero after an error-free migration. There is no general recommendation as to how many migration accounts you should use; it depends primarily on your personal preferences. It is definitely not advisable, however, to define vast numbers of migration accounts in order to make it easier to localize errors later on. You can achieve the same results if you use only one migration account, but different *document types* (i.e., depending on the situation) that you can then select for the migration account.

One or more migration accounts

Once the question of the data transfer account has been clarified, you can concentrate on the next subject, which is directly related to the migration of the accounting documents, namely, the *posting key* (PK). This is a two-digit numeric key that controls the recording of document items. Among other things, the posting key defines the account type, that is, whether a vendor account, a customer account, a G/L account posting, or a posting from Asset Management is involved. The posting key also indicates whether the specified account is posted to in credit or in debit. Posting keys are used whenever you use documents for posting, such as open credit items, in the standard SAP ERP transactions for document entry, especially Transaction FB01.

Posting keys

Returning to Example 1 above, typically, a data transfer document consists of two items. In addition to the vendor accounts (vendor 1, vendor 2), G/L accounts (migration account) are also included. Debit postings to G/L accounts must be assigned account key 40; credit postings to G/L accounts must be assigned posting key 50. You can differentiate further between debit and credit postings to vendor accounts, that is, you can choose from different debit and credit posting keys. We recommend using the standard SAP ERP posting keys

Reference to Example 1

for vendor invoices (31) and vendor credit memos (21), which would result in the following:

Vendor Invoice		
PK 40	Migration Account	100
PK 31	Vendor 1	100 (-)
Vendor Credit Memo		
PK 21	Vendor 1	50
PK 50	Migration Account	50 (-)

In the process, the SAP ERP system assigns a minus sign (-) to every credit posting, independently of the account type, so the document items always balance to zero when they are entered correctly. Therefore, the posting key controls whether an entered amount is interpreted as positive or negative.

Lastly, you must transfer customer open items and G/L account postings in a similar manner.

Customer Invoice		
PK 01	Customer 1	100
PK 50	Migration Account	100 (-)
Customer Credit Memo		
PK 40	Migration Account	50
PK 11	Customer 1	50 (-)
G/L Account Posting in Credit		
PK 40	Migration Account	200
PK 50	G/L Account	200 (-)
G/L Account Posting in Debit		
PK 40	G/L Account	100
PK 50	Migration Account	100 (-)

2.3 The Data Migration Process from the Project Perspective

Once you have finalized the considerations discussed in Section 2.2, you can begin to prepare for the actual data migration.

2.3.1 Basic Customizing

First, Customizing in SAP ERP must have progressed enough to enable execution of the basic processes that follow the data migration. For example, it doesn't make any sense to transfer open items if no payment terms have been previously defined in Customizing, which clearly indicates the due dates of the open items. In this example, the payment run would be a follow-up process, which would provide incorrect results if no exact due dates were available.

2.3.2 System Presentations in SAP ERP

Before they can provide the files with the necessary data from the legacy system, the involved user departments have to become familiar with and understand the process flows in the SAP ERP system. One way to impart this knowledge is to give theoretical presentations of the SAP ERP structures, their mutual dependencies, and the data flow that these structures create in an integrated system. This theoretical background makes it easier to understand and classify subsequent presentations in a live or simulated SAP ERP system. Throughout all these presentations, you should always ensure that the appropriate individuals are involved in order to enable them to ask the right questions.

Theoretical and system presentations

Ideally, after this initial meeting, the participating user departments will already be able to roughly determine which data has to be extracted from the legacy system in order to achieve the desired results in SAP ERP.

2.3.3 Business Reengineering

A far more difficult situation arises when the SAP ERP system and the legacy system are based on different logic and, therefore, the legacy system data cannot be migrated directly to SAP ERP. In this situation, the data must be processed prior to the transfer in order to

Paradigm shift

enable its subsequent use in SAP ERP. This process can be extremely time-consuming and, therefore, should not be underestimated. The SAP ERP system often requires information to map the business processes — called *required entry fields* — that does not necessarily exist in this form in the legacy system. Conversely, the legacy system may contain information in its data records that SAP ERP does not require due to differing application logic and possible organizational structures.

Organization follows software

The system knowledge described in Section 2.3.2 is particularly important in this framework, because, for the participating user departments, it is the foundation on which they can restructure and redesign their business processes. Therefore, the organization and data structures follow the demands of the new software. Because this *business reengineering* can take on extremely complex dimensions, you may once again want to discuss the extent to which you want to model the legacy system's history in the successor system (see Section 2.2.1).

2.3.4   Simulating the Data Migration

Once you have held the initial SAP ERP system presentations, and the user departments understand the logic of the SAP ERP system, you can intensify your focus on the activities associated with the data migration itself:

▶ Identify the ERP transactions that you want to use to migrate the legacy data to SAP ERP.

▶ Run these identified transactions manually in SAP ERP with test data from the legacy system and note which fields are required. There may be required entry fields that have no corresponding data fields in the legacy system.

Once the SAP transactions and the fields to be maintained are known, you can continue with the *mapping* phase.

2.3.5   Mapping (Field Matching)

Mapping

The field names in the legacy system agree with the corresponding terminology in the SAP ERP system only in the rarest of cases. If different naming conventions are used, the respective names must be recorded and assigned accordingly, theoretically at first, on a piece of paper. This procedure is usually referred to as *mapping*.

In the simplest case, the field names will be identical, which means the following equation applies:

1:1 relationships

> Field name (legacy system) = Field name (SAP ERP)

If the fields differ merely in their terminology, but not their content, this relationship still holds true.

If different designs are involved, however, the fields from the legacy system must be transformed upfront — because SAP ERP does not recognize them in their source format — and then assigned to the corresponding fields in SAP ERP. The legacy system doesn't necessarily have to work with posting keys, which are control parameters from Financial Accounting that control the account type, among other things, and determine whether a debit posting or a credit posting is involved. Similarly, you may discover that the legacy system uses a different logic to categorize its postings. In such cases, the individual fields of the legacy system, which control whether the postings to the respective accounts are listed under credits or debits, must be transformed to the appropriate posting keys in keeping with the ERP philosophy.

Transformations

In general, the following applies:

> Field name(s) (legacy system) → Transformation → Field name(s) (SAP ERP)

First, consider the example of the posting keys. If you assume that the legacy system generally flags invoices with "I" and credit memos with "C", the following transformation process is required:

Example

	Flag in Legacy System	Posting Key in SAP ERP System
Vendor Invoices and Credit Memos	I	31
	C	21
Customer Invoices and Credit Memos	I	01
	C	11

If a field is mandatory in SAP ERP (*required entry field*), but the legacy system doesn't have an equivalent field, the existing structures in the

Required entry fields

legacy system will have to be reworked — in an auxiliary system such as Microsoft Excel, for example — and adapted to the requirements of the new system landscape (see Section 2.3.3). Alternatively, you can set the field to a constant (solely for the data migration), or change the field to an *optional entry field* in Customizing.

At the end of this step, every SAP ERP field that is required for data migration must be assigned a corresponding field from the legacy system, either by direct assignment or through a transformation process.

2.3.6 Data Extraction from the Legacy System

Text files | Once the legacy system fields have been mapped to the corresponding SAP ERP fields, at least theoretically (see Section 2.3.5), the next step involves extracting all the fields that are required to model the business processes in SAP ERP and their contents from the legacy system.

When extracting the data from the legacy system, you should ensure that the data is provided in one or more text files; this makes it much easier to postprocess the data manually with a spreadsheet program (see Section 2.3.7).

2.3.7 Manual Postprocessing of the Extracted Data

Only rarely will the field mapping between the legacy system and the SAP ERP system deliver results that don't require manual postprocessing of the extracted data. In most cases, the data records must be adapted or transformed — due to a changed system landscape or business reengineering — to enable their processing in the SAP ERP system.

Therefore, your objective in this manual postprocessing is to create a file that the SAP ERP system can process without any further transformations or adjustments. This file is the result of the mapping performed in a previous step. The elimination of data that is no longer needed is also part of this process (see Section 2.2.2).

Using spreadsheet programs | Conventional spreadsheet programs such as Microsoft Excel will help you to achieve this objective, with their various calculation, filtering, and replacement functions. If your intention is to *avoid pro-*

gramming, you must ensure that this step is properly addressed within the process chain. As we mentioned previously, because one of our main goals in writing this book is to show you how to enable data migration without using custom programming, in Chapter 9, we describe several ways in which you can format your dataset in advance to avoid time-intensive programming during the subsequent migration phase.

2.3.8 Selecting a Data Migration Technique

When selecting the migration techniques, you must weigh your data security needs against the speed with which the data has to be migrated to the SAP ERP system. You should be aware that speed always comes at the expense of data security; it is almost impossible to achieve both goals simultaneously.

Speed versus security

After you learn about the individual methods for data migration, in Chapter 10 we will assess the various techniques and describe which procedures are optimal for certain situations. Chapter 11 contains a similar assessment of the various techniques for migrating asset values.

2.3.9 Uploading the Data in SAP ERP

The data upload to SAP ERP is a strictly technical process that you perform in accordance with the selected migration procedure (see Section 2.3.8). Chapters 4 to 7 describe which preparation steps are required in SAP ERP.

Upload according to migration technique

Problems that occur during the data upload are usually the direct result of an insufficient or erroneous data basis (see Section 2.3.7). Should the upload process terminate, you will have to analyze the data basis in depth and adjust it accordingly, and then repeat the upload. Any changes made to the database in the interim will have to be undone in order to avoid falsifying the results, which is yet another reason for you to pay particular attention to the activities described in Section 2.3.7.

Troubleshooting

> **Note**
>
> Unfortunately, not all the application areas in the SAP ERP system provide functions for deleting specific data. In such cases, you will have to back up your data prior to migration and restore the backup if your initial migration fails.

Dependencies and order of activities

To be thorough, you should take into account many dependencies during the migration. These dependencies require you to perform certain activities in a specific order, for example:

- Master data before transaction data
- General ledger before subledger (e.g., reconciliation account before vendor)
- Purchase orders before goods receipt postings
- Material master data before bill of material (BOMs)

2.3.10 Testing the Business Processes in SAP ERP

Quantitative completeness

Once you have transferred your dataset to the SAP ERP system — without program terminations — you must ensure that the migrated data is quantitatively complete. If transaction data is involved, you can compare the totals between the data in the upload file and the results in SAP ERP for an initial assessment. If no variances are detected, you can then analyze several random data records to ensure that all the fields in SAP ERP have been filled as expected according to the mapping (see Section 2.3.5). If differences occur between the expected and actual results, however, we recommend localizing the difference through a targeted analysis in SAP ERP. This will help you to determine whether the data basis was insufficient, or whether the problems are due to a systematic error related to the selected migration procedure. Depending on the result, you will have to analyze the data basis or the selected data migration procedure again and change it if necessary.

Testing the business processes

However, verifying that the data is quantitatively complete won't suffice. You must ensure that the data contains all the information required to model the subsequent business processes in SAP ERP. To do so, the migrated data must be processed further in the SAP ERP system, because this data is used as the foundation for testing the business processes. As you can see, you can't look at a data migration in isolation; you should always view it in the context of system tests as well.

If the data basis fails this system test because required information is missing, you will have to migrate additional fields from the legacy system to SAP ERP. Consequently, you will have to revise the mapping that you developed in Section 2.3.5. This new information then serves as the foundation for extracting and postprocessing the data again, as described in Sections 2.3.6 and 2.3.7, and then importing it into SAP ERP (after you have deleted the old, incorrect dataset). You have to continue this iterative process until you achieve the desired results in SAP ERP.

Iterative process

Figure 2.1 provides an overview of the full data migration process, as described in this section.

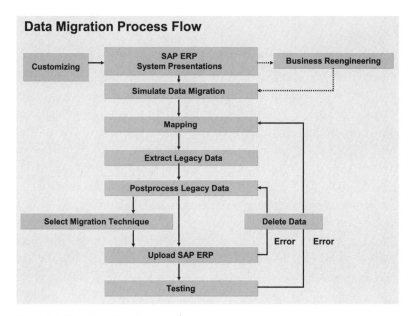

Figure 2.1 Data Migration Process Flow

This chapter introduces you to the basic concepts that you need to understand during any data migration, regardless of which technique you select. It also describes the major process steps involved in data migration from a technical perspective.

3 Technical Basics for Migrating Data to SAP ERP

3.1 Basic Terminology

The following terms will appear throughout this book:

▶ **Data migration, migration**
The term *data migration* refers to the transfer of business data (master and transaction data) from any application system to an SAP ERP system. The term *migration* is used as a synonym. Please note that this term is also used in other contexts, such as migrating from one technical platform to another; however, this is not the intended meaning here.

Data migration is sometimes also referred to as *data transfer*.

▶ **Legacy system**
The application system that contains the data to be transferred before the migration is referred to as the *legacy system* (or source system).

▶ **Legacy data**
The data that is to be migrated from a legacy system to the SAP ERP system is referred to as *legacy data* (or *source data*).

▶ **Data object, business data object, business object**
A data migration is usually based on data objects. A *data object* is a business data unit such as a customer master, material master, an FI document, and so on. Such objects are sometimes called *business data objects* or simply *business objects*.

▶ **Data migration object, object**
When data objects are mentioned in the context of data migration, the terms *data migration object* or simply *object* refer to a data object that has additional attributes that are relevant for the data migration, for example, the structure of the data object in the legacy system and the SAP ERP system, along with the mapping that connects the two structures.

▶ **File, text file, table-like file, sequential file**
All of the data migration techniques described in this book assume that the legacy data is available in one or more files. These files are usually *text files*, that is, files that are divided into several lines. The structure of these lines is differentiated as follows: If all the lines in a file have the same structure, that file is called a *table-like file*. In this case, the sequence of the lines in the file is usually not important for data migration. If all the lines in the file don't have the same structure (header and item records, for example), the file is called a *sequential file* (see Section 7.2.9).

▶ **Frontend, SAP Application Server**
In the SAP ERP system, files can be saved in one of two places: either on a *frontend*, that is, the end user's workstation, or on an *SAP Application Server*, the computer that runs the application logic of the SAP ERP system (or a storage medium accessible to the SAP Application Server).

3.2 The Data Migration Process from a Technical Perspective

Regardless of which migration procedure you select, every data migration project involves certain basic technical steps. The following five steps are characteristic of almost every data migration procedure.

3.2.1 Exporting the Data

First, the data you want to transfer to the SAP ERP system (i.e., the legacy data) has to be exported from the legacy system. This step is also referred to as *extracting* or *unloading* the legacy data.

The data migration procedures introduced in this book don't provide any support for exporting the legacy data from legacy systems. You will need to determine whether your legacy system offers functions for this purpose. If not, you will need to write suitable programs for data extraction in the legacy system.

Data extraction is the responsibility of the legacy system

In the process of exporting data, you must define how you want to store the legacy data. In particular, you must decide whether you want to group all the legacy data together in one file or divide it into several smaller files. You'll also need to define whether you want to write the legacy data to table-like files or to sequential files.

3.2.2 Reading the Data

Technically speaking, the legacy data exported from a legacy system can be saved in different files (see Section 7.2.9). It may therefore make sense to transform the data to a technically standardized format initially. However, most of the data migration procedures don't support this option. Instead, it is assumed that the legacy data will be provided in a predefined format.

Transforming the data to a technically standardized format

Of all the data migration procedures introduced in this book, only the *Legacy System Migration Workbench* (LSM Workbench) offers this option. In this case, the files, which can exist in different formats, are merged into a single sequential file. For more information, see Section 7.2.9.

3.2.3 Converting the Data

Application systems can model business data in many ways. You cannot assume that the data you export from a legacy system can be easily imported into an SAP ERP system without additional processing. Consequently, you usually have to convert the exported data to the appropriate format.

Converting the legacy data to SAP format

> **Note**
>
> The term *convert* is used synonymously with *transform*. The terms *data conversion* and *data transformation* are also used in this context, as well as *mapping*, *field mapping*, and *transformation*.

The data conversion can be as complex as is necessary. The effort required depends on how different the source and target formats are from one another. In order to make the work less cumbersome, however, you can define typical conversion tasks that must be performed repeatedly.

Value conversion

▶ Value conversion involves translating a known set of possible field values to a different set of values. This can apply to the country codes, for example, if the legacy data stores this information in a one-place field ("D" for Germany, "U" for the U.S., "I" for Italy, etc.), while the SAP ERP system uses ISO codes that can be up to three places long ("DE" for Germany, "USA" for the U.S., "IT" for Italy, etc.). In this case, the following conversion must be defined:

  ▶ D → DE

  ▶ U → US

  ▶ I → IT

  ▶ And so on

  This process is also referred to as translation.

Converting
field attributes

▶ The conversion of field attributes involves changing the representation of certain field contents. Let's assume, for example, that your legacy system saves date values in the format DDMMYY (such as 311295), while the SAP ERP system expects these values in the format YYYYMMDD (such as 19951231). You must convert these values accordingly. You can do so with custom programming, or by using a tool that supports such standard cases at the touch of a button.

Default field values

▶ You may also need to define default values for certain field values. You should always keep the following fact in mind: The data objects in the SAP ERP system are usually quite extensive. In most cases, your legacy system will contain only a fraction of the fields that are available in the SAP ERP system for a given data object. Frequently, you'll encounter situations in which the SAP ERP system expects a value for a field, but your legacy system doesn't have an equivalent for that field; for example, the company code used in the SAP ERP system is a variable that is unknown in many legacy systems.

There are two basic ways of dealing with such situations:

▷ If the desired value can be derived from other available data, then you can fall back on a simple conversion of values (translation).

▷ If the desired value is always constant (or at least for long periods), you can set it to a constant. The technique of using fixed values, which provides a greater degree of flexibility than working with constants, is introduced in Chapter 7, together with the LSM Workbench (see Section 7.2.8).

▶ In some cases, you must not only convert field contents and field attributes on the way from the legacy system to the SAP ERP system, but also change the overall structure of the data object.

Converting structures

For example, let's assume that a legacy system can save a maximum of three contact persons for a customer. Let's also assume that these (maximum) three contact persons are saved in the header record of the customer master record. You can define any number of contact persons in the SAP ERP system. A separate table record is created for each contact person. Therefore, in this case, you must convert the structure as shown in Figure 3.1.

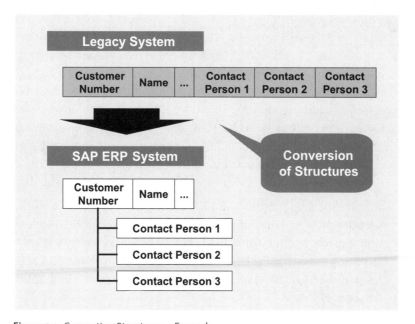

Figure 3.1 Converting Structures – Example

3.2.4 Importing the Data

All the previous steps serve to successively convert the legacy data into a format that the SAP ERP system can process. The next logical step is to transfer this converted legacy data to the database of the SAP ERP system. In addition to *importing data*, the term *loading data* is also used, as well as *uploading to SAP ERP*. There are generally two options for importing data:

Direct writing to the database

If you fully understand how the structure of database tables works in the SAP ERP system, you can use an ABAP program to write the legacy data directly to the database tables, at least theoretically. When it comes to throughput — the number of data records processed in any given time unit — this method is unbeatable. However, we don't recommend using this procedure because of the incalculable risk involved, namely, if this technique is used, that the database of the SAP ERP system could be filled with data that is inconsistent according to the rules of the SAP application. Consequently, you might not be able to process it further, or even display it, in the SAP ERP system.

Using standard ERP interfaces

All the procedures introduced here employ a different method. They are based exclusively on the interfaces provided in the SAP ERP system. In the following sections, these interfaces are called *standard ERP interfaces*. The standard ERP interfaces used in this book are outlined below.

▶ **Batch input**
Batch input refers to both a standard ERP interface and a procedure for data migration. This mature, proven technology "feeds" dialog transactions with the provided data (usually in the background). This ensures that all input checks are run, ensuring that all data imported with batch input is correct and consistent in the SAP ERP system. Of course, this certainty has its price: The data checks reduce throughput.

▶ **Direct input**
Because throughput from batch input is not always sufficient, direct input programs have been written for some data objects. In a sense, direct input involves the controlled, direct writing to the database of the SAP ERP system.

▶ **BAPI**

Business Application Programming Interfaces (BAPIs) were originally developed to open the SAP ERP system for external access. Data objects usually have read and write BAPIs. The latter can also be used to transfer data to the database of the SAP ERP system during a data migration.

▶ **IDoc**

Intermediate Documents (IDocs) come from the Electronic Data Interchange (EDI) environment. The challenge here is to transfer documents (such as purchase orders) electronically from one application system to another, possibly very remote, system. To do so, the structures of these documents first had to be defined for business purposes. This resulted in the development of IDocs, or more precisely, IDoc types. Secondly, a technique for processing these documents in the SAP ERP system had to be developed, namely, inbound processing. As you'll see in Chapter 7, you can also use this technique for data migration.

An important connection exists between BAPIs and IDocs. At the touch of a button, you can generate an IDoc type from a BAPI in the SAP ERP system. SAP already supplies the generated IDoc types for some BAPIs. In general, inbound processing of IDocs involves the following sequence: The data received in an IDoc is passed on to the corresponding BAPI, which updates the data in the SAP ERP system. This process is described in more detail in Chapter 7.

Connection between BAPIs and IDocs

3.2.5 Verifying the Data

Of course, once the legacy data has been imported into the SAP ERP system, you want to ensure that the process is complete and accurate. Unfortunately, there is no blanket solution for measuring the success of a data migration.

No blanket solution

Ultimately, you will have to rely on random samples and plausibility checks, such as comparing key figures (balances, for example), or comparing the number of records between the legacy system and the SAP ERP system.

3.3 Overview of Technical Procedures for Data Migration

This chapter concludes with a summary of the major data migration techniques introduced in this book.

3.3.1 Batch Input

As mentioned in Section 3.2.4, *batch input* is both a type of standard ERP interface and a procedure for data migration. Batch input can be used for data migration in two ways:

▶ **Standard batch input programs**
The SAP ERP system contains various batch input programs that transform prepared legacy data into a format that dialog transactions can process. These programs are called *standard batch input programs*.

▶ **Batch input recording**
In addition to the standard programs, the SAP ERP system enables you to record the process flow of a dialog transaction and generate an ABAP program from this recording at the touch of a button. While these generated programs theoretically work just like standard batch input programs, they lack the flexibility to react to changing screen sequences. The clear benefit of a batch input recording is that you deal only with the input fields of a dialog transaction that are relevant for your specific case. You can ignore all other input fields.

3.3.2 Extended Computer Aided Test Tool

Migrating data with the test tool

The *Extended Computer Aided Test Tool* (eCATT) is a tool that was originally developed to test business processes. Technically, a business process always consists of a sequence of dialog transactions. To avoid having to enter each transaction manually, the eCATT enables you to automate transaction processing and supply the transactions with appropriate values. Ultimately, the data generated in this manner forms the foundation for the system, integration, and mass tests that are essential to every ERP implementation project.

But, where is the connection to data migration? Data migration also involves creating data records with a specific transaction — such as

Transaction FK01 (*Create Vendor*) — and copying them automatically to SAP ERP. If you use the eCATT for data migration, you aren't interested in whether the dialog transactions respond accordingly with your expectations; you simply assume that this is where things are in the migration process. At this point, you are concerned only with transferring the legacy data to SAP ERP automatically, simply, and reliably.

3.3.3 Legacy System Migration Workbench

The *Legacy System Migration Workbench* (LSM Workbench) is an ERP-based tool for the one-time or periodic transfer of data from legacy systems to SAP ERP systems. It provides easy-to-use functions to convert legacy data and import it into the SAP ERP system, using standard ERP interfaces. The LSM Workbench is based on the following principles:

▶ Business data objects are migrated, not individual tables or field contents.

▶ The most frequent conversion tasks (see Section 3.2.3) are predefined and available at the touch of a button. Conversions can be added via the suitable ABAP statements.

▶ No ready-made conversion programs are provided. Instead, the conversion programs are generated from the defined conversion rules.

▶ Quality and consistency of the data imported into the SAP ERP system are more important than speed and throughput. Therefore, only the standard ERP interfaces are used.

▶ Conversion rules that have been defined once can be reused.

Principles of the LSM Workbench

These three techniques are introduced in exact detail in the following chapters.

This chapter introduces you to one of the basic techniques for entering data in the SAP ERP system. Using this technique, you can copy the data to be entered in the screen templates of an SAP transaction. You'll also learn several ways in which you can use this data entry technique for data migration.

4   Batch Input

4.1   What Is Batch Input Processing?

Batch input processing is a term derived from the early days of mainframe computing.

In the initial releases of SAP ERP, batch input processing was the only technique available to transfer external data to the SAP ERP system. Eventually, other techniques (BAPIs, IDocs) also became available. Yet, even today, batch input processing is still the most frequently used method for data migration. The reasons include the obvious similarities between batch input and dialog transactions, as well as the wide range of support available to users in the SAP ERP system. Both aspects are discussed in more detail in the next sections.

The most frequently used method for data migration

The basic principle of batch input processing is to "feed" the input fields in the screen templates (*dynpros*) of ERP dialog transactions with the provided data in the background. This ensures that the same input checks and authorization checks that would occur during manual entry are performed. Therefore, data imported via batch input is guaranteed to be just as accurate and consistent as the manually entered data.

Basic principle

4.2   How Does Batch Input Work?

This section describes the batch input technique in greater detail. First, we focus on the central concept of a batch input session and how it works. Then, we provide you with a way in which you can generate and process a batch input session.

4.2.1 What Is a Batch Input Session?

The main object in batch input processing is the *batch input session*. A batch input session consists of one or more calls of SAP transactions and the data to be processed by the transaction. The value for each field is specified for each transaction call, screen template, and input field. You can think of a batch input session as an ordered sequence of instructions for the SAP ERP system: "Supply value A to field X in screen template Y of transaction Z." In other words, a batch input session lets you control the SAP ERP system.

ABAP Dictionary structure BDCDATA

In the SAP ERP system, batch input sessions are saved according to ABAP Dictionary structure BDCDATA. This structure has the following composition:

1. PROGRAM: This field contains the name of the ABAP program to which the current dynpro (screen) belongs.

2. DYNPRO: This field contains the four-digit number of the current screen; i.e., it is saved here.

3. DYNBEGIN: This field indicates whether a new screen template (value "X") or a new transaction (value "T") starts.

4. FNAM: This field contains the technical name of the input field.

5. FVAL: This field contains the input value.

The following table, which shows an excerpt of a batch input session, gives you an idea of the structure. In the example, SAP Transaction FK01 (*Create Vendor*) is called and supplied with data:

No.	PROGRAM	DYNPRO	DYNBEGIN	FNAM	FVAL
01		0000	T	FK01	BS
02	SAPMF02K	0105	X		
03		0000		BDC_CURSOR	RF02K-KTOKK
04		0000		BDC_OKCODE	/00
05		0000		RF02K-LIFNR	34567

Table 4.1 Excerpt from a Batch Input Session

No.	PROGRAM	DYNPRO	DYNBEGIN	FNAM	FVAL
06		0000		RF02K-BUKRS	1000
07		0000		RF02K-KTOKK	0001
08	SAPMF02K	0110	X		
09		0000		BDC_CURSOR	LFA1-LAND1
10		0000		BDC_OKCODE	=VW
11		0000		LFA1-ANRED	Company
12		0000		LFA1-NAME1	Smith Jones Inc.
13		0000		LFA1-SORTL	WG
14		0000		LFA1-STRAS	123 Main St.
15		0000		LFA1-ORT01	Anytown
16		0000		LFA1-PSTLZ	55555
17		0000		LFA1-LAND1	USA
...					
18	SAPMF02K	0130	X		
19		0000		BDC_CURSOR	LFBK-BANKS(01)
20		0000		BDC_OKCODE	=VW
21	SAPMF02K	0210	X		
22		0000		BDC_CURSOR	LFB1-FDGRV
23		0000		BDC_OKCODE	=UPDA
24		0000		LFB1-AKONT	196300
25		0000		LFB1-FDGRV	A1

Table 4.1 Excerpt from a Batch Input Session (cont.)

In detail, lines 01 to 25 mean the following:

No.	Explanation
01	Transaction FK01 is called.
02	Screen 0105 from program SAPMF02K is called.

Table 4.2 Explanation of the Batch Input Session from Table 4.1

No.	Explanation
03	The cursor is positioned on field RF02K-KTOKK (account group).
04	Function code (OK code) 00 is triggered. This is equivalent to pressing the **Enter** key.[1]
05	The value 34567 is entered in field RF02K-LIFNR (vendor).
06	The value 1000 is entered in field RF02K-BUKRS (company code).
07	The value 0001 is entered in field RF02K-KTOKK (account group).
08	Screen 0110 from program SAPMF02K is called.
09	The cursor is positioned on field LFA1-LAND1 (country).
10	Function code (OK code) VW (continue) is triggered.
11	The value Company is entered in field LFA1-ANRED (form of address).
12	The value Smith Jones Inc. is entered in field LFA1-NAME1 (name).
13	The value WG is entered in field LFA1-SORTL (sort key).
14	The value 123 Main St. Is entered in field LFA1-STRAS (street).
15	The value Anytown is entered in field LFA1-ORT01 (city).
16	The value 55555 is entered in field LFA1-PSTLZ (zip code).
17	The value USA is entered in field LFA1-LAND1 (country).
18	Screen 0130 from program SAPMF02K is called.
19	The cursor is positioned in the table in row 01 and column LFBK-BANKS (bank key).
20	Function code (OK code) VW (continue) is triggered.
21	Screen 0210 from program SAPMF02K is called.
22	The cursor is positioned on field LFB1-FDGRV (cash management group).
23	Function code (OK code) UPDA (save)is triggered.
24	The value 196300 is entered in field LFB1-AKONT (reconciliation account).
25	The value A1 is entered in field LFB1-FDGRV (cash management group).

Table 4.2 Explanation of the Batch Input Session from Table 4.1 (cont.)

---

1 Of course, the function code (OK code) is not triggered until the input fields of the screen have been supplied with a value (i.e., after line 07).

You now have an idea of what a batch input session can do and how it is structured. Next, we come to the following two important questions:

▸ How do you create a batch input session?

▸ How do you process a batch input session?

Let's start with the simpler of the two questions, "How do you process a batch input session?"

4.2.2 How Do I Process a Batch Input Session?

In addition to *process*, the terms *run* and *play* are sometimes used in the context of processing batch input sessions. The SAP ERP system offers three different options (modes) for processing or running a batch input session:

Modes for batch input processing

▸ **Process in foreground**
In this mode, each screen is displayed with its configured data. You press the **Enter** key to go to the next screen. Any incorrect transactions can be corrected interactively. Use OK code /n to exit the current transaction and go to the next one. Use OK code /bend to cancel processing of the batch input session and resume it later (if desired).

It should be apparent that this mode is not suitable for large numbers of transactions.

▸ **Display errors only**
This mode is similar to the foreground processing mode, with one exception: transactions that are free of errors aren't processed interactively; instead, they are processed in the background. If an error occurs, background processing is interrupted and the screen where the error occurred is displayed. Once the error is corrected, processing switches from dialog back to background processing and remains there, until the next error occurs or the batch input session is processed.

▸ **In the background**
In this mode, batch input sessions are scheduled for processing in the background.

Principles of batch input processing The following basic principles apply to the processing of a batch input session (see Figure 4.1):

- ▶ Transactions that are processed successfully are removed from the batch input session.

- ▶ Incorrect transactions remain in the batch input session and must be corrected manually and processed again.

- ▶ Once all the transactions in a batch input session have been procesed successfully, the entire batch input session is deleted.

- ▶ When you create a batch input session, you can indicate that you want that session to be *retained*. In this case, the batch input session remains in the overview even after it is processed successfully. This can be useful for documentation purposes. However, even in this case, every batch input session can be processed only once.

- ▶ The processing of a batch input session is recorded in a detailed log.

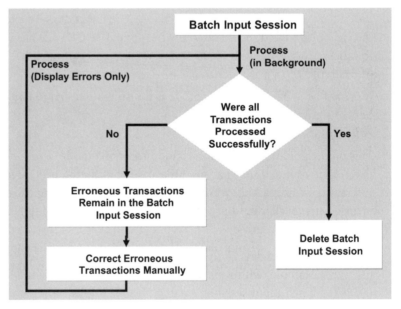

Figure 4.1 Processing Batch Input Sessions

Status   The status of a batch input session tells you the state of its processing at a glance. The following status values are possible:

► **New**
Batch input sessions with this status are ready for processing, but have not been processed yet.

► **Error**
If a batch input session has this status, this means that processing either couldn't be performed completely due to incorrect transactions, or was cancelled prematurely in foreground processing, that is, **Process in foreground** or **Display errors only**.

► **Processed**
As previously mentioned, successfully processed batch input sessions are usually deleted. If the **Retain Session** option is set for a batch input session, however, and that session is processed successfully, it is assigned this status. Processed batch input sessions are retained in the SAP ERP system until they're deleted by a periodic reorganization run.

These reorganization runs don't affect erroneous batch input sessions.

► **In process**
Batch input sessions have this status while they're being processed.

► **In background**
Batch input sessions have this status while they're being processed in the background.

► **Blocked**
This status means that you can block a batch input session to protect it against unintended processing.

Additional control options, which are available for processing batch input sessions, are briefly described here:

More options

► **Processing batch input sessions automatically**
When you migrate data to the SAP ERP system regularly — every night, for example, within the framework of a periodic data transfer — the batch input sessions created by the corresponding programs should generally be processed automatically. This automatic processing of one or more batch input sessions is achieved via a call of ABAP program RSBDCSUB. You can set the following selection parameters for this program:

   ► Name(s) of the batch input session(s)

> ▷ Creation date and time

> ▷ Status (ready for processing or error)

▶ **Deleting batch input sessions**
If you no longer need a batch input session in the list, you can delete it manually. You should not delete batch input sessions that still have unprocessed transactions, however, that is, sessions with status **New** or **Error**. In such cases, you must correct the transactions first and then continue processing, or enter the transaction data in the SAP ERP system in some other way.

▶ **Blocking and releasing batch input sessions**
You can block a batch input session to prevent the system from processing it before a specified date.

Transaction SM35   These (and other) functions involving batch input sessions are located in Transaction SM35 (batch input overview). You can also reach this transaction via the following menu path: **System • Services • Batch Input • Sessions**.

Let us now turn to the more difficult of the two questions we asked regarding batch input sessions.

4.2.3   How Do I Create a Batch Input Session?

There are three basic ways in which to create a batch input session (see Figure 4.2).

Batch input session from recording   ▶ You can use the SAP Transaction Recorder to record transaction flows. These are called *batch input recordings* or simply *recordings*. You can use these recordings to create a batch input session at the touch of a button. This option is described in more detail in Section 4.5.

Batch input session from program   ▶ You can use any suitable ABAP program to create batch input sessions. We differentiate between two different types of programs:

> ▷ The SAP ERP system provides an option for generating an ABAP program from a batch input recording at the touch of a button. Programs created in this manner usually must be revised manually. This technique is introduced in Section 4.4.

> ▷ In addition, the SAP ERP system comes with various *standard batch input programs*. These programs are described in detail in the next section.

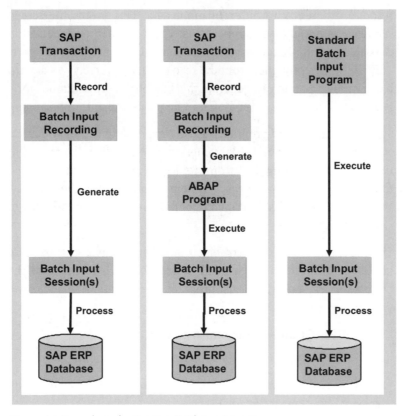

Figure 4.2 Procedures for Creating Batch Input Sessions

The three procedures for generating batch input sessions are contrasted in Figure 4.2.

4.3   Standard Batch Input Programs

The SAP ERP system comes with a variety of batch input programs, which are called *standard batch input programs*.

Standard batch input programs aren't generated automatically; they're programmed manually, and they're usually much more complex than automatically generated batch input programs for the following reason:

Manual programming

A program that is generated from a recording models the process flow of that recording precisely. SAP transactions, however, can respond differently to different input data. This means the screen sequence is not always identical; instead, it frequently depends on the selected input data. A generated batch input program supports only the screen sequence from the recording. Conversely, a standard batch input program can generate the suitable screen sequence for a given set of input data, enabling it to be processed without errors.

Specially structured file as input

Standard batch input programs usually expect input files to have a special structure. From the data migration perspective, the trick is to transform the existing data from the legacy system to this required format. Tools such as the Legacy System Migration Workbench (LSM Workbench), which is described in detail in Chapter 7, can help you with this task.

The most important standard batch input programs are introduced briefly below. For more detailed information, please refer to the online documentation for each program.

4.3.1 RFBIDE00 – Customer Master

Batch input program RFBIDE00 supports the following functions:

- Create customer master data, including credit limit data and bank master data (Transaction XD01)
- Change customer master data, including credit limit data and bank master data (Transaction XD02)
- Block and unblock customers (Transaction XD05)
- Set and reset deletion flag for customers (Transaction XD06)
- Maintain credit limit (Transaction FD32)

Any lock fields or deletion indicators passed on during the creation (Transaction XD01) and modification (Transaction XD02) of customer master data transactions are also processed.

The RFBIDE00 program is the foundation of the detailed example used in Chapter 7.

4.3.2 RFBIKR00 – Vendor Master

Batch input program RFBIKR00 supports the following functions:

▶ Create vendor master data (Transaction XK01)

▶ Change vendor master data (Transaction XK02)

▶ Block and unblock vendors (Transaction XK05)

▶ Set and reset deletion flag for vendors (Transaction XK06)

Any lock fields or deletion indicators passed on during the creation (Transaction XK01) and modification (Transaction XK02) of vendor master data transactions are also processed.

4.3.3 RFBISA00 – G/L Account Master

Batch input program RFBISA00 supports the following functions:

▶ Create G/L account master data (Transaction FS01)

▶ Change G/L account master data (Transaction FS02)

▶ Block and unblock G/L account master data (Transaction FS05)

▶ Set and reset deletion flag for G/L account master data (Transaction FS06)

4.3.4 RFBIBL00 – Financial Documents

Batch input program RFBIBL00 supports the following functions:

▶ Post document (Transaction FB01)

▶ Foreign currency valuation (Transaction FBB1)

▶ Enter accrual/deferral document (Transaction FBS1)

▶ Park document (Transaction FBV1)

▶ Post with clearing (Transaction FB05)

The RFBIBL00 program is primarily intended to create batch input sessions. However, you can also use the Type of Data Transfer parameter to create documents immediately with Call Transaction (see Section 4.4.5) or Direct Input.

4.3.5 RCSBI010, RCSBI020, RCSBI030, RCSBI040 – Material BOMs

Batch input program RCSBI010 supports the creation of BOMs (bill of materials) without long texts. You can create document structures, equipment BOMs, material BOMs, standard objects, and BOMs for functional locations. The following transactions are supported:

▶ Create document structures (Transaction CV11)

▶ Create equipment BOMs (Transaction IB01)

▶ Create material BOMs (Transaction CS01)

▶ Create standard objects (Transaction CS51)

▶ Create BOMs for functional locations (Transaction IB11)

Batch input program RCSBI020 permits changes to BOMs without long texts. You can change document structures, equipment BOMs, material BOMs, standard objects, and BOMs for functional locations. The following transactions are available:

▶ Change document structures (Transaction CV12)

▶ Change equipment BOMs (Transaction IB02)

▶ Change material BOMs (Transaction CS02)

▶ Change standard objects (Transaction CS52)

▶ Change BOMs for functional locations (Transaction IB12)

Two other batch input programs, RCSBI030 and RCSBI040, which let you create variant BOMs without long texts and BOMs with long texts (respectively) and support the same transactions as RCSBI010, are also available.

4.3.6 RM06BBI0 – Purchase Requisitions

Batch input program RM06BBI0 enables you to create purchase requisitions in the SAP ERP system.

You don't have to select a transaction for this program because the program automatically selects it.

4.3.7 RM07MMBL – Material Documents

You can use program RM07MMBL to create batch input sessions for goods movements. The data used to create the batch input session must have the same structure as ABAP Dictionary structure BMSEG.

4.4 Batch Input Recording: General Approach

The following sections describe how you can use the batch input technique to migrate legacy data to SAP ERP, based on the example of open debit items. The procedure can be divided into the following steps:

Steps for data migration

1. Identify the transaction that you want to use to transfer the legacy data to the SAP ERP system.

2. Implement this transaction with a typical data record and record it with the ERP transaction recorder.

3. Use the recording to create the ABAP source code with the appropriate pushbutton.

4. Although the ABAP program created in this manner is the foundation for the data migration, you will still have to customize it to meet specific requirements.

4.4.1 Creating the Batch Input Recording

Once you've decided which transaction you want to use to migrate your open debit items to SAP ERP — Transaction FB01 in this case — you can simulate the data migration with a sample data record. To do so, use the transaction recorder. You can access it via the following menu path: **System • Services • Batch Input • Overview** (Transaction SM35). Then, choose **Recording** and then **New Recording**. The dialog box shown in Figure 4.3 opens.

Creating the recording

Enter a name for the recording along with the transaction code that you want to use to transfer the open debit items to SAP ERP (Transaction FB01). To make it easier to manage your various recordings, we recommend that you include the transaction code in the name of the recording in some way (for example, Z_FB01). After you've maintained both fields, click the **Start recording** button to start entering a sample data record.

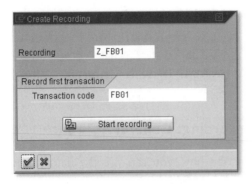

Figure 4.3 Creating a Recording

Immediately, you'll see the same screen template that you would otherwise see in the first screen for document entry in Transaction FB01. You can maintain the document header data here (see Figure 4.4).

Maintaining data During data entry, you should maintain all the mandatory fields — or *required entry fields* in the SAP terminology — and all the fields that you want to provide for the data migration in your input file. Using this approach, you can ensure that the recording will contain all the information required for the data migration.

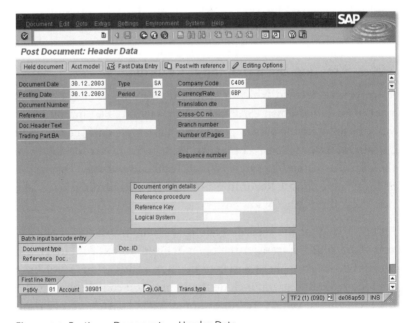

Figure 4.4 Posting a Document — Header Data

To avoid confusion, you should note that a recording with the transaction recorder is almost identical to dialog processing. This means that you must navigate through the respective entry templates for the transaction as usual and make your entries, which you complete by posting. The session does not merely simulate a transaction; the update triggers a change in the database. The only difference with strict dialog processing is that the data entry is recorded in the transaction recorder simultaneously. Its activities are documented by occasional messages in the status bar.

Change in the database

Once you've specified your entries in the document header, set posting key (**PstKy**) 01 to indicate that the next **Account** to be posted to, account 28306, is a customer account, that a debit posting is involved, and that it represents an invoice. When you press **Enter**, the screen shown in Figure 4.5 displays.

Customer item

To keep things simple, maintain only the **Amount** field, which reflects the gross amount of the sales invoice. The offsetting posting is made in credit to G/L account 999990, which was configured especially for the data migration, as indicated by posting key 50 (see Section 2.2.5). Pressing **Enter** displays the screen shown in Figure 4.6, where you also have to maintain the **Amount** field. Because this is the last line item, you can enter "*" instead of the amount. The SAP ERP system calculates the remaining amount automatically in this case.

G/L account item

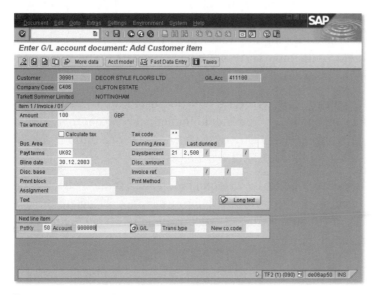

Figure 4.5 Posting a Document — Customer Item

65

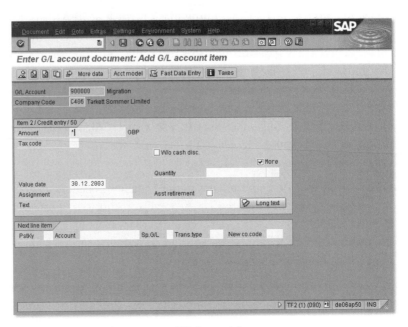

Figure 4.6 Posting a Document — G/L Account Item

The **Post** button triggers both a change to the database and the end of the recording. You go directly to the editor of the transaction recorder, which is shown in Figure 4.7.

Editor The transaction recorder provides information on the **program used for the transaction** you just recorded and which screens (**dynpros**) were processed during the transaction. You also see a list of all the table fields with their corresponding content that you maintained during the recording.

If you compare this recording with the batch input session introduced in Section 4.2.1, you should immediately recognize a similarity, which also explains why, at the mere touch of a button, you can create a batch input session from a recording.

Cancel If you want to conduct the data migration later, in the same client in which you made the recording, you must cancel or delete the data record that you just created in order to avoid falsifying the results of the data migration.

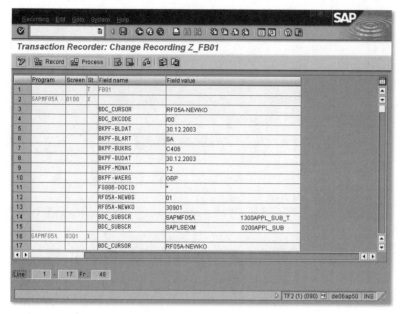

Figure 4.7 End of Recording — Transaction Recorder

There are several rules that you should follow when recording transactions:

Rules for recording

▶ Before you start the recording, ensure that you know how the transaction works.

▶ Don't toggle unnecessarily between screens.

▶ Don't double-click on lists.

▶ Don't trigger any error messages during the recording.

▶ Once you've finished the recording, don't make any customizing changes that alter the screens or their sequence within the transaction.

Once you have pressed **Save** to save the recording, you can generate the ABAP source code in the next step.

Generating
the program

4.4.2 Generating an ABAP Program from a Batch Input Recording

To do so, press **F3** to return to the recording overview and then choose **Create Program** (see Figure 4.8).

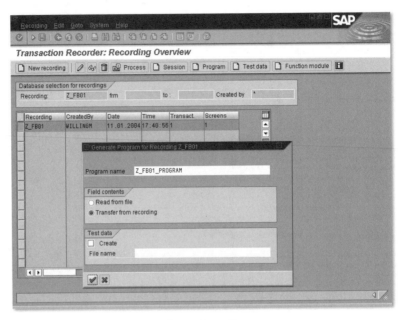

Figure 4.8 Generating a Program from a Recording

Enter a **program name**, such as Z_FB01 _PROGRAM.

Options for field contents

The **Field Contents** section provides two options:

▸ **Read from file**
The field contents from the recording can be replaced by the technical ERP field texts.

▸ **Transfer from recording**
The field contents from the recording can be used in the program to be generated.

To make the connection between the recording and the programming immediately apparent, the option **Transfer from recording** was selected here, even though the other option may involve less manual intervention during the subsequent revision of the program.

In the next dialog boxes, you're prompted to enter a **Title**, a **Package**, and a **Transport Request** for the program.

ABAP program

The result is a program with the following logic:

```
1  REPORT Z_FB01_PROGRAM NO STANDARD PAGE HEADING LINE-SIZE
   255.
2  INCLUDE bdcrecx1.
```

```
 3  START-OF-SELECTION.
 4  PERFORM open_group.
 5  PERFORM bdc_dynpro      USING 'SAPMF05A' '0100'.
 6  PERFORM bdc_field       USING 'BDC_CURSOR'
 7                                'RF05A-NEWKO'.
 8  PERFORM bdc_field       USING 'BDC_OKCODE'
 9                                '/00'.
10  PERFORM bdc_field       USING 'BKPF-BLDAT'
11                                '31.01.2007'.
12  PERFORM bdc_field       USING 'BKPF-BLART'
13                                'SA'.
14  PERFORM bdc_field       USING 'BKPF-BUKRS'
15                                '1000'.
16  PERFORM bdc_field       USING 'BKPF-BUDAT'
17                                '31.01.2007'.
18  PERFORM bdc_field       USING 'BKPF-WAERS'
19                                'EUR'.
20  PERFORM bdc_field       USING 'RF05A-NEWBS'
21                                '01'.
22  PERFORM bdc_field       USING 'RF05A-NEWKO'
23                                '10101'.
24  PERFORM bdc_dynpro      USING 'SAPMF05A' '0301'.
25  PERFORM bdc_field       USING 'BDC_CURSOR'
26                                'RF05A-NEWKO'.
27  PERFORM bdc_field       USING 'BDC_OKCODE'
28                                '/00'.
29  PERFORM bdc_field       USING 'BSEG-WRBTR'
30                                '100'.
31  PERFORM bdc_field       USING 'RF05A-NEWBS'
32                                '50'.
33  PERFORM bdc_field       USING 'RF05A-NEWKO'
34                                '900001'.
35  PERFORM bdc_dynpro      USING 'SAPMF05A' '0300'.
36  PERFORM bdc_field       USING 'BDC_CURSOR'
37                                'BSEG-WRBTR'.
38  PERFORM bdc_field       USING 'BDC_OKCODE'
39                                '/00'.
40  PERFORM bdc_field       USING 'BSEG-WRBTR'
41                                '100'.
42  PERFORM bdc_field       USING 'BDC_OKCODE'
43                                '=BU'.
44  PERFORM bdc_transaction USING 'FB01'.
45  PERFORM close_group.
```

Listing 4.1 Z_FB01_PROGRAM — ABAP Program Generated from a Recording

<table>
<tr><td>Basis for data migration</td><td>This automatically generated program already contains most of the commands and subroutines required for the subsequent data migration. Therefore, we recommend that you use this fragment as the basis for the actual data migration program and adapt it accordingly.</td></tr>
</table>

Basis for data migration | This automatically generated program already contains most of the commands and subroutines required for the subsequent data migration. Therefore, we recommend that you use this fragment as the basis for the actual data migration program and adapt it accordingly.

What does this program logic do?

PERFORM open_group | Simply put, the PERFORM open_group command in line 4 opens a batch input session. Later in the program, this batch input session is filled with the screens (dynpros) and field contents that resulted from the prior recording of Transaction FB01. To underscore this fact, let's analyze program lines 5, 10, and 11 more precisely.

PERFORM bdc_dynpro | PERFORM bdc_dynpro USING 'SAPMF05A' '0100' initially means that a subroutine named bdc_dynpro is called with the PERFORM command. The USING supplement passes the two parameters in single quotation marks to subroutine bdc_dynpro. This involves screen 0100 (see Figure 4.4) of program SAPMF05A. Program SAPMF05A is the main Financial Accounting program and the basis for Transaction FB01. You have now defined which screen template has to be processed, along with the corresponding field contents.

PERFORM bdc_field | PERFORM bdc_field USING 'BKPF-BLDAT' '31.01.2007' calls another subroutine, bdc_field, which is also assigned two parameters. The first parameter is the **Document Date** field, BLDAT, which appears in document header table BKPF and can be referenced using BKPF-BLDAT. The second passed parameter is the format of the document date resulting from the recording (31.01.2007 in this case). This way, it is clearly indicated that the document data of the open debit item is January 31 2007.

The situation in program lines 12 and 13 is analogous: PERFORM bdc_field USING 'BKPF-BLART' 'SA' dictates that the open item should be posted with document type "SA".

bdc_dynpro and bdc_field | As you can see from this brief explanation, the interaction between PERFORM bdc_dynpro and PERFORM bdc_field ultimately determines which screen (dynpro) and which fields are assigned values. Program lines 5 through 23 all refer to screen 0100, the document header. The information for the customer item (see Figure 4.5) is determined in program lines 24 through 34. The last screen to fill, 0300, is the G/L account line item (see Figure 4.6) and is determined by program lines 35 through 43.

Once all the document information is known, PERFORM bdc_transac-tion USING 'FB01' calls a subroutine named bdc_transaction, which uses Transaction FB01 to post the document passed on in the parameters. Therefore, PERFORM bdc_transaction concludes the transaction with a posting and is *de facto* the last statement in the batch input session (see program line 44).

PERFORM bdc_transaction

Before you can process a batch input session, however, you must first close the open session. You do this with PERFORM close_group, which doesn't require any parameters because the currently opened session is closed automatically (see program line 45).

PERFORM close_group

Now that you have read the above, you may be wondering exactly what the individual subroutines do. So far, all you know is that these subroutines — also called *form routines* — are assigned parameters. Simply put, these form routines themselves consist of *function modules*, subroutines with a clearly defined interface that can be called by any ABAP program. These function modules continue to process the parameters previously passed onto the form routine in order to enable their subsequent placement in an executable batch input session.

The advantage of this approach is that you don't have to worry about any of these technical details. The flow logic of all the form routines and the function modules they use is summarized in program line 2: include bdcrecx1 calls the additional ABAP code of program bdcrecx1, which is responsible for the overall batch input control. Among other things, this program defines how the data records will be processed. When the program starts, for example, you can choose whether you want to create a batch input session, which will then be processed with Transaction SM35, or whether you want to process the data records with the *call transaction* procedure, which posts the data records directly. Chapter 10 addresses the advantages and disadvantages of both procedures.

include bdcrecx1

Because the included program bdcrecx1 is not essential and this book is not a programming manual, we won't discuss this program in any detail here. For more information, you can examine this program in greater detail in the SAP ERP system.

You can summarize your activities up to this point as follows: the automatically generated ABAP program can apply the batch input method to create a batch input session, which can then be processed.

Conclusion

Alternatively, processing can also take place using the *call transaction* procedure.

This program, however, cannot be used for data migration in its current form for the following reasons:

- It can only process a single data record.
- It permits only the constant values from the recording.

Because both the number of data records and the instances of the field contents are variable during data migration, however, the program logic must be modified accordingly to take these factors into account.

4.4.3 Modifying the Generated ABAP Program

Migration file

Before you modify the coding of the program from Section 4.4.2 to meet the requirements of data migration, you should first create a table-like file containing the open debit items that you want to migrate. Because you maintained only the required entry fields when recording Transaction FB01 in Section 4.4.1, this information should be available for all the data records you have to migrate. This file, opened with Microsoft Excel, could resemble Figure 4.9:

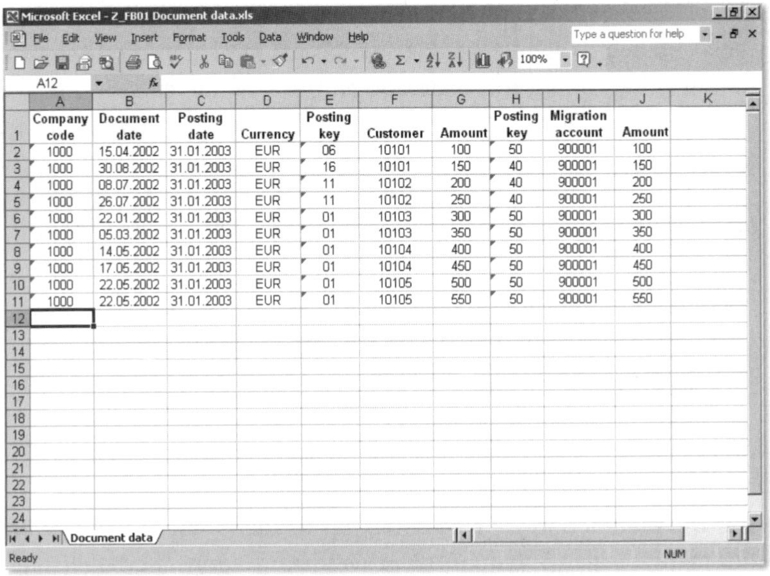

Company code	Document date	Posting date	Currency	Posting key	Customer	Amount	Posting key	Migration account	Amount
1000	15.04.2002	31.01.2003	EUR	06	10101	100	50	900001	100
1000	30.08.2002	31.01.2003	EUR	16	10101	150	40	900001	150
1000	08.07.2002	31.01.2003	EUR	11	10102	200	40	900001	200
1000	26.07.2002	31.01.2003	EUR	11	10102	250	40	900001	250
1000	22.01.2002	31.01.2003	EUR	01	10103	300	50	900001	300
1000	05.03.2002	31.01.2003	EUR	01	10103	350	50	900001	350
1000	14.05.2002	31.01.2003	EUR	01	10104	400	50	900001	400
1000	17.05.2002	31.01.2003	EUR	01	10104	450	50	900001	450
1000	22.05.2002	31.01.2003	EUR	01	10105	500	50	900001	500
1000	22.05.2002	31.01.2003	EUR	01	10105	550	50	900001	550

Figure 4.9 Requirements of the Supplied Data

Missing data

In other situations, it is entirely possible that you won't be able to provide values for every field in every data record you maintained during the recording. Consider the phone numbers during a master data migration, for example. In such situations, you must supply the field contents that are required during the recording (required entry fields). If necessary, you can also change the attribute of the respective fields from *required entry* to *optional entry* in Customizing, and then change it back after the migration.

Data requirements

The task at hand is to import the data shown in Figure 4.9 into the SAP ERP system and process it there. To do so, a local file should already be saved on your computer. Because the SAP ERP system can process text files more easily than other formats, you should save the migration file in **Text (Tab-Delimited) (*.txt)** format. To avoid complicating the program unnecessarily, ensure that the file doesn't contain any blank lines, since special program logic would be required to deal with the resulting exception situations. The same applies to the first line of the file, which is usually reserved for the field names. Delete this line to ensure that all the data records have the same structure; therefore, the program won't have to handle any one line differently (see Figure 4.10).

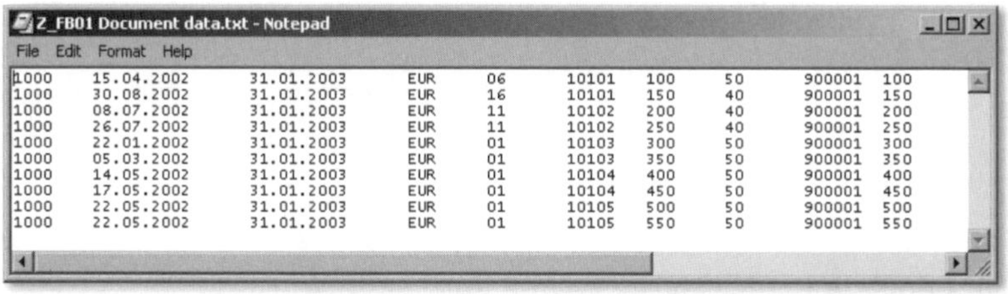

1000	15.04.2002	31.01.2003	EUR	06	10101	100	50	900001	100
1000	30.08.2002	31.01.2003	EUR	16	10101	150	40	900001	150
1000	08.07.2002	31.01.2003	EUR	11	10102	200	40	900001	200
1000	26.07.2002	31.01.2003	EUR	11	10102	250	40	900001	250
1000	22.01.2002	31.01.2003	EUR	01	10103	300	50	900001	300
1000	05.03.2002	31.01.2003	EUR	01	10103	350	50	900001	350
1000	14.05.2002	31.01.2003	EUR	01	10104	400	50	900001	400
1000	17.05.2002	31.01.2003	EUR	01	10104	450	50	900001	450
1000	22.05.2002	31.01.2003	EUR	01	10105	500	50	900001	500
1000	22.05.2002	31.01.2003	EUR	01	10105	550	50	900001	550

Figure 4.10 Text File for Upload

How can you load a text file into the SAP ERP system?

Subroutine load_data

Once again, we recommend that you use the *subroutine technique* to provide for a clear program structure. A subroutine (form routine), `load_data`, which is assigned the path of the migration file on your PC as a parameter, is responsible for loading the data to the SAP ERP system and adheres to the following logic:

```
FORM LOAD_DATA USING FILE.
CALL FUNCTION 'GUI_UPLOAD'
  EXPORTING
```

```
4        FILENAME                = FILE
5        FILETYPE                = 'ASC'
6        HAS_FIELD_SEPARATOR     = 'X'
7     TABLES
8        DATA_TAB                = ITAB
9     EXCEPTIONS
10       FILE_OPEN_ERROR         = 1
11       FILE_READ_ERROR         = 2
12       NO_BATCH                = 3
13       GUI_REFUSE_FILETRANSFER = 4
14       INVALID_TYPE            = 5
15       NO_AUTHORITY            = 6
16       UNKNOWN_ERROR           = 7
17       BAD_DATA_FORMAT         = 8
18       HEADER_NOT_ALLOWED      = 9
19       SEPARATOR_NOT_ALLOWED   = 10
20       HEADER_TOO_LONG         = 11
21       UNKNOWN_DP_ERROR        = 12
22       ACCESS_DENIED           = 13
23       DP_OUT_OF_MEMORY        = 14
24       DISK_FULL               = 15
25       DP_TIMEOUT              = 16
26       OTHERS                  = 17.
27 ENDFORM.
```

Listing 4.2 Subroutine LOAD_DATA with Function Module UPLOAD

Function module GUI_Upload

As program line 2 indicates, the subroutine shown in Listing 4.2 uses CALL FUNCTION 'GUI_UPLOAD' to call a function module named GUI_UPLOAD, which, in turn, is assigned various parameters for processing with EXPORTING. Specifically, these parameters are the file name, represented by the FILE placeholder, and the file format ASC, as well as the flag that specifies that the fields in the file are divided by separators.

Furthermore, the function module is assigned an internal table, ITAB, via TABLES.

The logic of the function module now places the migration file, FILE, in internal table ITAB, which is then accessed later on in the program.

Internal table ITAB

To ensure proper results, ITAB must have the same structure as the migration file. Specifically, this means the company code, which is contained in the first column of the migration file (see Figures 4.9 and 4.10), must also be displayed in the first column of the internal

74

table. Similarly, the document date and posting date, which appear in columns 2 and 3 of the migration file, must also be displayed in columns 2 and 3 of the internal table. The same applies to the remaining fields. If you declare internal table ITAB as shown below, you will have a one-to-one match with the migration file, ensuring the correct transformation of the field contents:

```
DATA: BEGIN OF ITAB OCCURS 0,
      BUKRS  LIKE BKPF-BUKRS,
      BLDAT  LIKE BKPF-BLDAT,
      BUDAT  LIKE BKPF-BUDAT,
      WAERS  LIKE BKPF-WAERS,
      BSCHL1 LIKE BSEG-BSCHL,
      KUNNR  LIKE BSEG-KUNNR,
      WRBTR1(8),
      BSCHL2 LIKE BSEG-BSCHL,
      HKONT  LIKE BSEG-HKONT,
      WRBTR2(8),
      END OF ITAB.
```

Listing 4.3 Declaration of Internal Table ITAB

The field names of internal table ITAB are based on the respective field names in the SAP ERP system and their *data types* are assigned accordingly, except for the amount fields WRBTR1 and WRBTR2. These fields are defined as eight-place character fields, because batch input processing would not fill the amount fields if the declaration were like BSEG-WRBTR, which means the migration data could not be processed.

Defining amount fields as characters

As you can see from program lines 9 to 26, the function module can also deal with exceptions. An exception occurs whenever the function module has calls with parameters that cause an error. The **Exceptions** enable the function module to catch such errors and inform the calling program of their cause. This helps you avoid runtime errors. Because your data migration program does not support error handling, this component of the function module is not discussed here.

Error detection

With the modifications you have made, you can now load your dataset into SAP ERP. To process it, however, you will need to make further changes to the automatically generated program from Section 4.4.2.

Replacing
constants with
variables
As previously mentioned, this program can process only data records
whose values are constant and determined by the underlying recording. You now have to replace these fixed values with *variables* in
order to process a number of different data records.

After the upload, all of the data records to be migrated are already
contained in internal table ITAB, which you now have to process
sequentially, that is, data record by data record. Therefore, ITAB has
to be included in a *loop* that reads all the data records in sequence
and places them in a batch input session accordingly. You can process an internal table in the SAP ERP system with the statement LOOP
AT ITAB ... ENDLOOP.

```
LOOP AT ITAB.
  PERFORM bdc_dynpro      USING 'SAPMF05A' '0100'.
  PERFORM bdc_field       USING 'BDC_CURSOR'
                                'RF05A-NEWKO'.
  PERFORM bdc_field       USING 'BDC_OKCODE'
                                '/00'.
  PERFORM bdc_field       USING 'BKPF-BLDAT'
                                ITAB-BLDAT.
  PERFORM bdc_field       USING 'BKPF-BLART'
                                'SA'.
  PERFORM bdc_field       USING 'BKPF-BUKRS'
                                ITAB-BUKRS.
  PERFORM bdc_field       USING 'BKPF-BUDAT'
                                ITAB-BUDAT.
  PERFORM bdc_field       USING 'BKPF-WAERS'
                                ITAB-WAERS.
  PERFORM bdc_field       USING 'RF05A-NEWBS'
                                ITAB-BSCHL1.
  PERFORM bdc_field       USING 'RF05A-NEWKO'
                                ITAB-KUNNR.
  PERFORM bdc_dynpro      USING 'SAPMF05A' '0301'.
  PERFORM bdc_field       USING 'BDC_CURSOR'
                                'RF05A-NEWKO'.
  PERFORM bdc_field       USING 'BDC_OKCODE'
                                '/00'.
  PERFORM bdc_field       USING 'BSEG-WRBTR'
                                ITAB-WRBTR1.
  PERFORM bdc_field       USING 'RF05A-NEWBS'
                                ITAB-BSCHL2.
  PERFORM bdc_field       USING 'RF05A-NEWKO'
                                ITAB-HKONT.
  PERFORM bdc_dynpro      USING 'SAPMF05A' '0300'.
  PERFORM bdc_field       USING 'BDC_CURSOR'
                                'BSEG-WRBTR'.
  PERFORM bdc_field       USING 'BDC_OKCODE'
                                '/00'.
```

```
     PERFORM bdc_field      USING 'BSEG-WRBTR'
                                  ITAB-WRBTR2.
     PERFORM bdc_field      USING 'BDC_OKCODE'
                                  '=BU'.
     PERFORM BDC_TRANSACTION USING 'FB01'.
ENDLOOP.
```

Listing 4.4 LOOP Statement for Processing Internal Table ITAB

The coding above is nearly identical to the coding from Section 4.4.2.   **Loop processing**
The only difference is that the constant field values — such as
"31.01.2007" for the document date and "1000" for the company
code — have now been replaced by the variable contents of internal
table ITAB, ITAB-BLDAT, and ITAB-BUKRS. Consequently, you can process different field values from the ITAB table during each loop pass.
To reiterate: Passing the loop once fills all the screens — document
header, customer line, and G/L account line item — with the current
field values of table ITAB and places them in the open batch input
session. Each pass is concluded with the statement to post the document with Transaction FB01. Therefore, the number of loop passes
determines the number of documents to be posted. Once the last
data record in the internal table ITAB has been processed, the batch
input session can be closed.

Before you see the complete data migration program, you should   **Special program**
first learn about several special details that you have to deal with   **modifications**
when testing the program: When you record a transaction with the
transaction recorder, the *cursor position* in the current screen is
always recorded as well. Because the cursor position is irrelevant for
the data migration in this example — even though it can have a negative impact in rare cases — the relevant passages have been com-
mented out with an asterisk (*) in the program.

```
REPORT Z_FB01_PROGRAM.
************************Declarations *******************
TABLES: BSEG,BKPF.
INCLUDE BDCRECX1.
DATA: BEGIN OF BDC_DATA OCCURS 0.
      INCLUDE STRUCTURE BDCDATA.
DATA: END OF BDC_DATA.
DATA: BEGIN OF ITAB OCCURS 0,
      BUKRS  LIKE BKPF-BUKRS,
      BLDAT  LIKE BKPF-BLDAT,
      BUDAT  LIKE BKPF-BUDAT,
      WAERS  LIKE BKPF-WAERS,
```

```
               BSCHL1 LIKE BSEG-BSCHL,
               KUNNR  LIKE BSEG-KUNNR,
               WRBTR1(8),
               BSCHL2 LIKE BSEG-BSCHL,
               HKONT  LIKE BSEG-HKONT,
               WRBTR2(8),
               END OF ITAB.
********************** Initializations **************
START-OF-SELECTION.
  CLEAR BDC_DATA.
  REFRESH BDC_DATA.
*********************** Upload **********************
  PERFORM load_data USING
  'C:\_Willinger\Data for FB01.txt'.
**** Call Transaction / Batch input in case of error *****
  PERFORM OPEN_GROUP.   "Open batch input file
  LOOP AT ITAB.

  PERFORM bdc_dynpro       USING 'SAPMF05A' '0100'.
  *PERFORM bdc_field       USING 'BDC_CURSOR'
  *                              'RF05A-NEWKO'.
  PERFORM bdc_field        USING 'BDC_OKCODE'
                                 '/00'.
  PERFORM bdc_field        USING 'BKPF-BLDAT'
                                 ITAB-BLDAT.
  PERFORM bdc_field        USING 'BKPF-BLART'
                                 'SA'.
  PERFORM bdc_field        USING 'BKPF-BUKRS'
                                 ITAB-BUKRS.
  PERFORM bdc_field        USING 'BKPF-BUDAT'
                                 ITAB-BUDAT.
  PERFORM bdc_field        USING 'BKPF-WAERS'
                                 ITAB-WAERS.
  PERFORM bdc_field        USING 'RF05A-NEWBS'
                                 ITAB-BSCHL1.
  PERFORM bdc_field        USING 'RF05A-NEWKO'
                                 ITAB-KUNNR.
  PERFORM bdc_dynpro       USING 'SAPMF05A' '0301'.
  *PERFORM bdc_field       USING 'BDC_CURSOR'
  *                              'RF05A-NEWKO'.
  PERFORM bdc_field        USING 'BDC_OKCODE'
                                 '/00'.
  PERFORM bdc_field        USING 'BSEG-WRBTR'
                                 ITAB-WRBTR1.
  PERFORM bdc_field        USING 'RF05A-NEWBS'
                                 ITAB-BSCHL2.
  PERFORM bdc_field        USING 'RF05A-NEWKO'
                                 ITAB-HKONT.
  PERFORM bdc_dynpro       USING 'SAPMF05A' '0300'.
  *PERFORM bdc_field       USING 'BDC_CURSOR'
  *                              'BSEG-WRBTR'.
  PERFORM bdc_field        USING 'BDC_OKCODE'
```

```
                                     '/00'.
    PERFORM bdc_field        USING 'BSEG-WRBTR'
                                    ITAB-WRBTR2.
    PERFORM bdc_field        USING 'BDC_OKCODE'
                                    '=BU'.
    PERFORM BDC_TRANSACTION USING 'FB01'.
ENDLOOP.
PERFORM CLOSE_GROUP.
**************************** Forms ******************
FORM load_data USING FILE.
   CALL FUNCTION 'GUI_UPLOAD'
      EXPORTING
         FILENAME                = FILE
         FILETYPE                = 'ASC'
         HAS_FIELD_SEPARATOR     = 'X'
      TABLES
         DATA_TAB                = ITAB
      EXCEPTIONS
         FILE_OPEN_ERROR         = 1
         FILE_READ_ERROR         = 2
         NO_BATCH                = 3
         GUI_REFUSE_FILETRANSFER = 4
         INVALID_TYPE            = 5
         NO_AUTHORITY            = 6
         UNKNOWN_ERROR           = 7
         BAD_DATA_FORMAT         = 8
         HEADER_NOT_ALLOWED      = 9
         SEPARATOR_NOT_ALLOWED   = 10
         HEADER_TOO_LONG         = 11
         UNKNOWN_DP_ERROR        = 12
         ACCESS_DENIED           = 13
         DP_OUT_OF_MEMORY        = 14
         DISK_FULL               = 15
         DP_TIMEOUT              = 16
         OTHERS                  = 17.
ENDFORM.
```

Listing 4.5 LOOP Statement for Processing Internal Table ITAB

If you run the program shown in Listing 4.5 via menu path **System • Services • Reporting** (or alternatively using Transaction Code SE38 or SA38), you can determine whether you want to use the batch input technique or **Call transaction** (see Figure 4.11).

Executing the program

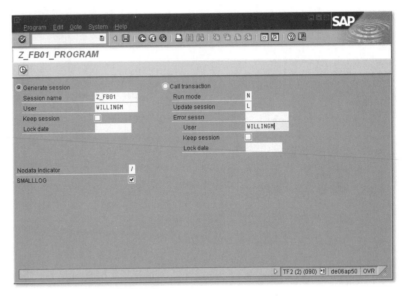

Figure 4.11 Selection Screen of Program Z_FB01_PROGRAM

4.4.4 Creating and Processing the Batch Input Session

If you use the batch input technique to process the data, only the left side of the selection screen from Figure 4.11 is relevant.

Selection fields

Therefore, select **Create Session** and choose a **Session name** for the generated session. As soon as program Z_FB01_PROGRAM is finished, the session will appear with this name — Z_FB01 in this case — in the session overview (Transaction SM35). In the **User** field, enter the name of an SAP user whose authorizations you want to use to process the session. This field is set to your user name by default, but can be overwritten. If you want to retain correctly processed sessions in the SAP ERP system — for logging purposes, for example — you must check the **Keep session** checkbox. If you enter a date in the **Lock date** field, the session cannot be processed before the specified date. This flag can help you to organize large data migration projects with multiple batch input sessions, because you can prevent the sessions from being processed before the final data transfer is complete. Use the **Nodata indicator** to define which character will be written to the batch input session when the system identifies missing data. The "/" character is proposed by default. You can then select whether you want a small log or summary log of the data transfer.

Generating and processing the batch input session

Once you have set all the parameters, pressing **Execute** immediately generates a batch input session, which appears in the batch input overview (Transaction SM35) under the session name you specified previously (i.e., Z_FB01). When you select this session and click on **Execute**, you can select the processing options in the dialog box that subsequently opens.

Because the duration of batch input processing is primarily determined by the data volume, you should always select background processing for sessions involving 1,000 or more data records. When smaller data volumes are involved, you can interactively correct any errors that occur immediately, which is supported in the **Display errors only** mode. Here, the **Process in foreground** mode is not recommended. You should use this mode only if you want to test the data migration with a few example data records.

The process described above is illustrated schematically in Figure 4.12.

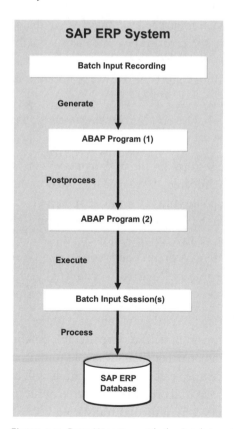

Figure 4.12 Data Migration with the Batch Input Procedure

4.4.5 Call Transaction and Batch Input Session in Case of Error

If you choose the call transaction method for performance reasons, the right side of the selection screen from Figure 4.11 is relevant. Chapter 10 assesses the various techniques and reviews the advantages and disadvantages of these methods.

Selection fields First, choose the **Call transaction** option. Then, select the **Processing Mode**, which determines whether the session will be processed in dialog or in the background. Three options are available:

▶ Processing mode "A" means display all. Because every screen template is displayed, this option is feasible for testing only individual data records. It isn't a practical alternative for data migration.

▶ Processing mode "E" displays only the errors in dialog, while error-free transactions are run in the background. Background processing continues until an error is encountered. If an error is encountered, the call transaction procedure changes to dialog processing in order to enable the error to be corrected manually. Once the data is corrected, the system switches back to background processing and continues until the next error occurs, or processing is complete.

▶ Processing mode "N" is pure background processing without any dialog.

Update mode In the next step, you define the settings for the **update mode**; that is, you define how the data will be updated. "S" stands for synchronous update, "A" for asynchronous update, and "L" for local update. If you want to update error-free transactions with **Call transaction**, but place erroneous transactions in a batch input session for subsequent processing, which is explicitly recommended for background processing, you must enter a name in the **Error session** field with which you can identify and process the error session in the session overview (Transaction SM35).

If you don't specify an error session here, the system won't be able to collect erroneous transactions or make them available for subsequent interactive processing. Instead, error-free transactions will be posted as expected. Erroneous data records are merely recorded in the log, however, and are excluded from the data migration.

The fields **User**, **Lock date**, and **Session** were introduced in Section 4.4.2 and have the same meanings here.

The following parameters are recommended for data migrations based on the call transaction procedure: **processing mode** "N," **update mode** "L," **error session** "X," **user** "Y."

Parameterization

Once you have maintained the selection fields, click on **Execute** to start updating the data with **Call Transaction**.

Figure 4.13 shows a schematic diagram of the call transaction procedure.

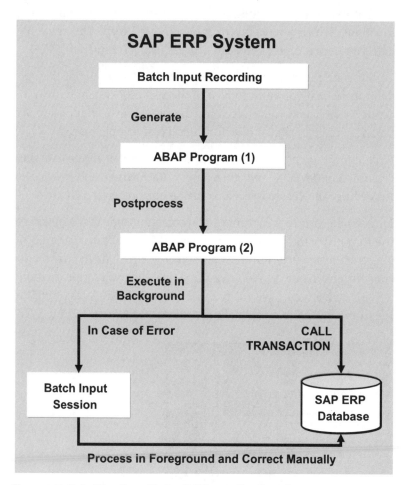

Figure 4.13 Data Migration with the Call Transaction Procedure

4.5 Batch Input Recording Combined with Microsoft Word Mail Merge Processing

Avoiding programming

In Section 4.4, you learned how to use a batch input recording to generate an ABAP program, which you then revise, import as a local file from the PC, and process as a batch input session. But, because this procedure requires programming skills, which contradicts the objectives of this book, it should be avoided whenever possible.

The following sections introduce you to a procedure that will enable you to reach the same goal in a much more user-friendly manner. In this approach, a batch input recording is combined with mail merge functions, which you know from Microsoft Word. The result is a batch input session that you can process using Transaction SM35.

Example: FB01

To illustrate this procedure, let's return to the example of the open debit items that you want to post to the SAP ERP system with Transaction FB01. The first part, creating the recording, is identical to Section 4.4, and is repeated here for the sake of completeness.

First, choose menu path **System • Services • Batch Input • Sessions** (Transaction SM35), and then press **Recording**, and then **New Recording**. The **Create Recording** dialog box opens (see Figure 4.14).

Creating the recording

Enter a name for the recording and transaction code that you want to use to transfer the open debit items to SAP ERP (Transaction FB01). For structuring purposes, we suggest that you include the transaction code in the name of the recording in some way (for example, Z_FB01). Once you have maintained the two fields, press the **Start recording** button to create your recording (see Figures 4.15 to 4.18).

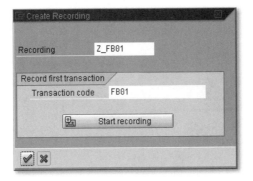

Figure 4.14 Creating a Recording

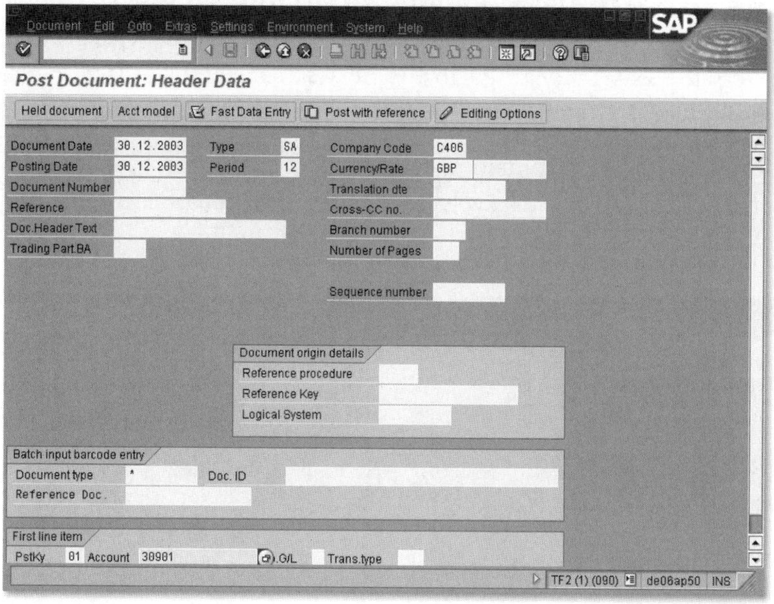

Figure 4.15 FB01 — Document Header

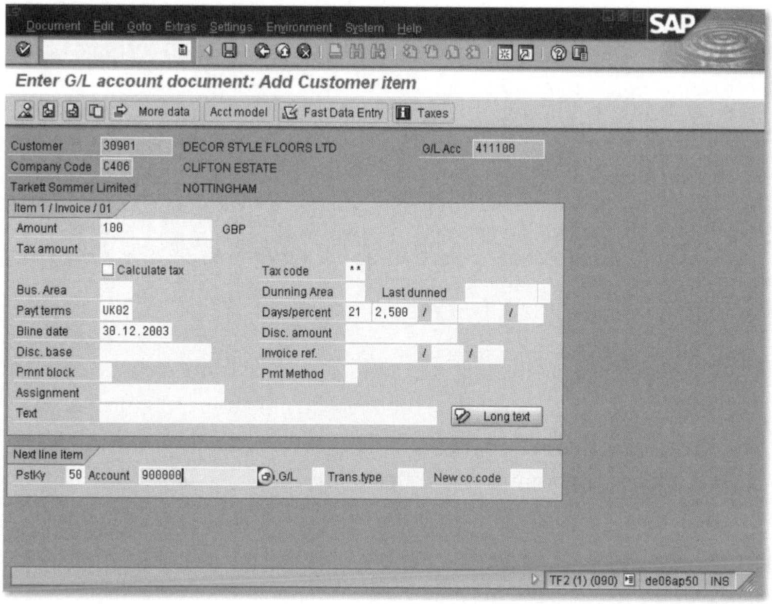

Figure 4.16 FB01 — Line Item 1

Document header and customer line

Maintain the fields in Figure 4.15 as if you were using regular online processing, without the transaction recorder in the background. Press the **Enter** key to go to the next screen template (see Figure 4.16), where you can enter the information for the first line item.

The next line item contains a balance sheet account (see Figure 4.17) that was created exclusively to migrate the transaction data, and which accepts all the open debit items accordingly.

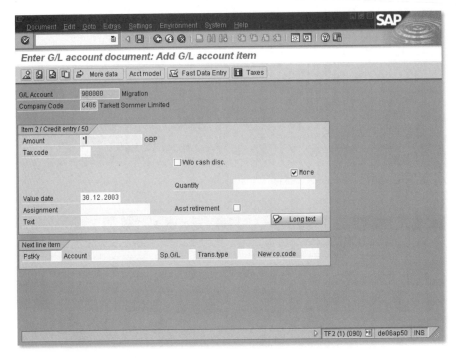

Figure 4.17 FB01 — Line Item 2

G/L account line

You can usually set the **Amount** field of the last line item to "*". The SAP ERP system then calculates the remaining amount automatically. The **Post** button ends the recording, creates a document in the database, and returns you to the transaction recorder screen (see Figure 4.18).

Now, you see information on the program used for the transaction that you just recorded and which screens (dynpros) were processed during the transaction. You also see a list of all the table fields, with their corresponding content that you maintained during the recording.

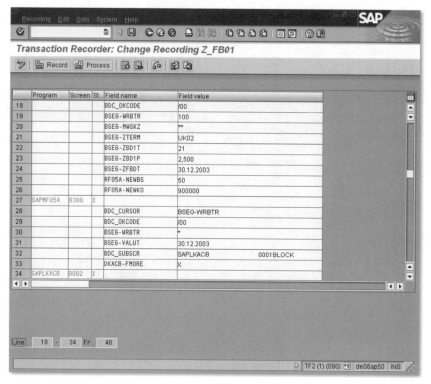

Figure 4.18 Transaction Recorder — Result of the Recording

Use menu path **Recording · Export** (or, alternatively, the **Export** button) to export the transaction you just recorded (see Figure 4.19).

Exporting the recording

Figure 4.19 Exporting the Recording

Choose a file name and the file format "DAT," which corresponds to the **Text (Tab-Delimited) (*.txt)** format.

As a result, the text file you just generated contains the same data record you created during the recording of Transaction FB01 (see Figure 4.20).

```
Z_FB01 Recording.txt - Notepad
File  Edit  Format  Help
          0000        T           FB01      BS
SAPMF05A              0100        X
          0000                    BDC_CURSOR          RF05A-NEWKO
          0000                    BDC_OKCODE          /00
          0000                    BKPF-BLDAT          16.03.2003
          0000                    BKPF-BLART          SA
          0000                    BKPF-BUKRS          1000
          0000                    BKPF-BUDAT          16.03.2003
          0000                    BKPF-MONAT          3
          0000                    BKPF-WAERS          EUR
          0000                    FS006-DOCID         *
          0000                    RF05A-NEWBS         01
          0000                    RF05A-NEWKO         10101
SAPMF05A              0301        X
          0000                    BDC_CURSOR          RF05A-NEWKO
          0000                    BDC_OKCODE          =AB
          0000                    BSEG-WRBTR          100
          0000                    BSEG-MWSKZ          **
          0000                    BSEG-ZFBDT          16.03.2003
          0000                    RF05A-NEWBS         50
          0000                    RF05A-NEWKO         900001
SAPMF05A              0300        X
          0000                    BDC_CURSOR          BSEG-WRBTR
          0000                    BDC_OKCODE          =BU
          0000                    BSEG-WRBTR          *
          0000                    BSEG-VALUT          16.03.2003
          0000                    BDC_SUBSCR          SAPLKACB
          0000                    DKACB-FMORE         X
SAPLKACB              0002        X
          0000                    BDC_CURSOR          COBL-GSBER
          0000                    BDC_OKCODE          =ENTE
          0000                    BDC_SUBSCR          SAPLKACB
```

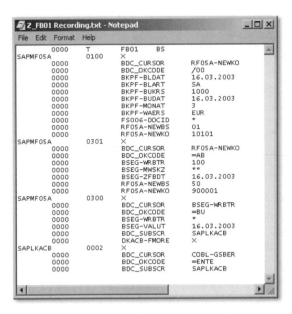

Figure 4.20 Viewing the Recording as a Text File in a Text Editor

Concurrently, prepare the open debit items that you want to migrate, preferably with Microsoft Excel (see Figure 4.21). Here, the order of the columns is not important.

Company code	Document date	Posting date	Reference	Document header text	Currency	Posting key	Customer	Amount	Posting key	Migration account	Amount
1000	15.04.2002	31.01.2003	6000001	Reference 6000001	EUR	06	10101	100	50	900001	100
1000	30.08.2002	31.01.2003	6000002	Reference 6000002	EUR	16	10101	150	40	900001	150
1000	08.07.2002	31.01.2003	6000003	Reference 6000003	EUR	11	10102	200	40	900001	200
1000	26.07.2002	31.01.2003	6000004	Reference 6000004	EUR	11	10102	250	40	900001	250
1000	22.01.2002	31.01.2003	6000005	Reference 6000005	EUR	01	10103	300	50	900001	300
1000	05.03.2002	31.01.2003	6000006	Reference 6000006	EUR	01	10103	350	50	900001	350
1000	14.05.2002	31.01.2003	6000007	Reference 6000007	EUR	01	10104	400	50	900001	400
1000	17.05.2002	31.01.2003	6000008	Reference 6000008	EUR	01	10104	450	50	900001	450
1000	22.05.2002	31.01.2003	6000009	Reference 6000009	EUR	01	10105	500	50	900001	500
1000	22.05.2002	31.01.2003	6000010	Reference 6000010	EUR	01	10105	550	50	900001	550

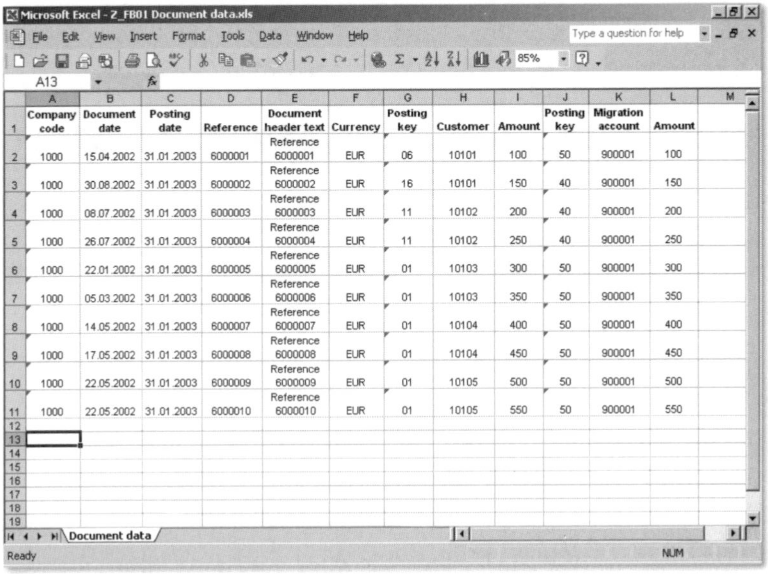

Figure 4.21 Document Data in Microsoft Excel

The Excel file must consist of a single worksheet. You also must have one table row for each data record, with row 1 of the table reserved for the field names. To improve clarity, we recommend that you set the field names to the corresponding names. Then, you can arrange the field contents for migration starting in row 2, according to the field names from row 1.

Format of the Excel file

Note that you should avoid using rows and columns in the worksheet where you have no data. However, you can fill a row or column for individual records, but not for each record.

Once you have completed the preparations for the data migration, you can now open the text file you generated from the recording with Microsoft Word, as shown in Figure 4.22.

Mail merge

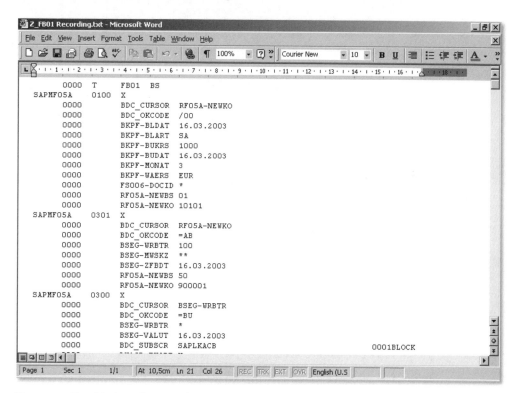

Figure 4.22 Text File from the Recording, Opened with Microsoft Word

To use the mail merge functions for the data migration, choose **Tools • Letters and Mailings • Mail Merge Wizard...** in the open document in Microsoft Word (see Figure 4.23).

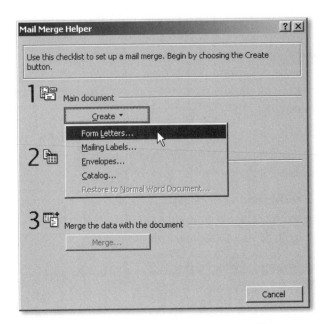

Figure 4.23 Microsoft Word — Mail Merge Wizard (1)

Then click on **Next: Starting document**. The wizard now guides you through the individual mail merge steps (see Figure 4.24).

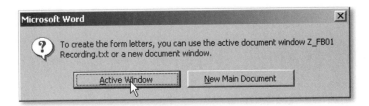

Figure 4.24 Microsoft Word — Mail Merge Wizard (2)

You can use the predefined settings shown in Figure 4.24 by clicking on **Next: Select recipients**. The system then displays the screen shown in Figure 4.25.

Then you must import the Microsoft Excel file you prepared previously (see Figure 4.21 above), that is, the recordings, into the text file opened in Microsoft Word by clicking on **Browse...** (see Figures 4.26 to 4.28). You can always use the default settings in the individual screens by clicking **OK**.

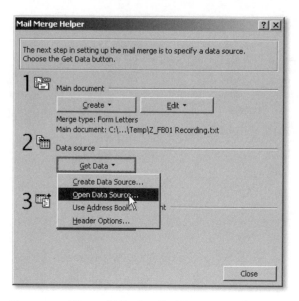

Figure 4.25 Microsoft Word — Mail Merge Wizard (3)

Once you have imported the data source, you can continue by clicking on **Next: Write your letter**. The system now displays the screen
shown in Figure 4.29.

Figure 4.26 Microsoft Word — Mail Merge Wizard (4)

Figure 4.27 Microsoft Word — Mail Merge Wizard (5)

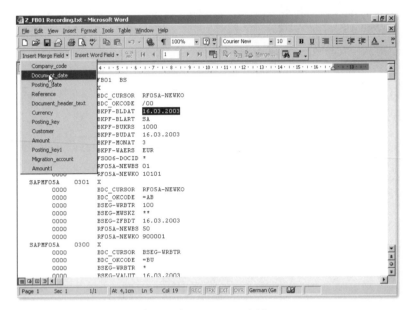

Figure 4.28 Microsoft Word — Mail Merge Wizard (6)

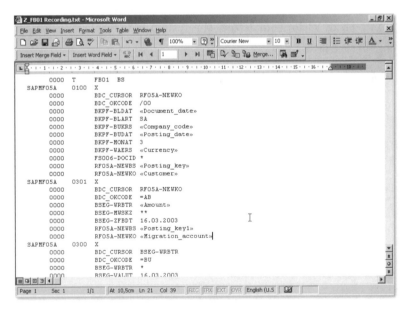

Figure 4.29 Microsoft Word — Mail Merge Wizard (7)

You now have to replace all the constants that resulted from your
original recording with the corresponding field names, wherever the
field contents of the Excel file can vary. For example, select the doc-

ument date, 31.01.2007, and click on the **More items...** button. The system displays the dialog box shown in Figure 4.30, which contains all column headers from the Microsoft Excel file.

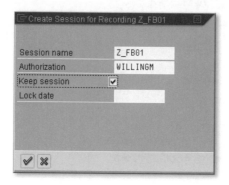

Figure 4.30 Microsoft Word — Mail Merge Wizard (8)

For the document date example, you must now select the **Document Date** and confirm this selection by clicking on **Insert**. You must repeat this procedure, which is described for the field "document date" for all other fields of the Excel file until you have assigned all values of the recording. The system displays the screen shown in Figure 4.31.

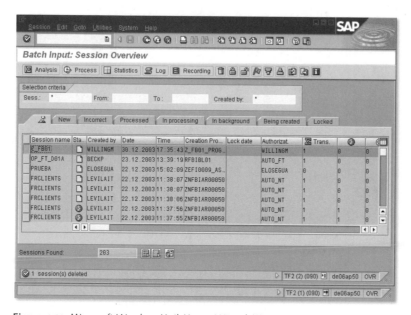

Figure 4.31 Microsoft Word — Mail Merge Wizard (9)

Click on **Next: Preview your letters**. The system displays the dialog box shown in Figure 4.32.

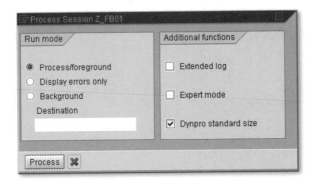

Figure 4.32 Microsoft Word — Mail Merge Wizard (10)

You can use the arrow buttons (**>>**, **<<**) shown in Figure 4.32 to view the individual data records of the Microsoft Excel file — transformed into the format of the recording — prior to actually starting the mail merge process by clicking on **Next: Complete the merge**. The system now displays the dialog box shown in Figure 4.33.

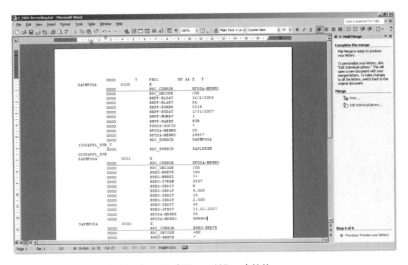

Figure 4.33 Microsoft Word — Mail Merge Wizard (11)

You can now print the mail merge or, as is required in our data migration case, process it further. The **Edit individual letters...** button enables you to personalize your letters. Confirm the dialog box that appears next (see Figure 4.34) by clicking **OK**. This will take you to the screen shown in Figure 4.35, which represents the end of the mail merge process.

Figure 4.34 Microsoft Word — Mail Merge Wizard (12)

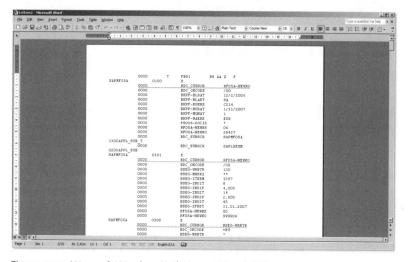

Figure 4.35 Microsoft Word — Mail Merge Wizard (13)

This process has modified every data record according to the structure of the exported recording (see Figure 4.31), and has thus enabled the SAP ERP system to process these records. Save the file again as a text file (**Text Only (*.txt)**) and close the file.

Now that the data is available in a format supported by SAP ERP, you can switch back to the SAP ERP system and start Transaction SM35 there. Click the **Recording** button to display a list of all the recordings and then select the relevant one. If you press **Change**, the recording editor is displayed (see Figure 4.18 above). Now, choose menu path **Recording • Import** to import the recording that you modified with the mail merge function back into the SAP ERP system.

Importing the recording

Generating the
batch input session

Save the modified recording and press **F3** to return to the recording overview. Select your recording and then choose **Edit • Create Session** to create a batch input session called Z_FB01 from recording Z_FB01 (see Figure 4.36), which you can then process.

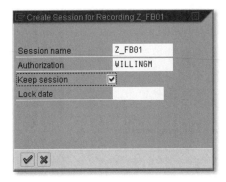

Figure 4.36 Creating a Batch Input Session

You should activate the **Retain Session** option for logging purposes. Sessions that have been processed correctly will continue to be listed in the session overview.

As soon as you press **Enter** to confirm your entries, the SAP ERP system creates a batch input session and displays it in the batch input session overview (Transaction SM35, see Figure 4.37).

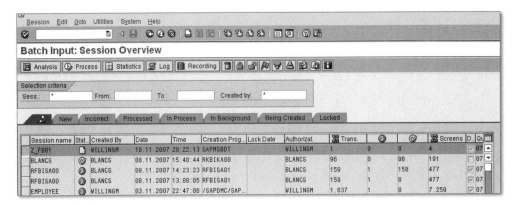

Figure 4.37 Batch Input Session Overview

Processing the
batch input session

You can now use the familiar processing modes to process your new session Z_FB01 (see Figure 4.38).

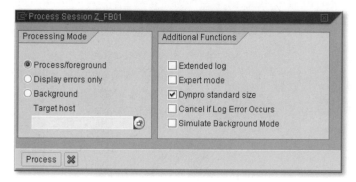

Figure 4.38 Processing the Batch Input Session

Finally, the data migration procedure utilizing Microsoft Word mail merge processing is summarized in a schematic diagram (see Figure 4.39).

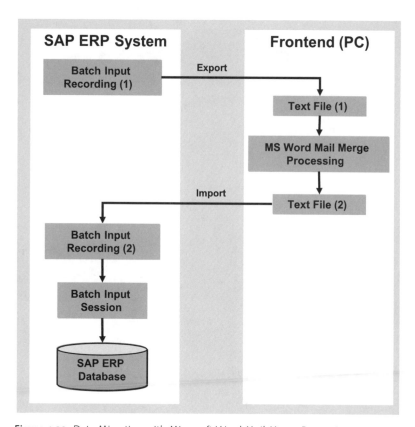

Figure 4.39 Data Migration with Microsoft Word Mail Merge Processing

This chapter describes how the Extended Computer Aided Test Tool (eCATT) was developed to test business processes for data migration. The major benefits of the eCATT are that it can be used in nearly all applications and that it enables you to avoid programming during data migration.

5 Extended Computer Aided Test Tool (eCATT)

5.1 What Is the eCATT?

As its name implies, the Extended Computer Aided Test Tool (eCATT) is intended to support the testing of business processes. Because testing is an essential activity, albeit a time-consuming and cost-intensive process as well, many users asked for a way to reduce the amount of time required for testing, while simultaneously maintaining the quantity and quality of the tests. The answer to these demands was to automate test scenarios with the eCATT. At the same time, the eCATT also made it much easier to document and analyze the test results. Ultimately, using the eCATT significantly increases productivity during the testing phase.

Purpose and objective

5.2 History of the eCATT

The eCATT is a further development of the Computer Aided Test Tool (CATT), which has been available since SAP R/3 Release 3.0 and therefore its functionality is slightly restricted in some respects.

Advanced development of the CATT

The CATT technique only enables you to process transactions that are based on the standard SAP GUI, for example. Figure 5.1 shows a sample screen template that meets this requirement.

Standard SAP GUI

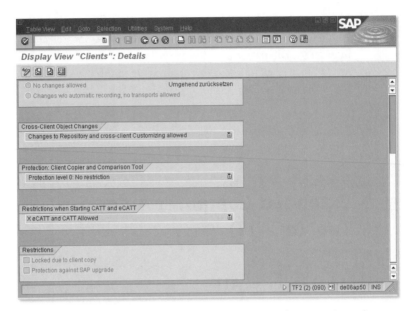

Figure 5.1 Example of a Standard SAP GUI Transaction without GUI Controls (MM02 — Change Material)

GUI control technology

This means that none of the transactions that employ the GUI control technology can be used for automated tests with the CATT. Such transactions include the following:

▶ Expanding a tree and selecting a node

▶ Calling the context menu via right-click and selecting an entry

▶ Clicking on a hyperlink

Figure 5.2 shows a transaction based on the GUI control technology.

Non-SAP GUI

In this context, we should also mention that external applications — such as Internet-based applications that are started in a browser and that communicate with the SAP ERP system — cannot be included in test scenarios, because the CATT doesn't support processing of non-SAP GUIs. Because of the increasing popularity of this type of application, this situation has to be corrected (see Figure 5.3).

With this in mind, a new procedure was needed that maintained the proven advantages of the CATT, yet also supported all SAP transactions — regardless of whether or not they used GUI controls — and moreover could integrate external applications as part of the process chain in test scenarios.

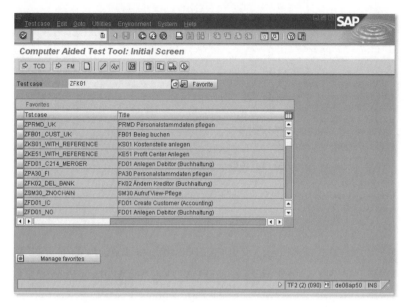

Figure 5.2 Example of a Standard SAP GUI Transaction with GUI Controls (CRM Marketing Planner)

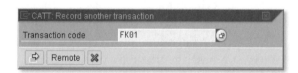

Figure 5.3 Example of an Internet Application — SAP CRM E-Selling

5.3 Availability and Functionality of eCATT and CATT

Table 5.1 provides a brief overview of the SAP Basis and NetWeaver releases in which the CATT and eCATT are available, as well as the functional scope that is supported in the respective release statuses.

Availability and functionality based on the release status

SAP Basis Release	≤ 6.10	6.20	6.40	≥ 7.0
SAP NetWeaver Release	n/a	n/a	NW 04	NW 7.0
SAP R/3 Release or SAP ERP Release	R/3 4.6C, CRM 3.0	R/3 Enterprise (4.7)	ERP 2004	ERP 6.0

Table 5.1 Availability of CATT and eCATT

SAP Basis Release	≤ 6.10	6.20	6.40	≥ 7.0
CATT: Full support	Yes	Yes	No	No
CATT: Creating new CATTs	Yes	Yes	No	No
CATT: Changing existing CATTs	Yes	Yes	Yes	No
eCATT available?	No	Yes	Yes	Yes
Migration of CATTs to eCATT	n/a	Yes	Yes	Yes
eCATT: Loading data from local files	n/a	No	Yes	Yes

Table 5.1 Availability of CATT and eCATT (cont.)

In summary, this table contains the following information:

- You cannot create any new CATTs as of SAP Basis Release 6.40.
- You cannot change any existing CATTs as of SAP Basis Release 7.0.
- You can use the eCATT for data migration as of SAP Basis Release 6.40.

The chapter is intended for users of SAP Basis Release 6.40 or higher

Because the following descriptions clearly focus on using the eCATT for data migration purposes, this chapter addresses readers who use SAP Basis Release 6.40 or higher. Those of you who have earlier releases must use the CATT for data migration, provided you want to use such a tool at all. Chapter 6 describes the relevant processes for using the CATT.

5.4   Preparing the System for Using the eCATT

The term *test script* means that the transactions of multiple different clients are recorded and that these recordings can generally be created in any client. You can use the client table, **T000**, to define whether or not test scripts can be started in a specific client.

To do so, you must select **Tools • Administration • Administration • Client Administration • Maintain Clients** or, alternatively, enter Transaction Code SCC4.

Make sure the flag **eCATT and CATT Allowed** is selected in the detail view of the client, in group **CATT and eCATT Restrictions** (see Figure 5.4).

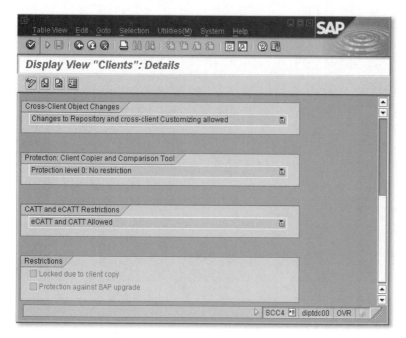

Figure 5.4 Display Clients — Details

In general, if you want to use the CATT or eCATT exclusively to test business processes, you should not allow CATT or eCATT runs in production clients. The test master and transaction data created as a result of using the tool would inevitably cause errors in a production system.

eCATT runs in production clients

However, if you want to use the eCATT functions for data migration projects, you must allow eCATT runs in all clients involved in the data migration, including production systems. Once the data migration is complete, you must reset the **eCATT and CATT Allowed** option in the production clients.

Furthermore, you must ensure that the *new GUI scripting* function is enabled in your SAP ERP system. To do so, use Transaction Code RZ11 with the parameter name `sapgui/user_scripting` (see Figure 5.5).

Enabling GUI scripting

Check the profile parameter settings by clicking on the **Display** button; the parameters should have the **TRUE** value, as shown in Figure 5.6. If the parameter values are different in your system, you can modify them by clicking on the **Change Value** button.

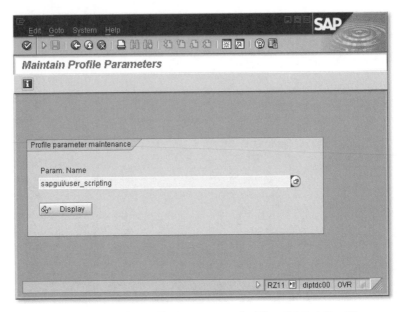

Figure 5.5 Maintaining the Profile Parameters — Enabling GUI Scripting (1)

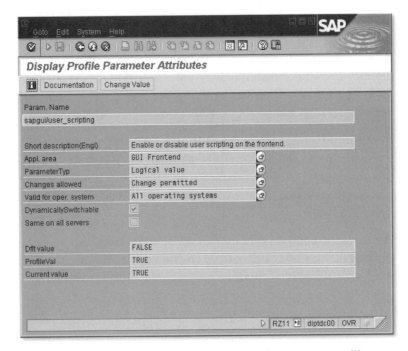

Figure 5.6 Maintaining the Profile Parameters — Enabling GUI Scripting (2)

This book is not intended to describe the full range of functions available in the eCATT. Instead, it will focus on the functions that are required during eCATT-supported data migration. If you need more detailed information on the eCATT, please refer to the pertinent documentation from SAP.

Functions for data migration

5.5 How Does the eCATT Work?

Instead of testing specific system processes manually, you use the eCATT to create a *test script* that contains the transactions to be tested. You can combine this test script with different input data and execute it as often as you like in order to examine the reliability of the system behavior with different parameter configurations.

With the eCATT, you need to develop and record a test for a specific transaction in the SAP ERP system only once, and can then run it again at any time, as per your requirements. You will notice that the term *test script* or *test configuration* is used in the remainder of this chapter instead of *test*; this is merely to conform to the exact SAP terminology. There is no intrinsic difference between these terms.

Test script

Creating a test script for a transaction hardly takes longer than performing a single, manual transaction in the SAP ERP system. This is because you simply execute the transaction to be tested within the eCATT, running through the same dynpros (screen templates) as you would when performing the transaction in the conventional manner. When you press **Enter**, all the entries you make are recorded in a transaction recorder. The recorded transactions form the test script. The test script is saved and can be used for functional and regression tests, because it can be reused at any time. When you execute the test script, the recorded transaction is actually performed, testing the system in its current configuration. You can either run the eCATT in full automatic mode or assume partial or complete control of the execution yourself. In either case, the result is a log, in which the test program run is documented, and a corresponding update in the database for each specific transaction that has been tested.

Transaction recorder

The functionality of the eCATT can be best demonstrated by using a simple example: *creating vendor master data*. Because the procedure is always identical, regardless of which application you want to test

Case example: creating a vendor

with the eCATT, the example can be applied to other application areas. The following sections will guide you through the individual steps involved in using the eCATT for data migration.

5.5.1   Recording a Test Script

Three options are available for accessing the initial screen of the eCATT (see Figure 5.7):

▸ **System · Services · eCATT · Record**

▸ **Tools · ABAP Workbench · Test · Test Workbench · Test Tools · Extended CATT**

▸ Transaction code: SECATT

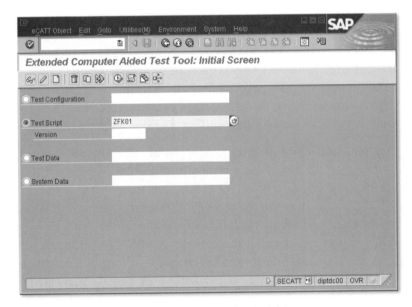

Figure 5.7 Extended Computer Aided Test Tool — Initial Screen

You must assign a name for the new test script in this initial screen. Remember that the name has to start with Y, Z, or your namespace prefix in the customer namespace. We recommend including the transaction code of the relevant transaction in the name of the test script. For example, you could call a test script for creating vendors ZFK01. With this approach, you can use the search help to easily check whether a test script already exists for the transaction you want to test. If so, you must clarify whether you can use this test script as is, or whether you need to adapt it to fit a different test situation (the latter case is discussed in more detail in Section 5.7.2).

Once you have defined the name of the test script, click on **Create**. The dialog box shown in Figure 5.8 appears.

Defining the test script attributes

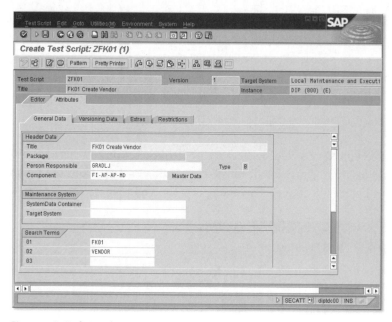

Figure 5.8 Defining the Test Script Attributes

Here, you must specify a title, which typically describes the transaction to be recorded, and assign the transaction to an SAP application in the **Component** field. By default, the system uses the author of the test script as the person responsible; however, you can overwrite this value if you wish. To facilitate finding the test script at a later stage, you can store up to 10 search terms, which you can use to search for the test script in the initial transaction (SECATT) on the basis of the match code.

The following two options are generally available to save your entries (see Figure 5.9): If you want to transport the test script to other systems, you must select a **Package** (not $TMP) that supports the transport process. Then, when saving the test script, the system prompts you for a transport request, which you need to create. If you only want the test script to be available in the current client, you must save it as a **Local Object** ($TMP package).

Test script can be transported

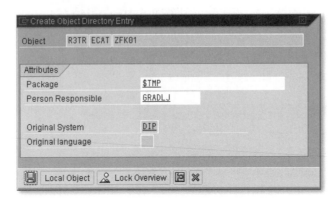

Figure 5.9 Creating an Object Directory Entry

Default settings for the recording

Once you have saved the test script attributes, you can start recording the transaction. To do this, select **Edit • Pattern** from the menu (see Figure 5.8 above). The dialog box shown in Figure 5.10 appears.

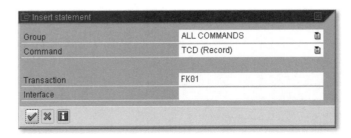

Figure 5.10 Inserting a Pattern (1)

Store all commands in the **Group** field and select the **TCD (Record)** command as well as **Transaction FK01** as the transaction to be recorded. If you don't know the transaction code, you can use the F4 input help. You can also navigate to the transaction through the menu tree that opens.

Once you confirm the entries by pressing **Enter**, a default value automatically displays in the **Interface** field; you can use this value (see Figure 5.11).

Executing the recording

Press **Enter** again to confirm your entries. The system now takes you through all screen templates of Transaction FK01 (see Figures 5.12 through 5.17).

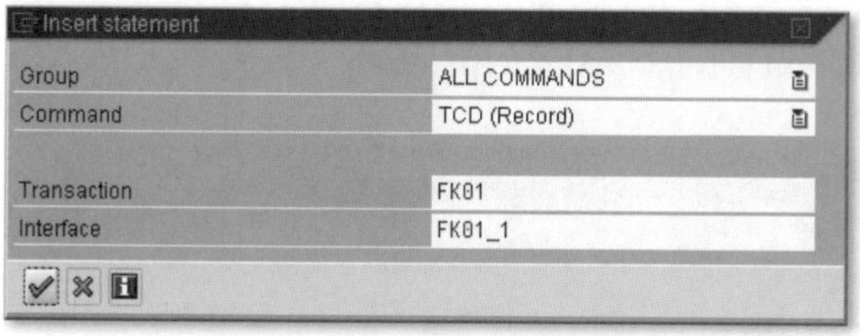

Figure 5.11 Inserting a Pattern (2)

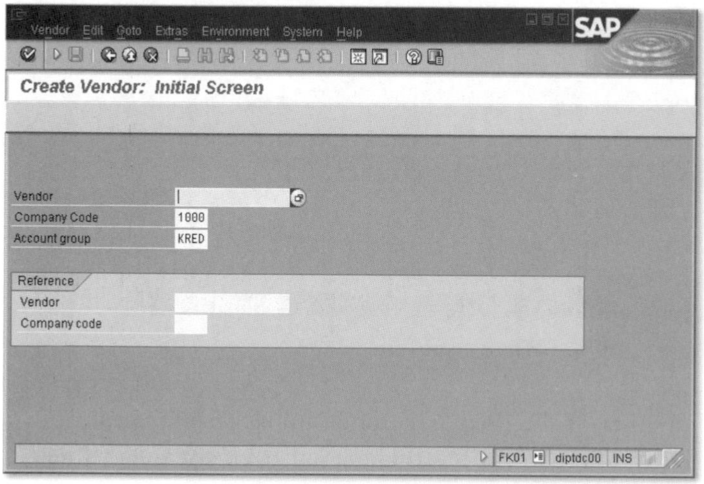

Figure 5.12 Creating a Vendor — Initial Screen

You now have to enter your values and navigate through the appropriate screens exactly as if you were performing the transaction manually, without the eCATT. The only indications that the eCATT is active and that the transaction recorder is recording the input in the background are the occasional messages in the status bar, which appear whenever you confirm your entries with **Enter** or navigate to the next screen.

The example assumes that a vendor with internal number assignment and account group **KRED** is involved, who has to be created in company code **1000**. In addition, his address and phone number, VAT registration number, the reconciliation account, the terms of payment, and the payment method should be entered.

Fields to fill

Therefore, you must enter the **Account group** and **Company code** in the initial screen.

Address data   When you click on **Enter**, the address data shown in Figure 5.13 is displayed, which you can maintain accordingly.

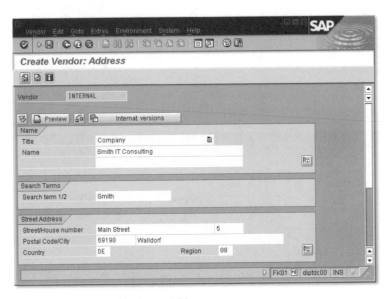

Figure 5.13 Creating a Vendor — Address

Control data   **Click on Enter** or the **Next Screen** button to reach the control data, and payment   followed by the general information on payment transactions, as transactions   shown in Figures 5.14 and 5.15.

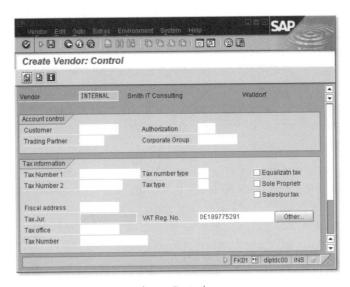

Figure 5.14 Creating a Vendor — Control

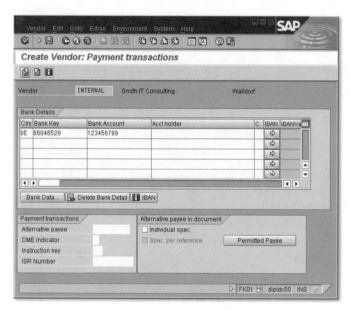

Figure 5.15 Creating a Vendor — Payment Transactions

Once you have maintained the general data for the vendor, you can continue with the company code-specific values (see Figures 5.16 and 5.17).

Company code-specific fields

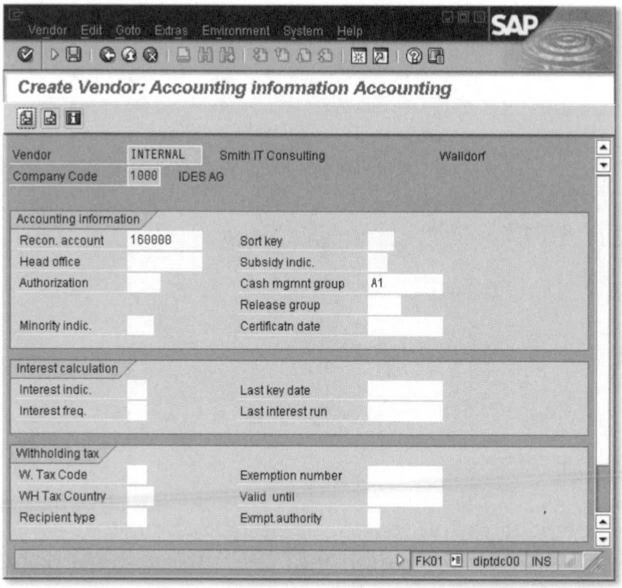

Figure 5.16 Creating a Vendor — Accounting Information, Accounting

Ending the
recording

Once you have entered all the data, click on the **Save** button to finish creating the vendor. Clicking on **Save** always ends the current transaction and saves the processed data record in the database. If you want to use the eCATT for data migration, you must delete the first data record that you created during the recording of the test script in order to avoid falsifying the migration results. A dialog box opens (see Figure 5.18), asking you whether you want to transfer the data. Click **Yes**.

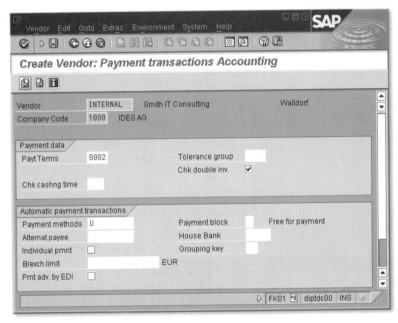

Figure 5.17 Creating a Vendor — Payment Transactions, Accounting

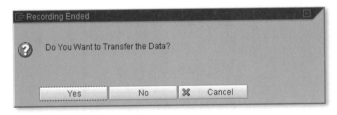

Figure 5.18 Recording Ended

Transferring the
test script

This task doesn't refer to transferring the data record, that is, the vendor you just created. That data record was already saved in the database when you clicked the **Save** button in the last screen template. Instead, the prompt refers to transferring the test script (i.e., transferring the individual screen templates, including the field contents that were used for creating the data record).

When you click on the **Yes** button in the dialog box shown in Figure 5.18, the system displays the screen shown in Figure 5.19, which allows you to save the transferred test script.

Saving the test script

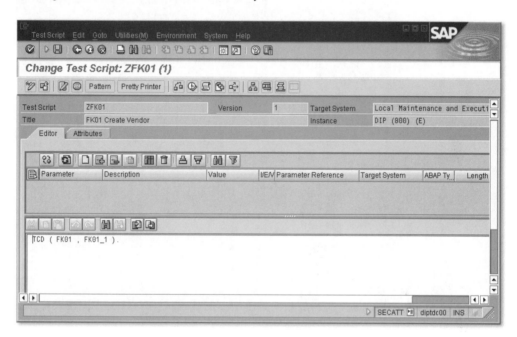

Figure 5.19 Changing the Test Script

This was the last activity involved in recording a test script. You can now use the test script for generating data in the SAP ERP system as often as you want. Up to this point, the procedure is identical, whether you plan to use the test script to generate test data, or to migrate data.

5.5.2 Executing a Test Script

Once the test script has been created, you can execute it immediately. From the initial screen of the eCATT (Transaction SECATT), you can specify the test script to execute and then click on the **Execute** button (F8). This takes you to the screen template shown in Figure 5.20.

Execution

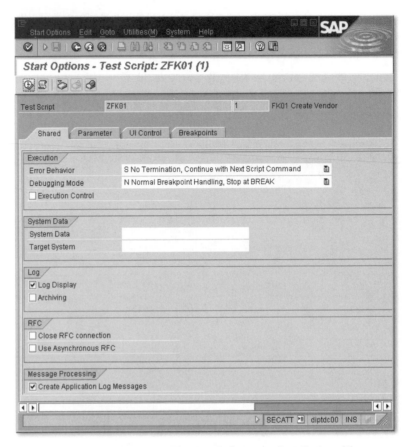

Figure 5.20 Executing Test Script ZFK01 — Defining the Start Options (1)

Select the **UI Control** tab in the screen shown in Figure 5.20, which takes you to the screen shown in Figure 5.21.

Here, you can store the following settings for the **Start Mode for Command TCD**, for example:

▸ **A Process in Foreground, Synchronous Local**
The test script is executed fully in dialog. In the process, you can change field inputs to influence the test results. Click on **Enter** to go to the next screen.

▸ **E Display Errors Only, Synchronous Local**
In this case, the transactions continue to be processed in the background until the first error or termination occurs. When an error situation occurs, the system switches to dialog mode, enabling you to change incorrect entries. Once you click on **Enter** to con-

firm the corrected entry, the system switches back to background processing and continues until the next error or termination occurs.

▸ **N Process in Background, Synchronous Local**
The transactions are executed in the background, without any dialog.

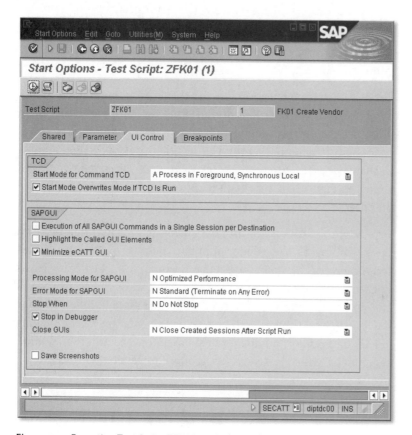

Figure 5.21 Executing Test Script ZFK01 — Defining the Start Options (2)

At this stage, you should note the available options provided by the **Error Behavior** field. These options are particularly useful when the test script is processed completely *in the background*:

Options for occurring errors

▸ **V – Termination, Continue with Next Variant**
If an error occurs during the processing of a data record, the processing of the current data record terminates, and the system continues with the processing of the next data record.

- ▸ **T – Termination, Continue with Next Test Configuration**
  The procedure described here uses only one test configuration. In this case, the error behavior "T – Termination, Continue with Next Test Configuration" is equivalent to "X – Termination of Start Process".

- ▸ **X – Termination of Start Process**
  The process terminates entirely if an error occurs.

- ▸ **S – No Termination, Continue with Next Script Command**
  In this case, the system tries to process the data record although an error occurred.

For demonstration purposes, we run the test script in the foreground by clicking on the **Execute** button **(F8)** (see Figure 5.21), that is, we don't use the default value here based on which the script would be processed in the background. All other default values remain unchanged. The system then takes you to the screen templates shown in Figures 5.22 through 5.28; confirm all screens by clicking on **Enter**.

Creating a vendor

Typically, the SAP system proposes using the account number from the recording as the vendor number. Because recording the test script caused a change in the database, vendor 100244 already exists. Consequently, if you execute the test script now, the system would attempt to create the vendor again under the same number, which is not possible. To migrate all the recorded data anyway, you must delete the vendor number that's based on the internal number assignment, which is easy in foreground processing with its interactive change options.

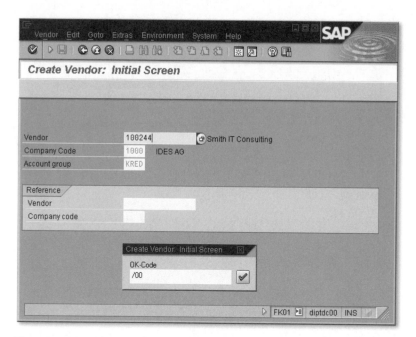

Figure 5.22 Creating a Vendor — Initial Screen

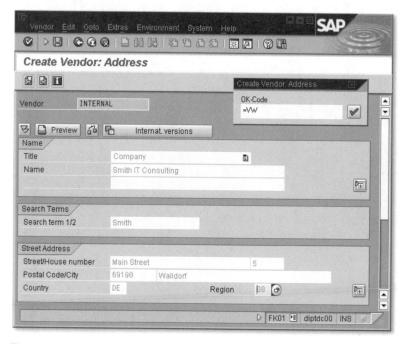

Figure 5.23 Creating a Vendor — Address

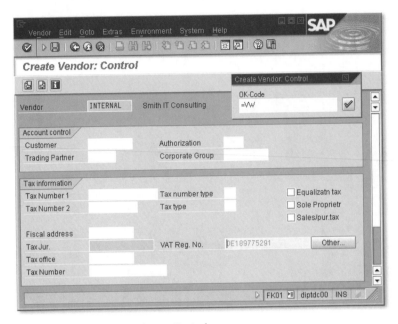

Figure 5.24 Creating a Vendor — Control

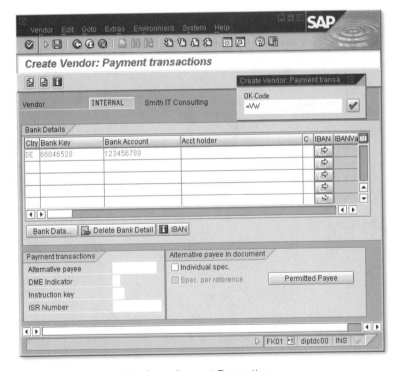

Figure 5.25 Creating a Vendor — Payment Transactions

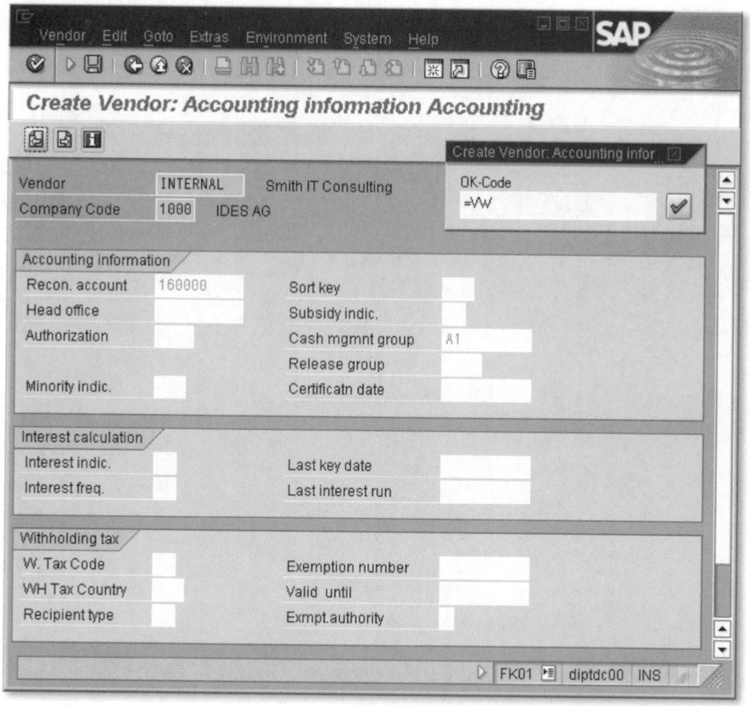

Figure 5.26 Creating a Vendor — Accounting Information, Accounting

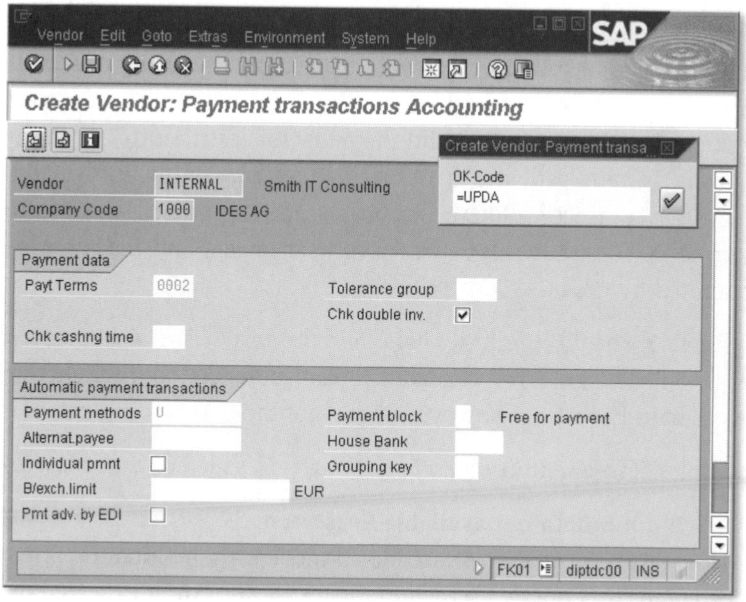

Figure 5.27 Creating a Vendor — Payment Transactions, Accounting

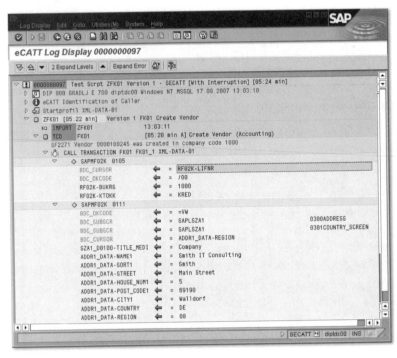

Figure 5.28 eCATT Log Display

The last screen template (see Figure 5.28) always displays a log of the last performed test script in a hierarchical structure. Among other things, the highest hierarchy level displays the **executing client**, the **date, time**, and **user ID** of the executing person as well as the name of the **test script**. If you expand the entry for test script ZFK01 in the log, the system provides a detailed view containing information about the Transaction FK01, the processed screen templates of program SAPMF02K, the entries that have been made, and the messages generated by the eCATT.

Frequent error messages Ultimately, the log indicates whether the test script was executed successfully. If an error occurred, the responsible components are highlighted in the log; however, that's not the case in our example.

Examples of frequently occurring error messages include the following:

▶ **Batch input data not available for screen ...**
The reason for this error can be an incorrectly maintained screen sequence or a missing screen in the test script. An unexpected dia-

log box during execution of the test script can also cause this error message.

▶ **Field <table-field_name> does not permit input**
An output field was assigned values, not an input field. The cause for this could be incorrect parameterization of the input fields. This possibility is discussed in detail later on (see Section 5.6.1).

▶ **Fill in all required fields**
This error message is displayed when no values have been specified for a required entry field.

So far, you've learned how to record and execute a test script. Each execution writes exactly one data record to the database. To generate five vendors, for example, you would have to start the test script five times. With the structure described above, these five vendors would even be identical aside from the vendor number, because the test script refers to the information defined during the recording each time and uses this information to create new vendors. To use the eCATT as a data migration tool, however, the input values have to be variable. In addition, you must be able to migrate the entire dataset (i.e., all the creditors) with one run of the test script. The following section describes how you can achieve this degree of flexibility.

Summary and outlook

5.6 How Can You Use the eCATT for Data Migration?

The answer to the preceding question is the core message of Chapter 5. For this purpose, we will once again use and extend the example of automatically creating vendors using the eCATT, which was introduced in Section 5.6.1.

Case example: creating a vendor

5.6.1 Parameterizing Input Fields

In all the business processes that you want to map in test scripts, you first enter the data in the SAP ERP input templates and fields. This data can be used to create master data, for example, as illustrated in the preceding section, or to generate transaction data. To make the test scripts flexible, which is an essential prerequisite if you want to use them for data migration, we recommend that you parameterize the input fields instead of using fixed values. This gives the input fields a variable character, enabling them to process different values for the migration.

The following sections clarify how you can achieve this parameterization.

In the initial screen of the eCATT (Transaction SECATT), first enter the test script you want to edit, ZFK01, and choose **Change**. The screen shown in Figure 5.29 opens.

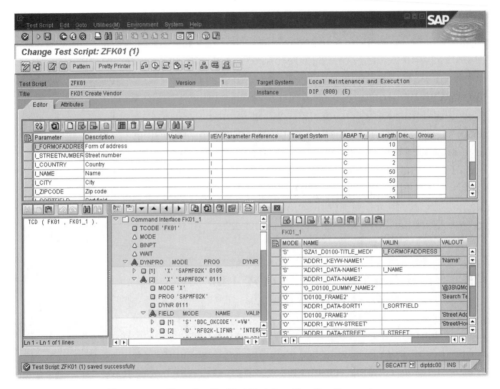

Figure 5.29 Changing the Test Script — Creating Parameters

Defining the parameters   Here, you must first identify all fields of the recording that can be variable in the context of the data migration, and define these fields as parameters. To do that, you must change from the **Command Interface** view to the **Parameter Interface** view, as shown in Figure 5.29. You can do so by clicking on the **Parameter <- -> Command Interface** button, which is represented by a red or green circle respectively. In this view, you can define the parameters via the **Attach Parameters** button.

The system then displays a line in which you can enter the **parameter name** and a **description**. In addition, you must specify that the parameters are import parameters, represented by the input value, "I". Furthermore, you must enter information about the **ABAP Type** of the parameters (i.e., about its field contents), which are all character type (C) parameters in our example, and you must specify their maximum **length**. The **Value** field allows you to store a default value for each parameter. During the data migration, the fields are filled with the default values whenever the respective data record doesn't provide corresponding field contents. If the field in question is not a required entry field, you might consider foregoing a default value altogether, which would result in a blank field in the corresponding data record. As you will see, it will be far easier to manage the migration if you use mnemonic names for the parameters, as was the case in the previous example.

Parameterization in detail

Repeat the procedure described above until all parameters of the recording have been defined.

At this point, you should note that we won't go into further detail on the numerous editing and control commands that are available during the editing of the test script, as this would exceed the scope of this book. Instead, we will focus on the functions that are required and used in the data migration process. If you need more information on the editing functions, please refer to the official SAP documentation.

Once you have defined the parameters, you must assign them to the corresponding fields of the individual screens (dynpros) in the next step. To do that, double-click on the **Dynpro** line in the central part of the lower screen half (see Figure 5.29). The tree that opens next contains all screen templates represented by the associated program name, SAPMF02K, which have been processed during the recording of the test script. Open these screen templates as well and navigate to the **Field** line. Double-click on this line to open it. In the lower right-hand section of your screen, the system now lists the individual fields of the currently selected screen containing the values from the recording.

Parameters are assigned fields

In the next step, you must distinguish which fields will be variable for the data migration and which fields should be assigned fixed values that apply to all the data records for migration. To make the test

Parameter versus fixed value

script as flexible and universally usable as possible, we recommend parameterizing as many fields as possible and thereby keeping them variable. Doing so causes the constant values of the recording to be overwritten with the parameters, as shown in Figure 5.29. The preset "S" mode may remain unchanged.

Once you have parameterized all fields of the screen that can have variable values, select the next screen in the central section of the bottom half of your screen and parameterize the individual fields in the manner described above. We recommend starting with the first screen and then running through all the others in sequence until the parameterization process is complete. To conclude this process step, you must save the data.

Thus far, you have learned that by parameterizing the fields of a test script, you can execute a test run not only statically, that is, with fixed values, but also with variable field contents that you transfer dynamically at runtime for each field and data record. This is essential for the data migration. The following sections describe how these different field contents are ultimately passed on.

5.6.2 Generating the File Format

Defining the file format for data migration

In this step, you define the file format of the dataset to be migrated. In this context, the term "file format" describes the structured arrangement of the fields to be transferred. On the one hand, the basis for this step is represented by the test script recording, which consists of the individual screen templates and field contents that were processed sequentially; on the other hand, the file format is also affected by the parameterization carried out in the previous step, because the parameters represent placeholders for fields or field contents and therefore determine the file format for the fields to be transferred. This means that fields that haven't been parameterized (fixed values) are not included in the structure of the file format. Consequently, you obtain a file that can be used for the data migration, provided you incorporate your dataset in this file and arrange it according to the file format.

As you'll see in the following section, you are currently performing the step of creating test data; however, this doesn't mean that you are creating specific data records that are supposed to be migrated at this point. This task is performed outside of the SAP system, primarily in Microsoft Excel, but based on the file format generated in this step.

But how do you generate the relevant file format? To do this, you must select the **Test Data** radio button in the initial screen of the eCATT (SECATT) and enter a relevant name, whose structure should be based on the name of the transaction, and a reference to a dataset (see Figure 5.30).

Details of the file format

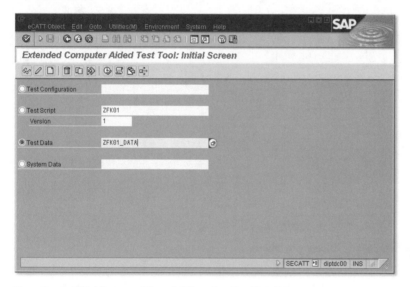

Figure 5.30 Initial Screen of the eCATT — Creating Test Data

After clicking the **Create** button, you can select the **Title** and **Person Responsible** fields as well as the **Component** to which you want to assign the dataset to be migrated (see Figure 5.31). By default, the system proposes the user who created the test data as the responsible person. With regard to the title of the test data, the descriptions of Section 5.5.1 apply in the same manner.

Defining attributes

Once you have maintained all data, go to the **Parameters** tab and select **Edit • Import Parameters** from the menu. The dialog box shown in Figure 5.32 appears.

Transferring parameters from the test script

In this dialog box, you must specify the test script you recorded previously, ZFK01, and then click **Get Parameter** in order to make its parameters available to the test data container, or rather, to the migration file you still need to generate. Finally, you must click on the **Attach** button, which is represented by the arrow pointing to the right (see Figure 5.32), to transfer the parameters to the test data container. Figure 5.33 shows the result of this step.

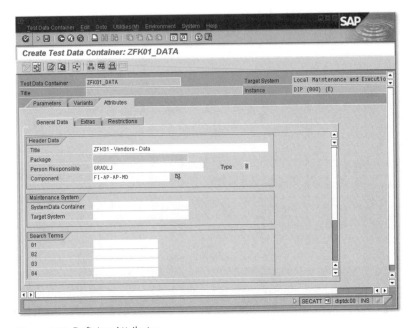

Figure 5.31 Defining Attributes

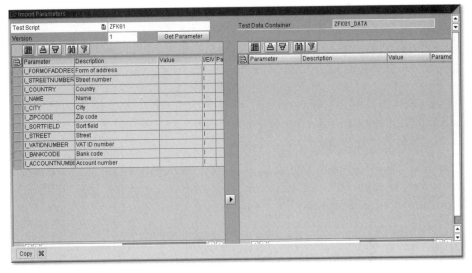

Figure 5.32 Importing Parameters (1)

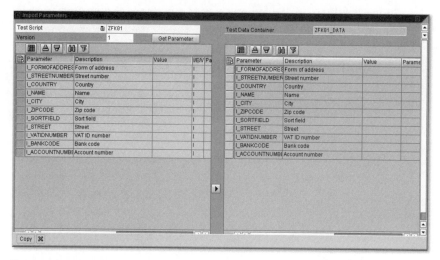

Figure 5.33 Importing Parameters (2)

Click on **Copy** to exit this dialog. The system then displays the screen shown in Figure 5.34, which allows you to save your entries.

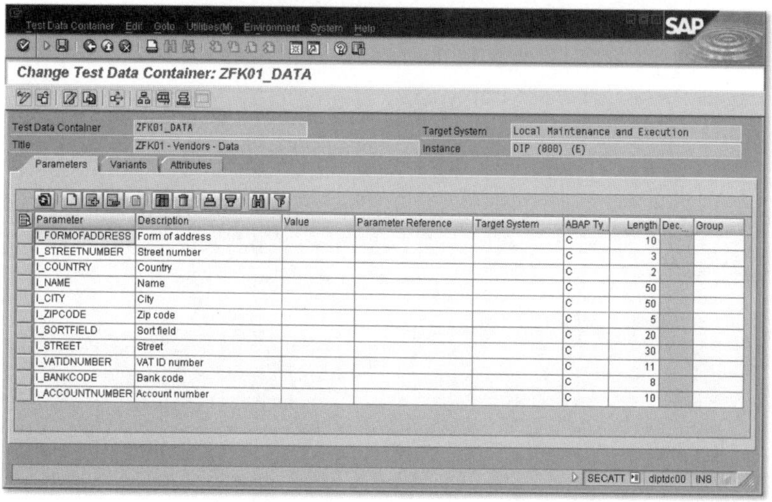

Figure 5.34 Importing Parameters (3)

Now you must generate the file format for the data migration, as already mentioned. To do that, go to the **Variants** tab (see Figure 5.34) and activate the **External Variants/Path** *radio button*. Then select **Utilities • Settings** from the menu and go to the **eCATT tab and then** the **External** tab. Figure 5.35 shows the result of this naviga-

Defining the path for downloading the file format

127

tion. The **Variants** field allows you to store a path, such as "C:_Data_Migration".

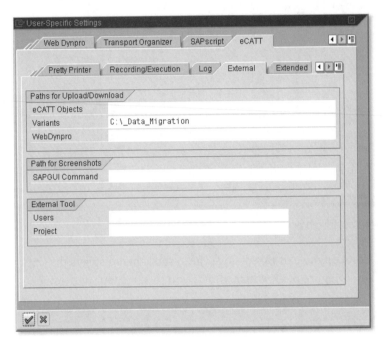

Figure 5.35 User-Specific Settings

Click **Enter** to navigate to the screen shown in Figure 5.36

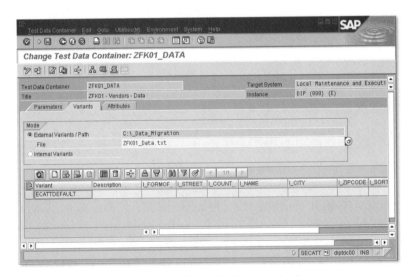

Figure 5.36 Proposed Path and File Names for the Download

This screen enables you to store the file format required for the data migration on your local hard disk by selecting **Edit • Variants • Download** from the menu. Note that for structuring reasons you should replace the suggested file name, VAR_ECTD_ZFK01_DATA.TXT, with ZFK01_DATA.TXT. The dialog shown in Figure 5.37 displays the path you specified previously as well as the file name, which you can confirm by clicking on **Save**. As a result, all transferred parameters of the test script will be saved in accordance with their declaration and including their names and default values. Note that the file is saved as a **Text file**, that is, it has the ending *.txt*. This means that the individual elements in the file have to be separated by tabs to enable processing.

Executing the download

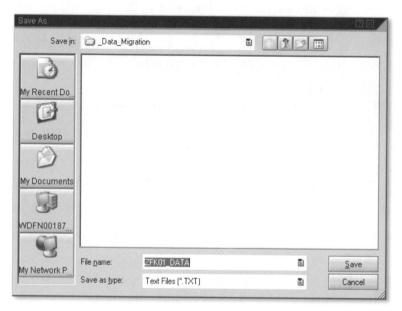

Figure 5.37 Downloading the File Format to the PC

5.6.3 Arranging the Data According to the File Format

Once you have saved the file format to your PC, it is useful to take a closer look at the contents of the file using the text editor, as shown in Figure 5.38.

File format

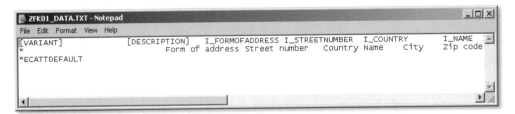

Figure 5.38 Format of File ZFK01_DATA.TXT

When you export the proposal, the SAP ERP system generates a three-line text file that consists of the following columns:

Columns
▶ [VARIANT]
This is the ID of a variant. In this context, the term "variant" represents the dataset to be migrated. As you will see later on in this chapter (see Figure 5.44), each data record must be assigned a corresponding ID in order to ensure uniqueness.

▶ [DESCRIPTION]
The DESCRIPTION can consist of a variant text.

▶ Parameters
The parameters represent the parameterized fields that were copied from the test script. The parameters listed in the text file must match the names of the parameters in the test script.

Lines
The individual lines contain the following information:

▶ The first line contains the column headers, as you defined them above.

▶ Below the column headers are the names that were defined for the parameters.

▶ Line 3 lists the default values of the parameters as you configured them during parameterization.

Processing external variants with Microsoft Excel
To ensure a seamless data migration, we recommend that you leave the structure of this file unchanged. It forms the basis for processing external variants, which you carry out using a spreadsheet program. Due to the popularity of Microsoft Excel, this program is used for the demonstration.

Start Microsoft Excel and open the text file ZFK01_DATA.TXT. The dialog box shown in Figure 5.39 opens.

Figure 5.39 Opening File ZFK01_DATA.TXT with Microsoft Excel

Files with type *.txt* are only displayed when you select **All Files (*.*)** for the file type. You can now select file ZFK01_DATA.TXT and click **Open**. The screen shown in Figure 5.40 opens.

Opening the text file

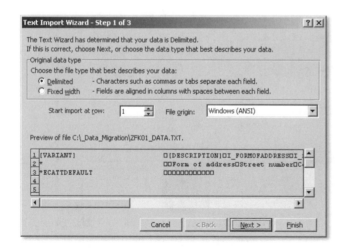

Figure 5.40 Microsoft Excel Text Import Wizard (1)

Microsoft Excel detects that the file you want to open is not an *xls* file and activates the Text Import Wizard. The wizard has already preset the appropriate parameters. Click on **Next** to continue. The screen shown in Figure 5.41 opens.

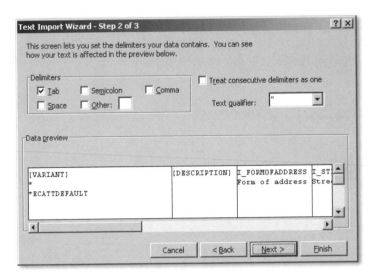

Figure 5.41 Microsoft Excel Text Import Wizard (2)

Once again, you can click on **Next** to use the default settings, because the elements of *.txt* files are always separated by tabs as described above. The dialog box shown in Figure 5.42 opens.

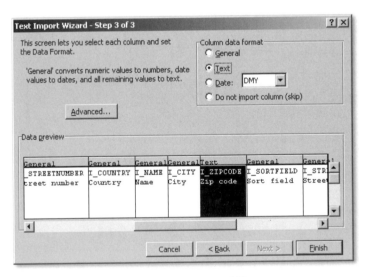

Figure 5.42 Microsoft Excel Text Import Wizard (3)

Column formatting   You define here which data format the individual columns will have. All columns/fields that can begin with a leading zero — such as phone, fax, region, or ZIP code — should be set to **Text** format. This ensures that Excel will protect the leading zeros. You can leave the remaining columns set to **Default**. Once you have formatted the columns, click on **Finish**. Microsoft Excel opens the text file in a screen similar to Figure 5.43.

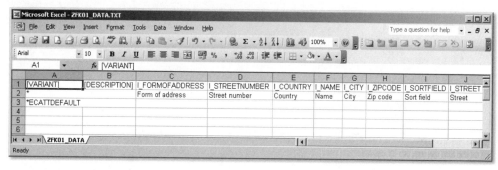

Figure 5.43 File ZFK01_DATA.TXT Opened in Microsoft Excel

You see the same data structure and contents from Figure 5.38. However, to make maintaining the variant more user-friendly, you open the file ZFK01_DATA.TXT with Excel. Once again, leave rows 1 to 3 unchanged, and maintain the variants starting with line 4. One row is reserved for each data record. Accordingly, the maximum number of data records is limited only by the maximum worksheet size in Excel.

To create a new data record for a vendor, start in row 4 and follow the structure specified in rows 1 to 2. Specifically, this means entering the name of the vendor in the appropriate column, and so on. As a reference, you can use the name of the parameter, I_NAME, or the default value from the parameter definition, provided it is available. Proceed accordingly for the rest of the fields in the data record. If no field contents are available, leave the corresponding field in row 4 blank. The result is that the field in question will be set to the default value from the recording. If no default value is available from the recording, as you can see from row 3, the field contents will remain empty for this data record. Once you have defined the first data record, you can continue with the next data record in row 5. The procedure is identical. File ZFK01_DATA.TXT, which consists of five data records, might look like the screen in Figure 5.44.

Further processing with Microsoft Excel

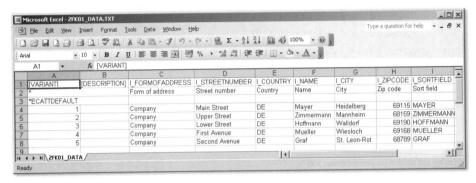

Figure 5.44 Processing the File with Microsoft Excel

Serial numbering of data records

You should particularly note the first column in Figure 5.44, **[VARI-ANT]**, which is used to distinguish the individual data records. This column must contain a *unique* value for each data record to be migrated. This means you must ensure that different data records are not assigned identical IDs. Because the distinction of the data records has a purely technical reason and doesn't affect the data migration result, it makes sense to assign serial numbers to the data records, starting with "1".

Saving the migration file in .txt format

Typically, the data to be migrated is stored in a sequential file, preferably in Microsoft Excel. You can therefore use the Excel functions **Copy** and **Paste** to transform your file to the structure required for data migration shown in Figure 5.44. Once all the data records for migration are present in ZFK01_DATA.TXT, you must save your changes. The important thing here is that you save the file as a text file again, as this is the only format that the eCATT supports. When you save the file, Excel will inform you that file ZFK01_DATA.TXT already exists and ask you whether you want to overwrite it. Confirm all prompts with **Yes**. In order to import file ZFK01_DATA.TXT to SAP ERP, you have to close it first. In the process, confirm all messages from Microsoft Excel with **Yes** or **OK**.

5.6.4 Loading Data

Creating the test configuration

Once you have completed all preliminary steps as described in the preceding sections, you can start loading the file ZFK01_DATA.TXT to SAP ERP. For this purpose, you must first create a test configuration by clicking on the **Create** button in the initial screen of the eCATT (SECATT). Figures 5.45 and 5.46 show this process.

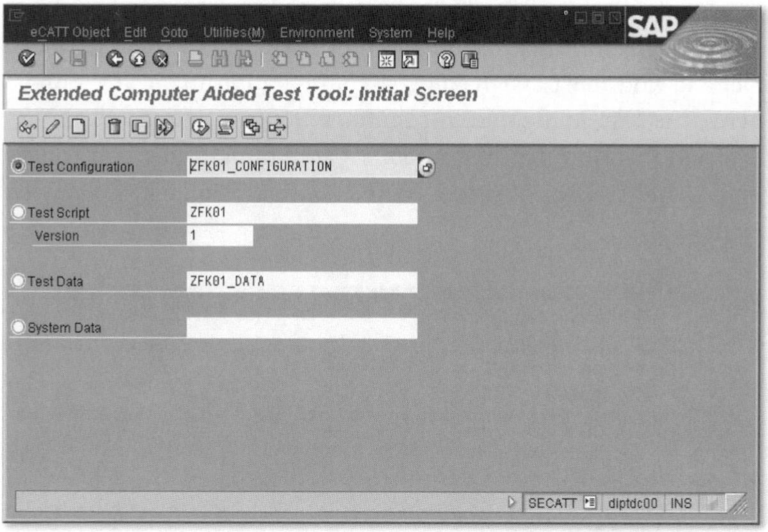

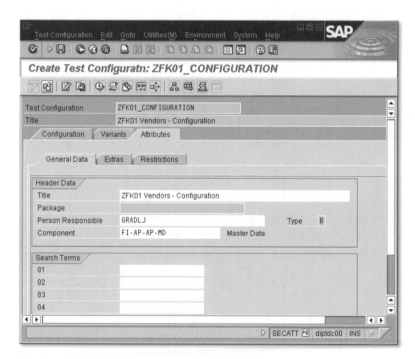

Figure 5.45 Initial Screen of the eCATT — Creating a Test Configuration

Figure 5.46 Test Configuration — Maintaining Attributes

Maintaining
attributes and
configuration

As already mentioned, when maintaining the attributes, you must define a **Title** for the test configuration as well as a **Person Responsible**, and you must assign the test configuration to an **SAP Component**. The test configuration combines the test script with the test data and therefore acts like an outer parenthesis, as it were. You can immediately see this if you select the **Configuration** tab, as shown in Figure 5.47.

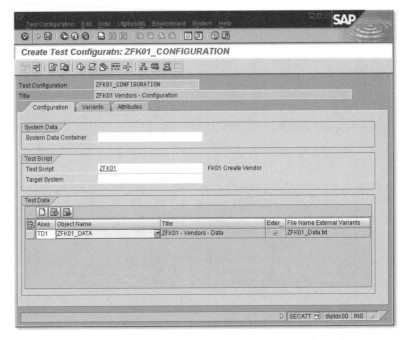

Figure 5.47 Test Configuration — Maintaining the Test Script and Test Data

Executing the test
configuration

Once you have entered the test script ZFK01 and the test data ZFK01_DATA as shown in Figure 5.47, you must save your entries so that you can start the actual data migration process. To do that, you must click on the **Execute** button. The system opens the dialog boxes shown in Figures 5.48 and 5.49.

Start options

The settings defined here ensure that the data migration process is carried out in the background and that the processing of the current data record terminates if an error occurs. In this case, the erroneous data record is skipped completely and the system continues by processing the next data record. The entire process is carried out in the background.

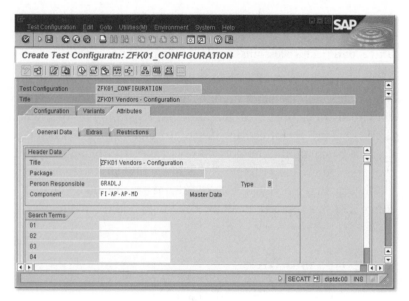

Figure 5.48 Executing the Test Configuration — Start Options (1)

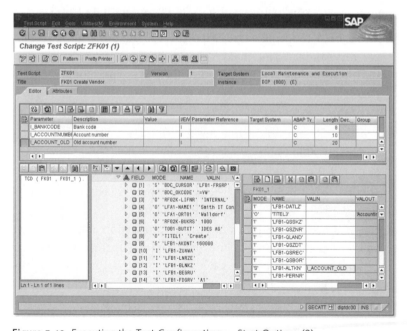

Figure 5.49 Executing the Test Configuration — Start Options (2)

The problem with this method is that data records containing errors won't be transferred, which may result in an incomplete data migration process. For this reason, we recommend that you analyze the log that is generated at the end of the data migration (see Figure 5.28 above) and postprocess missing data records, if necessary.

Brief appraisal

Where performance is concerned, this data migration procedure is comparable with the batch input technique, not only with regard to the screens to be processed, but also with regard to the consistency checks that are performed for the input values. A major advantage over the batch input technique, however, is that absolutely no ABAP coding is required, which makes this method accessible to less technically oriented individuals as well. Chapter 10 provides you with a comprehensive appraisal of all the data migration techniques.

5.7 Tips and Tricks

5.7.1 General Recommendations

This section contains several recommendations that will help you to simplify your work with the eCATT in data migration projects.

Use only familiar transactions

▸ You should only create test scripts for transactions with which you are very familiar. This ensures that you know the system response during recording and execution of the test script; moreover, your past experience with the transactions will enable you to deal with any error messages that may occur.

▸ Process only one transaction per test script, even though it is technically possible to process several transactions. This approach lets you split the overall data migration into smaller, transaction-specific packages, which will help you to allocate responsibilities for the migration within your enterprise.

▸ Use parameters to pass values to the transaction and avoid fixed values whenever possible in order to ensure that a test script can be applied as widely as possible.

▸ The universal character of the test script should also be considered when choosing its parameters and screen sequence.

▸ Avoid creating new test scripts when you can modify existing ones. For more information, see Section 5.7.2.

▸ Use the log that is generated at the end of the data migration as documentation, even in external audits.

► If you want to use transactions from other applications, you should use their specific test scripts and request their extension, if necessary (see Section 5.7.2).

5.7.2 Modifying Test Scripts

Often, you may have to deal with situations whereby someone else has already created a test script for a transaction that you now want to test yourself, or use for a data migration. On closer examination, however, it seems that the test script includes fields that you don't need for your own project, or that required fields are missing. In such cases, it doesn't make sense to create a new, redundant test script for the same transaction. Instead, you should modify the existing test script to address the changed situation, which may require coordination with the person responsible for the original test script.

To illustrate this problem, consider the example for creating a vendor (Transaction FK01) introduced in Section 5.5. In this example, the situation demands that the **Old Account Number** field be maintained, in addition to the fields that have already been filled or parameterized. This field contains the vendor number in the legacy accounting system, which will enable you to select and analyze reports based on this old number in SAP ERP as well.

To add additional information to an existing test script, you have to modify it. To do so, call the initial screen of the eCATT, enter test script ZFK01, and click on **Change**. The dialog box shown in Figure 5.50 opens.

Because the **Old Account Number** field can have a different value depending on the vendor, you must provide a parameter I_ACCOUNT_OLD for it, which you can define as described in Section 5.6.1.

Then go to the central pane in the bottom half of your screen (command interface) and navigate to the screen template that is represented by the SAP program name, SAPMF02K. This screen template contains the old account number field. Double-click on the screen template. The system then displays a screen similar to Figure 5.51. Here, you can assign the previously defined parameter, I_ACCOUNT_OLD, to the **Old account number** field. Click on **Save** to finish the modification of the test script.

Initial situation

Example

Procedure

Parameter definition

Parameter assignment

Figure 5.50 Modifying the Test Script — Creating Parameters

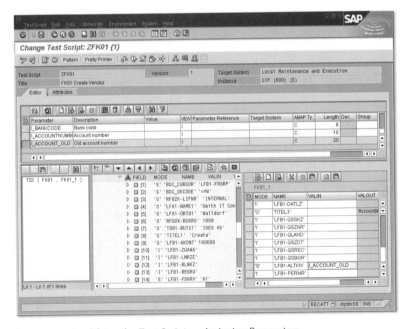

Figure 5.51 Modifying the Test Script — Assigning Parameters

In the next step, you must make sure to include the **Old account number** field in the file that is used for the data migration. For this reason, you must include the I_ACCOUNT_OLD parameter in the file format. You can do that by selecting the **Test Data** radio button in the initial screen of the eCATT, entering "ZFK01_DATA", and then clicking on **Change**.

Including parameters in the migration file

Then go to the **Parameters** tab and select **Edit • Import Parameters** from the menu. The system opens the dialog box shown in Figure 5.52 in which you must specify the associated test script, ZFK01. In addition, you can make its parameters available by clicking on the **Get Parameter** button.

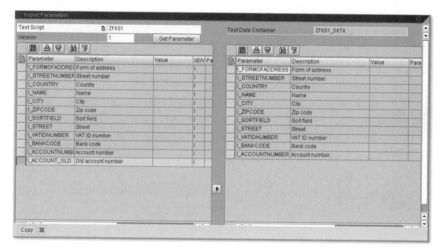

Figure 5.52 Importing Parameters

In contrast to Figure 5.32, Figure 5.52 displays the I_ACCOUNT_OLD parameter, which you have defined in the test script and assigned to a field after the step that was shown in Figure 5.32. The **Attach** and **Copy** buttons enable you to transfer the parameters to the test data container. Finally, click on **Save** to complete this step. Regarding the download of the modified file format to your PC, you should proceed as described in Section 5.6.2.

If you open the downloaded file in Microsoft Excel (see Figure 5.53), you will see that a new three-line file was created and that the I_ACCOUNT_OLD parameter was inserted in the last column of the file. You can now enter the data records for migration, as described in section 5.6.3, and then start the upload to SAP ERP.

Positioning the parameter in the migration file

Figure 5.53 Old Account Number as Parameter in ZFK01_DATA.TXT

Test configuration remains unchanged

At this point, you should note that the actual test configuration remains unchanged. However, because the test configuration acts as the outer parenthesis, which connects the test script with the test data, a modification of these components implicitly affects the test configuration as well.

Modifying the structure of the text file

Situations are also possible in which you have nearly completed your preparations for data migration, as far as recording the test script and maintaining the data in Microsoft Excel is concerned (see Section 5.6.3), but the user department then asks you to migrate additional fields to SAP ERP. In such situations, we recommend that you change the test script and test data, as described above, and add and parameterize the additional fields accordingly. You then have to generate the text file required for the data migration and save it, for example, as ZFK01_1.txt. The three-line ZFK01_1.txt file is merely an auxiliary file, because only its structure — particularly the columns with the added parameters — is relevant. Now, copy these additional columns from ZFK01_1.txt and insert them on the right border of your actual migration file, ZFK01.txt. In other words: The structure of ZFK01.txt must be identical to that of ZFK01_1.txt. You can then delete file ZFK01_1.txt and begin maintaining the values of the new parameters in ZFK01.txt, starting with line 4. Alternatively, you can also copy the data records from ZFK01.txt to ZFK01_1.txt and use ZFK01_1.txt as the migration file. It's completely up to your own preferences which of the two alternatives you should use.

5.7.3 Initializing Field Contents

Initial situation

When you execute a test script, you may get an error message indicating that a master record with the identical number already exists; however, you cannot create another master record with the same number. This error occurs because SAP ERP doesn't automatically initialize (that is, reset to blank) the field that identifies the master record (for example, the G/L account number) after it is created with the eCATT.

To learn how to resolve this problem, we'll return to the example of creating G/L accounts in the company code (Transaction FSS0).

Example

Call the initial transaction of the eCATT (SECATT) and record a test script called ZFSS0 for Transaction FSS0. To keep the example simple, maintain only the fields **G/L Account**, **Company Code**, and **Field Status** in the test script. Figure 5.54 shows an excerpt of the maintained values.

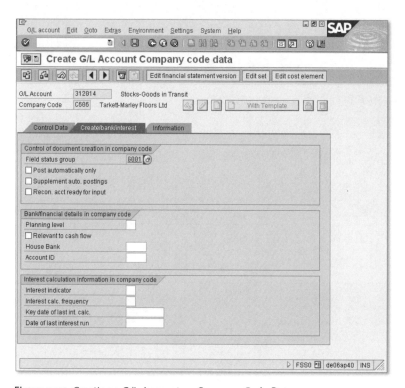

Figure 5.54 Creating a G/L Account — Company Code Data

As soon as you have maintained the **field status** and saved your data, as well as ensured that the transaction recorder is still active, initialize the **G/L Account** field. To do so, you can use an old function taken from SAP R/2. Position the cursor in the **G/L Account** field, preface the existing G/L account number with an exclamation point

Initialization

(!), and click on **Enter** to confirm your entries. The dialog box displayed in Figure 5.55 opens.

The transaction recorder records an entry for the initialization you just performed. Click on the green arrow (**F3**) to go back and end the recording. You can now start parameterizing the fields. The last recorded screen, which contains information about the initialization, is particularly important (see Figure 5.56).

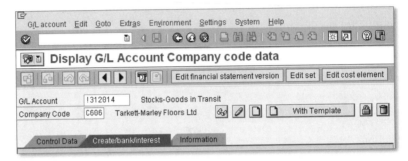

Figure 5.55 Initializing the G/L Account Field

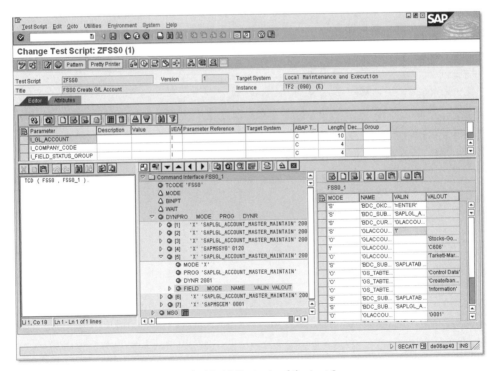

Figure 5.56 Recorded Field Contents of the Last Screen

As you can see in Figure 5.56, an exclamation point (!) was recorded in the last screen for the G/L account number. If you use this fixed value in the test script and execute the script of the test configuration, the G/L account number you previously defined will be removed before you create the next account. In this way you can eliminate the problem described at the start of this section. To ensure that we have covered everything here, we should mention that you must carry out the parameter definition for the remaining fields, including the field assignment as before, in order to generate the file format for the data migration in the next step. Because fixed values have the same value for all data records, the migration file doesn't contain any column that is provided for the initialization. The initialization is an integral component of the test script, which each data record must undergo in order to be processed.

Using a fixed value for initialization

5.7.4 Table Maintenance with the eCATT

You can also use the eCATT to maintain customer-specific tables, which once again underscores the cross-application character of this tool. If you want to use this option, the transaction to record is called **Extended Table Maintenance**; the corresponding transaction code is SM30. The procedure — recording the test script, parameterizing the fields, processing the migration file externally with Microsoft Excel, then merging the test script and migration file to form the test configuration and uploading the data to SAP ERP — is analogous to the descriptions in Sections 5.3 and 5.6 and is therefore not repeated here.

General approach

There is one special feature, however, which you won't encounter in any other application but table maintenance. This feature occurs whenever you want to record a test script for a blank table (i.e., one that doesn't have any entries yet). In this situation, this table receives its first entry when you record the test script. Because the screen sequence depends on the table entries, a different screen sequence is displayed when you record the test script (the table does not have any entries yet) than when you execute it (the table already has an entry), which will result in the error message **Batch input data not available for screen...** (see Section 5.5.2). This occurs regardless of whether customer-specific tables or Customizing tables are involved.

Differing screens

To avoid this problem, ensure that the tables have *at least two entries* before you begin recording the test script. This guarantees that the

Solution

system presents identical screen sequences during both the recording and the execution of the test script or test configuration, and prevents the initial error message from being displayed.

Maintaining Customizing tables As already mentioned, you can also use the eCATT to maintain Customizing tables. This approach is helpful whenever you have to enter similar entries that are already available in a sequential file and have to be imported into SAP ERP. Figure 5.57 shows a screen in which you can maintain accounting administrators for individual company codes as an example of a Customizing table.

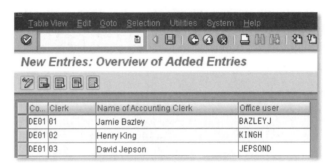

Figure 5.57 Customizing Table for Accounting Administrators

You should also take steps to prevent the creation of transport requests while recording a test script. Otherwise, the system will create an additional transport request for every imported data record. If you processed 100 data records, for example, 100 transport requests would have to be transported to the consolidation and production systems, which would be extremely time-consuming. In this case as well, it is better to create an entry in the corresponding Customizing table manually and then save it in a separate transport request. You can then refer to this transport request when you record the test script, which will prevent the creation of another transport request during recording.

Outlook If this chapter has taught you to appreciate the eCATT as an easy-to-use tool for data migration, it has served its purpose. If, however, your situation is more complex than what we have described here, thereby making the eCATT unsuitable to your needs, we suggest that you look at Chapter 7, which describes a tool specifically designed for cases of greater complexity, namely, the Legacy System Migration Workbench or LSM Workbench.

This chapter is intended for those of you who use an SAP ERP release lower than SAP ERP 2004. With those releases, you cannot use the eCATT for data migration projects. However, if you still want to benefit from the advantages of using the eCATT in your specific environment, we recommend using the traditional CATT.

6 Computer Aided Test Tool (CATT)

Why CATT?

The following descriptions are intended for users who have not yet upgraded to SAP ERP 2004 or a higher release status and, therefore, cannot use the eCATT as described in Chapter 5. Although the eCATT has been available since SAP R/3 Enterprise, you cannot use it for data migration purposes because that release doesn't support an essential function of the tool, namely, the uploading of a local file into the SAP system. However, you can circumvent this functional limitation by using the *traditional* CATT instead of the eCATT. The CATT provides all functions that are required for data migration and can be operated very easily.

6.1 Basic Terminology

Test case
and variant

When using the CATT instead of the eCATT, we no longer speak of a *test script*, *test data*, and a *test configuration*. Instead, these different work steps are summarized into a single work step, namely, the *test case*. The test case consists of the transaction recording and subsequent parameterization, as well as of the generation of the file format, which is required for the data migration and can be downloaded to a PC for external processing purposes (i.e., for the arrangement of data to be migrated).

Data records to be migrated are also referred to as *variants*. This applies to both the CATT and eCATT.

6.2 Preparing the System for Using the CATT

Test cases are cross-client and can generally be created in any defined client. You can use the client table, T000, to define whether test cases can be started in a specific client (see Figure 6.1).

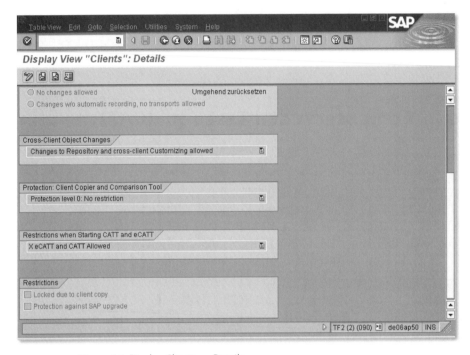

Figure 6.1 Display Clients — Details

To do so, you must select **Tools · Administration · Administration · Client Administration · Maintain Clients** or, alternatively, enter Transaction Code SCC4.

Make sure the flag **eCATT and CATT Allowed** is selected in the detail view of the client, in group **Restrictions when Starting CATT and eCATT**.

6.3 How Does the CATT Work?

Example: Posting an FI document

The functionality of the CATT can be demonstrated best by using a simple example: *entering an FI document*, or, to put it more precisely, entering an open vendor item.

6.3.1 Recording a Test Case

Initial transaction

Three options are available for accessing the initial screen of the CATT:

- **System · Services · CATT · Record**
- **Tools · ABAP Workbench · Test Workbench · CATT**
- Transaction Code SECATT

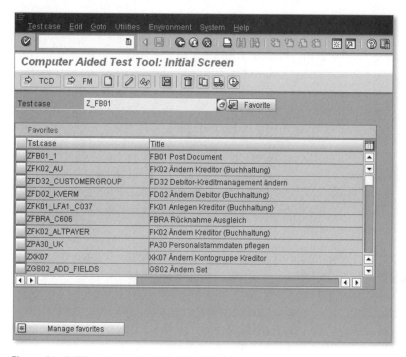

Figure 6.2 CATT — Computer Aided Test Tool: Initial Screen

Name assignment and transaction recording

You assign a **name** for the new test case in this initial screen (see Figure 6.2). Remember that the name must start with Y, Z, or your namespace prefix in the customer namespace. To help you structure your test cases later, we recommend that you include the transaction code of the relevant transaction in the name of the test case. For example, you could call a test case for entering open vendor items via Transaction FB01 Z_FB01. We decided to use Transaction FB01 because it allows you to easily design screens and define default values for fields, which provides us with a high degree of flexibility regarding the data entry.

Once you have defined the name of the test case, choose **Record Transaction**. In the process, a transaction recorder records all the input and triggered functions within a transaction run.

Figure 6.3 CATT — Recording a Transaction

Entering the transaction code and posting the FI document

You use the dialog box in Figure 6.3 to specify the **transaction code** of the transaction to be tested. If you don't know the transaction code, you can use the **F4** input help. You can also navigate to the transaction through the menu tree that opens. Position the cursor on the corresponding menu and select **Copy**.

If you know the transaction code, you can begin with the actual recording of the transaction. To do so, click on **Record**. Start Transaction FB01 — *Post Document* (see Figure 6.4) — and go through all screens that are relevant for the posting of a document (see Figures 6.4 through 6.7).

You now have to enter your values and navigate through the appropriate screens exactly as if you were performing the transaction manually, without the CATT. The only indications that the CATT is active and that the transaction recorder is recording the input in the background are the occasional messages in the status bar, which appear whenever you confirm your entries with **Enter** or navigate to the next screen.

Fields to fill

Our example assumes that we must provide the essential document information required for transferring an open vendor item. This information includes the **Document Date**, **Posting Date**, **Document Type**, **Company Code**, **Document Currency**, and **Translation Rate;** if the open item is specified in a foreign currency, we need to enter the **Reference** (Document Number). In addition, we need a **Posting Key** and the associated **Vendor Account**, the **Amount** of the open item, a **Posting Key** for the G/L account line, and the associated (transfer) **Account**.

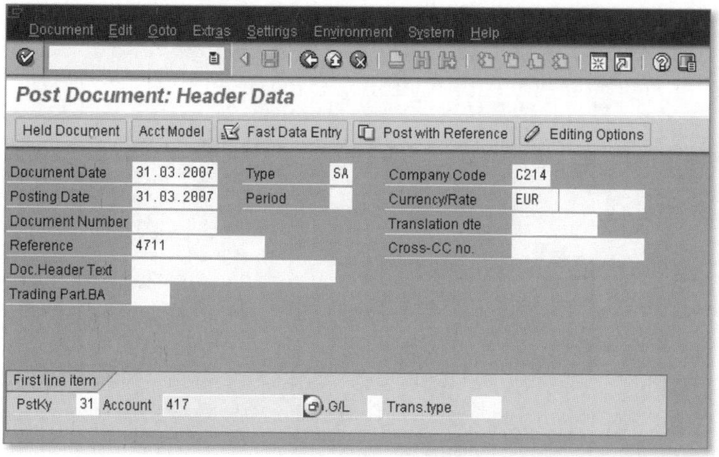

Figure 6.4 CATT — Posting an FI Document: Initial Screen

Once you have entered this information according to Figure 6.4, click **Enter** to go to the vendor line item shown in Figure 6.5. Here, you must enter the relevant information as well, and then click **Enter** to go to the G/L account line item in order to provide the relevant information (see Figure 6.6).

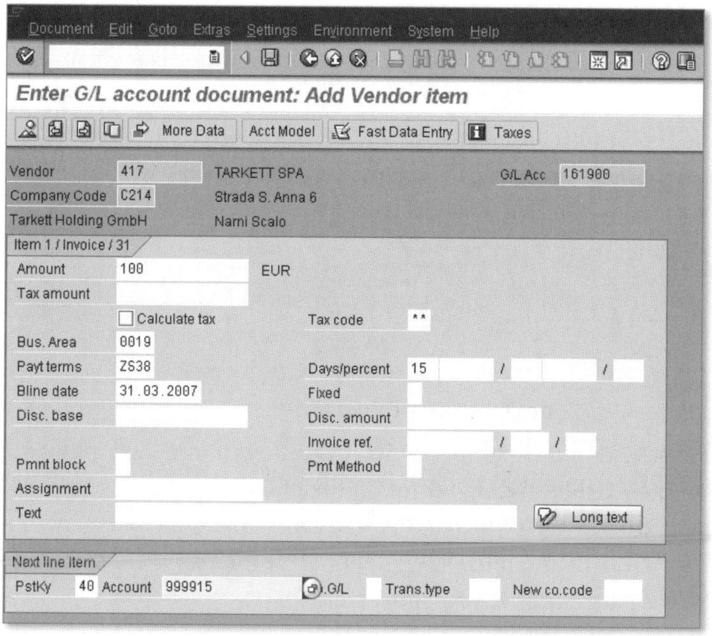

Figure 6.5 CATT — Posting a FI Document: Vendor Line Item

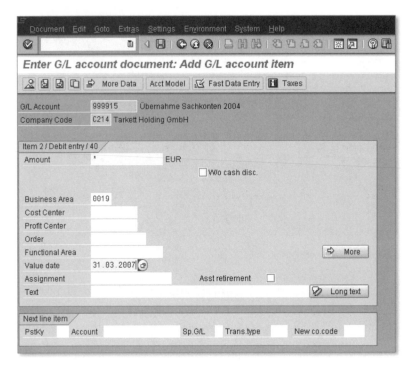

Figure 6.6 CATT — Posting a FI Document: G/L Account Line Item

Once you have **posted** the document you just entered, the system displays a message (see Figure 6.7), which you can confirm by clicking **Enter**.

Figure 6.7 CATT — FI Document Posted

Ending the recording

Because you don't want to record any other transaction, you can click on the **Exit Recording** button in the dialog shown in Figure 6.8. This takes you to the screen shown in Figure 6.9, which displays the parameters for maintaining the attributes of the test case. Maintaining test case attributes is your next step.

CATT: Record another transaction
Transaction code
FB01

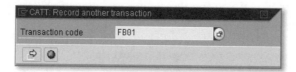

Figure 6.8 CATT — Ending the Recording

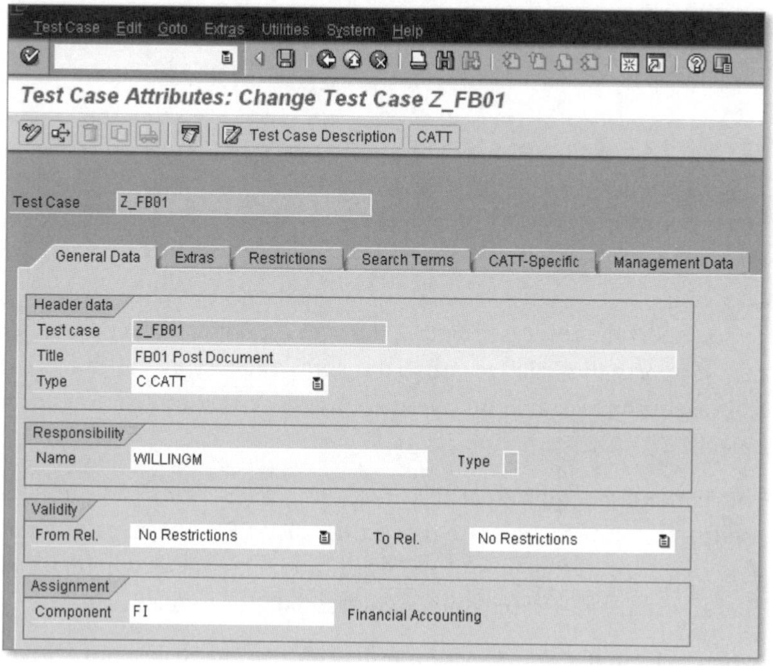
Test Case Edit Goto Extras Utilities System Help
Test Case Attributes: Change Test Case Z_FB01
Test Case Description
CATT
Test Case
Z_FB01
General Data
Extras
Restrictions
Search Terms
CATT-Specific
Management Data
Header data
Test case
Z_FB01
Title
FB01 Post Document
Type
C CATT
Responsibility
Name
WILLINGM
Type
Validity
From Rel.
No Restrictions
To Rel.
No Restrictions
Assignment
Component
FI
Financial Accounting

Figure 6.9 CATT — Maintaining the Test Case Attributes

Maintaining test case attributes

Default values are already proposed for a majority of the fields and you can use them unchanged. The name of the current test case appears in the **Test case** field and a short description of the test case appears in the **Title** field. The person who created the test case is automatically entered in the **Responsibility** section. If the person who created the test case is not the contact person, you must change this entry. The **Validity** of the test case provides information on the release statuses in which you can execute the test case. The validity is generally not restricted. The **Component** field contains the corresponding SAP ERP application component where the transaction you want to test is located.

Object directory entry Once you have finished maintaining the attributes, you can save the test case (see Figure 6.10).

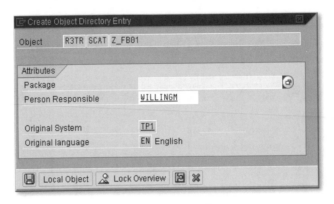

Figure 6.10 Creating an Object Directory Entry

Transport request To transport the test case to other systems, you must select a *package* that supports this, along with a transport request. If you want the test case to be available only in the current system, save it as a **local object**.

This is the last required task for recording a test case. You can now use the test case to generate data in the SAP ERP system as often as you want. Up to this point, the procedure is identical, whether you plan to use the test case to generate test data, or to migrate data.

When exiting the test case, you must confirm the dialog box shown in Figure 6.11 by clicking on the **Yes** button.

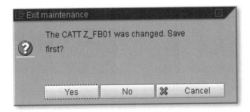

Figure 6.11 CATT — Exiting the Test Case Maintenance

6.3.2   Parameterizing the Input Values

Next, you have to set the parameters for the fields that need to have   Parameterization
variable contents for the data migration. To ensure that you can
reuse the test case at a later stage, you should parameterize as many
fields as possible. To do so, you must proceed as follows.

In the initial screen of the CATT (Transaction SCAT), enter the test
case you want to edit, Z_FB01, and select **Change**. The screen shown
in Figure 6.12 opens.

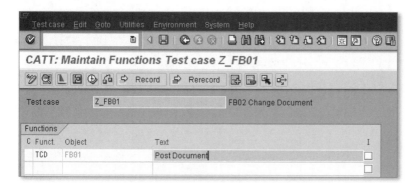

Figure 6.12 CATT — Functions for Test Case Z_FB01

Figure 6.12 displays the *Function Editor* of the CATT. The Function   Function Editor –
Editor uses the TCD function to define the transaction that will be   overview
executed in the test case. In our example, this is Transaction FB01,
which is used to post open vendor items. The numerous editing and
control commands available in the Function Editor aren't described
in any detail here. Instead, we'll focus on the functions that are
needed and used in the data migration process. If you need more
information on the Function Editor, please refer to the official SAP
documentation.

When you double-click to navigate to the detail view of this transac-   Function Editor –
tion (see Figure 6.13), you see a list of all the screen templates from   processed screens
Transaction FB01 that you processed during your recording.

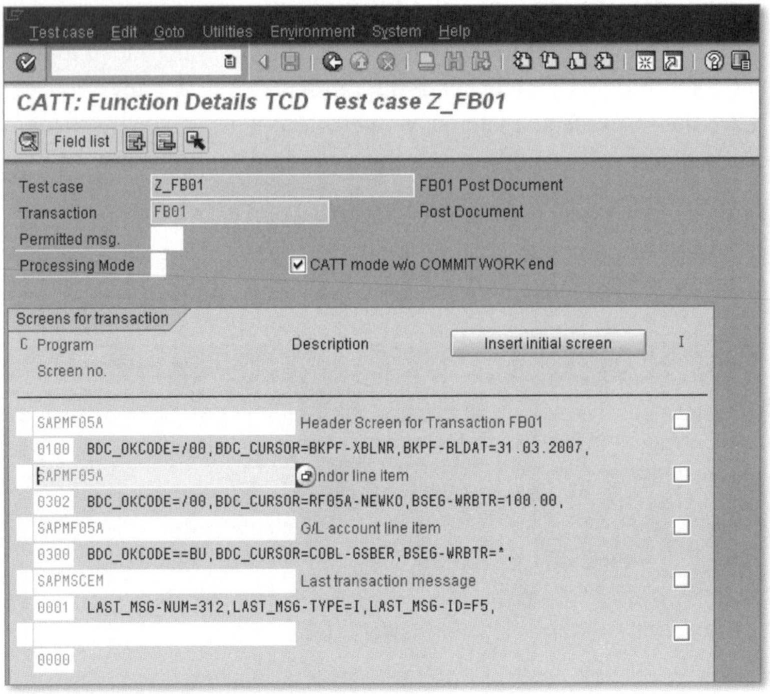

Figure 6.13 CATT — Details of Function TCD

Function Editor – processed screens: details

To display detailed information for the individual screens, position the cursor within a screen and double-click again. We recommend starting with the first screen and then sequentially running through all the other screens. The system displays the initial screen of Transaction FB01, as shown in Figure 6.14.

Function Editor – processed screens: parameterizing the input fields

As you can see in Figure 6.14, the system has filled all the input fields with the values you entered when you recorded the test case. In the next step, you must distinguish which fields will be variable for the data migration and which fields should be assigned fixed values that apply to all the data records for migration. To make the test case as flexible and universally applicable as possible, we recommend that you parameterize as many fields as possible. The procedure is extremely simple. Position the cursor on a field whose contents you want to define variably and double-click. If you choose the **Document Date** field, for example, a dialog box like the one shown in Figure 6.15 opens.

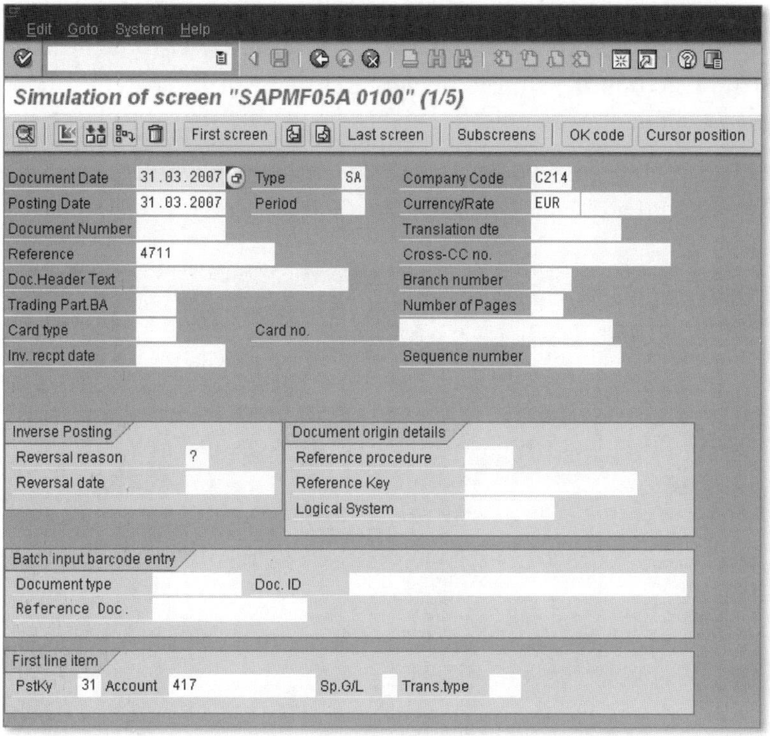

Figure 6.14 CATT — Simulation of the Header Data Screen

This dialog box consists of the **Parameter Name** and **Field Contents** fields. Define a parameter name, such as "Document_date", and a default value for the field.

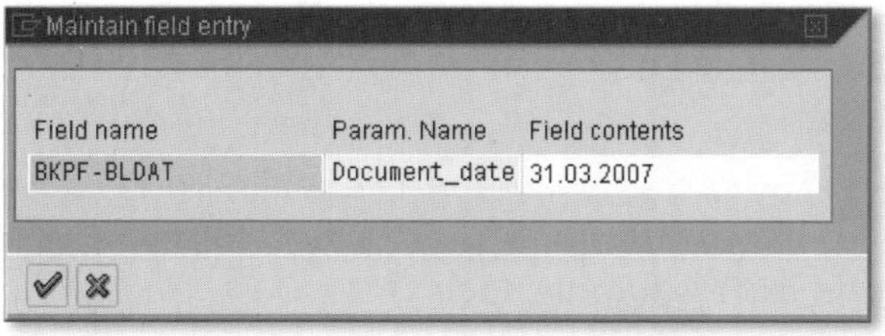

Figure 6.15 CATT — Parameterizing the "Document Date" Field

Usually, this default value is taken from the recording; however, you can overwrite it if necessary. During the data migration, the fields are filled with the default values whenever the respective data record doesn't provide corresponding field contents. If the field in question is not a required entry field, you might consider foregoing a default

value altogether, which would result in a blank field in the corresponding data record. As you'll see, it is much easier to manage the
data migration if you use mnemonic names for the parameters, as
was done in our example.

When you click on **Enter** to close the dialog box, you return to the
screen where you started (see Figure 6.16).

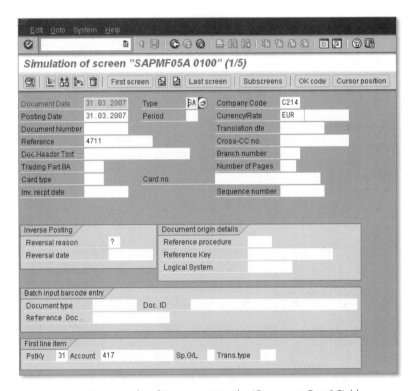

Figure 6.16 CATT — Results of Parameterizing the "Document Date" Field

As you can see in Figure 6.16, the screen field is no longer ready for
input after parameterization. Its contents are merely a default value.
When values are passed during the test case execution, it will be
overwritten and highlighted. Field contents for fields that are ready
for input are simply fixed values that are copied identically to the
corresponding fields of all the data records for migration. Consequently, you can determine which fields were assigned default values during the migration and which fields received variable contents.

Once you have defined all parameters of the first screen, the system
displays the results, which look similar to Figure 6.17.

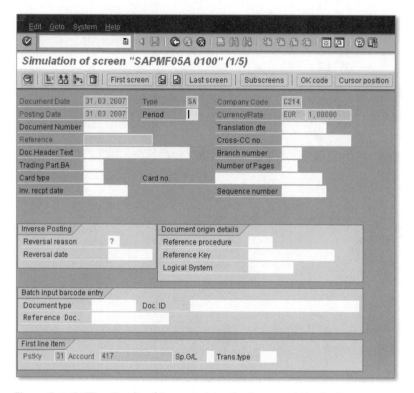

Figure 6.17 CATT — Results of Parameterizing the Document Header Data

Click on the **Next Screen** button in order to parameterize the fields contained in the subsequent screen. Repeat this iterative process, which is illustrated in Figures 6.18 and 6.19, until you have defined all parameters as required.

Parameter definition as an iterative process

As you can see in Figures 6.17 through 6.19, the following fields were parameterized:

▸ **Document Header**: document date, posting date, document type, company code, currency, rate, reference

▸ **Document Item 1**: (vendor) posting key, (vendor) account, amount

▸ **Document Item 2**: posting key (for G/L account posting), (G/L) account, amount, business area

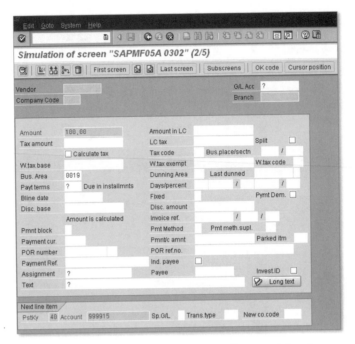

Figure 6.18 CATT — Results of Parameterizing Document Item 1

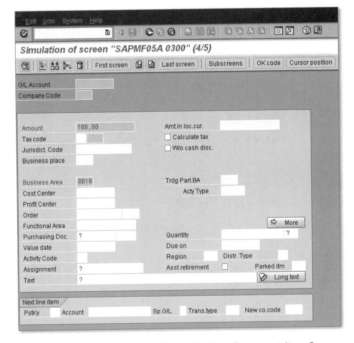

Figure 6.19 CATT — Results of Parameterizing Document Item 2

The last screen (see Figure 6.20) contains only messages relating to posting the FI document that don't require any further action. Here, you can click on the **Next Screen** button to return to Figure 6.13, then press **F3** to return to Figure 6.12, which enables you to **save** the changes you made and select **Goto • Variants • Export Proposal** from the menu in order to download the file format required for the data migration as text file Z_FB01.txt to your PC (see Figure 6.21).

Downloading the migration file

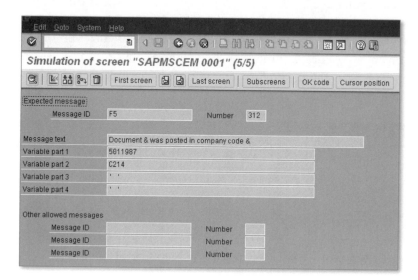

Figure 6.20 CATT — Messages Created During the Posting of the FI Document

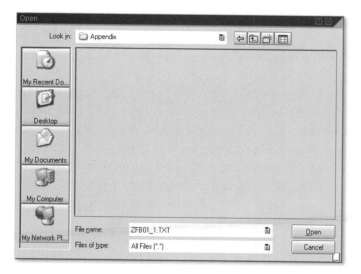

Figure 6.21 CATT — Downloading the Text File for the Data Migration

By default, the dialog shown in Figure 6.21 proposes the path, which is preset in your SAP GUI settings and can be overwritten easily. You should give the file a name similar to the name of the test case. This enables you to easily determine which files need to be processed with which test cases. Note, however, that the file format must always be a text file with the ending *.txt*.

Processing the migration file with MS Excel

When you open Z_FB01.txt in Microsoft Excel (see Figure 6.22), you can easily maintain the open vendor items to be migrated in accordance with the format predefined by the file. Note that you should not modify lines 1 through 4. From line 5 onwards, all lines are reserved for the data migration, with each line being provided for one complete data record.

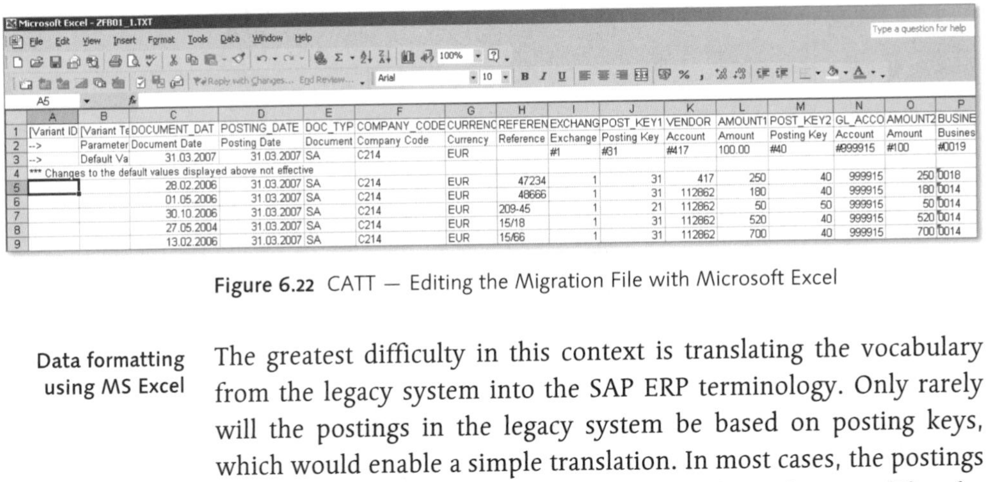

	A	B	C	D	E	F	G	H	I	J	K	L	M	N	O	P
1	[Variant ID	[Variant Te	DOCUMENT_DAT	POSTING_DATE	DOC_TYP	COMPANY_CODE	CURRENC	REFEREN	EXCHANG	POST_KEY1	VENDOR	AMOUNT1	POST_KEY2	GL_ACCO	AMOUNT2	BUSINE
2	-->	Parameter	Document Date	Posting Date	Document	Company Code	Currency	Reference	Exchange	Posting Key	Account	Amount	Posting Key	Account	Amount	Busines
3	-->	Default Va	31.03.2007	31.03.2007	SA	C214	EUR		#1	#31	#417	100.00	#40	#999915	#100	#0019
4	*** Changes to the default values displayed above not effective															
5			28.02.2006	31.03.2007	SA	C214	EUR	47234	1	31	417	250	40	999915	250	0018
6			01.05.2006	31.03.2007	SA	C214	EUR	48666	1	31	112862	180	40	999915	180	0014
7			30.10.2006	31.03.2007	SA	C214	EUR	209-45	1	21	112862	50	50	999915	50	0014
8			27.05.2004	31.03.2007	SA	C214	EUR	15/18	1	31	112862	520	40	999915	520	0014
9			13.02.2006	31.03.2007	SA	C214	EUR	15/66	1	31	112862	700	40	999915	700	0014

Figure 6.22 CATT — Editing the Migration File with Microsoft Excel

Data formatting using MS Excel

The greatest difficulty in this context is translating the vocabulary from the legacy system into the SAP ERP terminology. Only rarely will the postings in the legacy system be based on posting keys, which would enable a simple translation. In most cases, the postings in the legacy system will have an indicator that at least qualifies the posting in question as an invoice or credit memo. Of course, this indicator must be extracted from the legacy system along with the open items to enable you to assign appropriate SAP ERP posting keys. If the posting key for posting to the vendor account is known, you can directly derive the posting key for the G/L account line (data transfer account). Furthermore, SAP ERP does not support the entry of negative values. The posting key controls whether a value should be interpreted as positive or negative. The data extract from the legacy system might set all vendor credit memos with a minus sign, however, which would have to be removed prior to the data migration. As these brief examples show, you will have to format the data with Microsoft Excel in most cases before you can transfer this structured data with Z_FB01.txt. The versatile filter and copy options in Microsoft Excel make it an outstanding tool for this task. Note that you must save the formatted migration file as a text file (.*txt*) again in order to enable the SAP ERP system to process it.

6.3.3   Executing a Test Case

Once you have created the test case, parameterized all fields, and saved the migration file that is filled with data as a text file (.*txt*), you can start executing the test case and thus migrating the data. From the initial screen of the CATT (Transaction SCAT), you can specify the test script to execute and then click on the **Execute** button. This takes you to the screen shown in Figure 6.23.

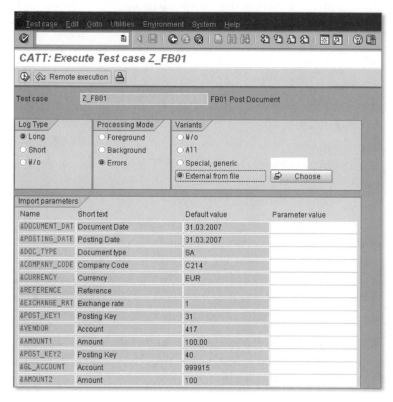

Figure 6.23 CATT — Starting Test Case Z_FB01

In the upper left-hand part of the screen, you can specify which type of log you want the CATT to generate. Three log type options are available:

Type of Log

▸ **Long**

All screen templates and input fields are recorded under this option; the input fields show the assigned values from the migration file. If an error occurs, the system automatically generates a long log, which starts with the component that contains the error. In that case, the long log is always created, even if you elected not to generate any log.

▸ **Short**

If no errors occur, the short log merely contains information about the functions called in the test case and the parameter contents.

▸ **No**

Processing modes   In the upper central part of the screen, you must define the mode in which you want to process the transactions. Three processing mode options are available:

▸ **Foreground**

The test case is executed fully in dialog. In the process, you can change field inputs to influence the test or data migration results. Clicking on **Enter** takes you to the next screen.

▸ **Background**

The transactions are executed in the background, without any dialog.

▸ **Errors**

In this case, the transactions continue to be processed in the background until the first error or termination occurs. When an error occurs, the system switches to dialog mode, enabling you to change incorrect entries. Once you click on **Enter** to confirm the corrected entry, the system switches back to background processing and continues until the next error or termination occurs.

Variants   In the right-hand part of the screen shown in Figure 6.23, you must specify the *variants*, that is, the data records to be migrated. Because these variants are contained in a text file outside of the SAP ERP system, you must select the **External from file** radio button and click **Choose**. In the dialog box that opens next, you can select your migration file (see Figure 6.24).

Migrating the data   Now start the data migration by clicking on the **Execute** button. Based on the settings shown in Figure 6.23, the system generates a hierarchically structured log once the migration process has completed. This log should look similar to the one shown in Figure 6.25.

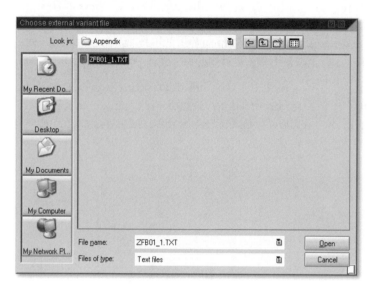

Figure 6.24 CATT — Selecting the Migration File

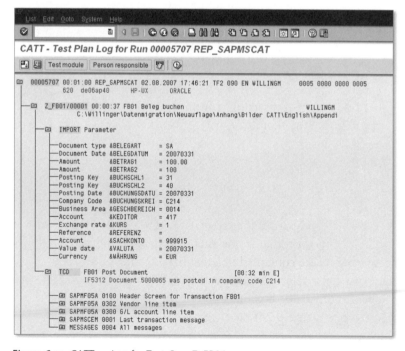

Figure 6.25 CATT — Log for Test Case Z_FB01

Log The example shown in Figure 6.25 represents a *long log*. The header section, which contains, among other things, the **executing client**, **date**, **time**, and **platform**, forms the top hierarchy level. The next level lists the test case used, Z_FB01, which is broken down further into the called transaction (Transaction FB01), the executed screens, SAPxxxxx, the inputs made, and the messages generated by the CATT.

Ultimately, the log indicates whether the test case was executed successfully. If an error occurred, the responsible components are highlighted in the log; however, that is not the case in our example.

In this chapter, you'll learn about a powerful, flexible tool that you can use to transfer data from non-SAP systems to an SAP ERP system with minimal programming. The Legacy System Migration Workbench (LSM Workbench) is useful whenever the structure of the legacy data differs widely from the structure in the SAP ERP system, thus making data conversion necessary.

7 Legacy System Migration Workbench

7.1 Overview of the LSM Workbench

The *Legacy System Migration Workbench* (also called the *LSM Workbench* and *LSMW*) has its roots in the R/2-R/3 Migration Workbench. The primary concepts and experience with R/2-R/3 migration influenced the development of the LSM Workbench.

History

The LSM Workbench is a powerful SAP NetWeaver technology-based tool that supports both one-time and periodic data transfer from non-SAP systems (*Legacy systems*) to SAP systems based on the SAP NetWeaver technology (*SAP systems* for short).

Features

The LSM Workbench features easy-to-use functions for *reading* data from files from non-SAP systems, *converting* this data to SAP formats, and *importing* the converted data into an SAP ERP system, using the following standard SAP interfaces: batch input, direct input, *BAPIs (Business Application Programming Interfaces)*, and *IDocs (Intermediate Documents)*.

The LSM Workbench also has functions for recording SAP transactions (similar to those in the eCATT). Consequently, you can record an entry or change transaction and use the resulting recording as the basis for your data migration.

Basic principles The LSM Workbench was based on the following principles:

▶ The LSM Workbench is not used to migrate individual tables or field contents; instead, it is used to migrate integral business data objects, such as customer masters, material masters, financial documents, and so on.

▶ The full functionality is contained within the SAP ERP system. There should not be a collection of scattered, unrelated, difficult-to-maintain programs on different platforms.

▶ The quality and consistency of the data imported into the SAP ERP system are more important than the speed of the data migration.

▶ No ready-made data conversion programs are provided. Instead, the necessary programs are generated from defined conversion rules.

▶ These conversion rules are reusable.

On this basis, a concept was developed that is illustrated in Figure 7.1.

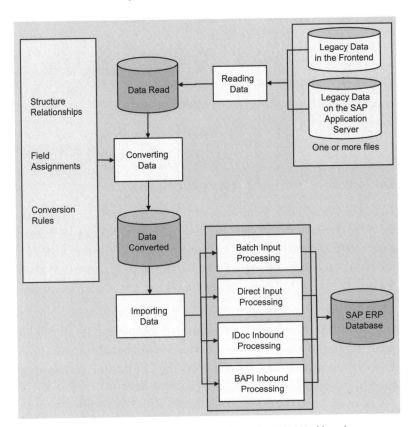

Figure 7.1 Flow Diagram of a Data Migration Using the LSM Workbench

The LSM Workbench has the following core functions:

▶ **Reading data**
Reading data from the legacy system, which is stored in files on the frontend or the SAP application server.

▶ **Converting data**
Converting the data to the SAP ERP format. The terms "converting data" and "translating data" are used synonymously.

▶ **Importing data**
Posting the data in the database of the SAP ERP system.

The main benefits of the LSM Workbench can be summarized as follows:

▶ The LSM Workbench is part of the SAP ERP system and is therefore platform-independent.

▶ It offers a wide range of technical data conversion options.

▶ It ensures data consistency via the use of standard SAP import techniques (standard interfaces).

▶ It generates ABAP programs from defined conversion rules.

▶ It offers clear user guidance.

▶ It supports reading the data from both the frontend and the application server.

▶ It can record an SAP ERP entry or change transaction and use the resulting recording as the basis for data migration.

▶ It is available to SAP customers and partners free of charge.

If you're already familiar with the *Data Transfer Workbench* (*DX Workbench*, Transaction Code SXDA) you can also use the LSM Workbench in this context. The Data Transfer Workbench is described in detail in Section 12.1, especially in combination with the LSM Workbench.

The LSM Workbench can be used in any SAP system with a Basis Release 4.0 or later, but is only a standard component starting in SAP Basis Release 6.20. Therefore, the LSM Workbench is available in SAP R/3 Enterprise, SAP ERP 2004, and SAP ERP 6.0. If your SAP system has an earlier Basis release, you will have to install the LSM Workbench separately. You can download the corresponding transport request free of charge from the SAP Service Marketplace (*https://service.sap.com/lsmw*). More information is also available at this site, along with the software itself.

7.2   Data Migration with the LSM Workbench

This section shows you, step by step and based on a specific example, how you can use the LSM Workbench to migrate data. Note that this is the most important section of the chapter.

Example: Migrating customer master data

In this example, the goal is to migrate customer master data from a legacy system to the SAP ERP system. The example assumes that you have already extracted the legacy data and saved it in two worksheets of an Excel file, *Customers.xls*:

▶ Worksheet *Customers_Headerrecord* contains a header record for every customer (see Figure 7.2).

▶ Worksheet *Customers_Contact* contains one or more records with contact person data for every customer (see Figure 7.3).

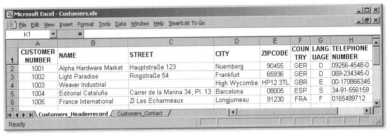

Figure 7.2 Example "Migrating Customer Master Data" — Header Records (Excerpt)

Figure 7.3 Example "Migrating Customer Master Data" — Contact Person Records (Excerpt)

7.2.1   Getting Started with the LSM Workbench

To start working with the LSM Workbench, use Transaction LSMW. **Initial transaction**
The first time you call the transaction, you'll see the "Welcome" message shown in Figure 7.4.

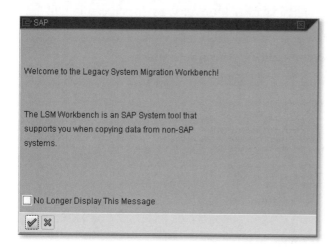

Figure 7.4 LSM Workbench — Welcome Message

When you confirm this dialog box, the initial screen opens (see Figure 7.5).

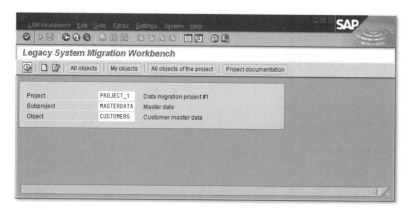

Figure 7.5 LSM Workbench — Initial Screen

As you can see in the initial screen, the data units to be migrated (also **Project, subproject**
called *data migration objects*) are organized by *projects* and *subprojects*
in the LSM Workbench. A project can contain any number of sub-

projects and a subproject can contain any number of data migration objects. You can apply this breakdown to your specific requirements.

There are no general guidelines for using these breakdown options. In this context, packing an extremely large data migration project into a single project makes as little sense as does creating hundreds of microprojects.

Example   Our example will use the following breakdown:

▶ **Project**
  ▹ ID: PROJECT_1
  ▹ Name: Data migration project #1

▶ **Subproject 1**
  ▹ ID: MASTERDATA
  ▹ Name: Master data

▶ **Subproject 2**
  ▹ ID: TRANSDATA
  ▹ Name: Transaction data

Alternatively, you could also use the following breakdown, independently of this example:

▶ **Project**
  ▹ ID: MASTERDATA
  ▹ Name: Master data

▶ **Subproject 1**
  ▹ ID: CUSTOMERS
  ▹ Name: Customer master data

▶ **Subproject 2**
  ▹ ID: VENDORS
  ▹ Name: Vendor master data

Object   A subproject can contain any number of *objects*. An object refers to a business unit of data (customer master, material master, financial documents, and so on), including all the definitions required for data migration (source, target, mapping, conversion rules, and so on).

Therefore, in this example, you must first create a project with ID PROJECT_1 and the name *Data migration project #1*. To do so, position the cursor in the **Project** field and click on **Create**. Enter the above data in the dialog box that opens (see Figure 7.6).

Creating a project/subproject/object

Figure 7.6 LSM Workbench — Creating a Project

Proceed in a similar fashion to create the subproject with ID MASTERDATA and the name *Master data*, as well as the object with ID CUSTOMERS and the name *Customer master data*.

You can choose any IDs for projects, subprojects, and objects up to the maximum permissible length of 10 characters (SAP Basis Release 6.20 and later: 15 characters).

Before you continue, you should first learn about a number of useful functions that are available in the initial screen of the LSM Workbench (see Figure 7.5):

Useful functions in the initial screen

- ▶ The **All objects** button displays an overview of all defined projects, subprojects, and objects.

- ▶ The **My objects** button displays an overview of all the objects you have created (under the current user ID).

- ▶ The **All objects of the project** button displays an overview of all subprojects and objects of the selected project. Figure 7.7 shows this display for your project, PROJECT_1, with all subprojects and objects.

- ▶ The **Project documentation** displays the full documentation, if any, that you have created for the individual dialog boxes and steps. You can print the project documentation, mail it, and save it in different file formats.

- ▶ The **Documentation** button enables you to enter your comments. After clicking on it, a popup appears in which you can write down your personal documentation.

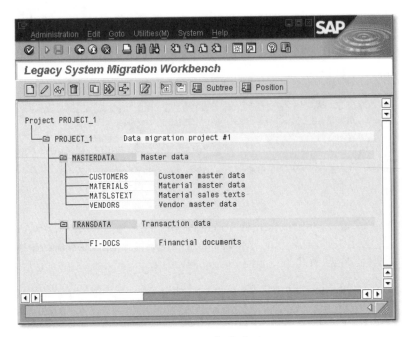

Figure 7.7 LSM Workbench — Overview of a Project

Version ▶ When you choose menu path **Extras • Display LSMW Version,** information about the installed version of the LSM Workbench is displayed (see Figure 7.8). If you need to contact SAP Support, you must always provide this version number.

Figure 7.8 LSM Workbench — Displaying Versions

Administration The **Administration** function goes one step further than **All objects of the project**. To start this function, choose menu path **Goto • Administration** from the initial screen. All the projects defined in the LSM Workbench are displayed in an overview.

From here, you can create, edit, display, delete, copy, or rename projects, subprojects, objects, and reusable rules (see Section 7.2.8). Double-click on an entry to navigate to the display or edit screen for that entry.

As its name implies, the administration function is used for the general administration of projects and their components.

When you position the cursor on an entry, you can click on the **Documentation** button to save a personal note. Each time an item is edited, the name of the person who made the last change and the date of the last change are saved.

Because the LSM Workbench manipulates data in the SAP ERP system, access to these functions must be restricted. Fortunately, this is a simple task because the LSM Workbench is integrated in the ERP authorization concept. You can use the four nested authorization profiles that are listed in Table 7.1.

Authorization concept

> **Note**
>
> These profiles are not contained in the standard profiles of the SAP ERP system in SAP Basis Release 4.6C and earlier. When the LSM Workbench is installed in such systems, they are created in client 000. Then, you must distribute them to the other clients.

Profile	Name	Authorizations
B_LSMW_SHOW	Display	Display projects and their steps without switching to edit mode
B_LSMW_EXEC	Execute	Authorizations of B_LSMW_SHOW; plus read, convert, and import data
B_LSMW_CHG	Change	Authorizations of B_LSMW_EXEC; plus create and change objects
B_LSMW_ALL	Administrate	Authorization for all functions of the LSM Workbench

Table 7.1 Authorization Profiles of the LSM Workbench

7.2.2   User Guidance: The Main Steps of Data Migration

Now that you have created or selected your project, subproject, and object, press **Enter** or **Nest** to display the user guidance for the LSM Workbench (see Figure 7.9).

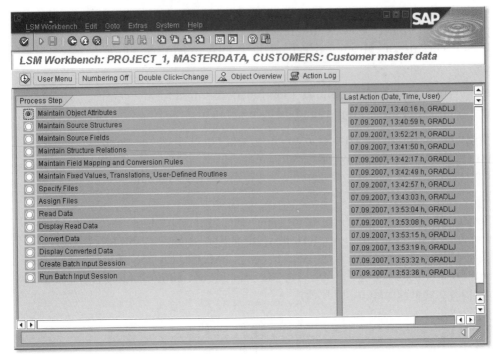

Figure 7.9 LSM Workbench — User Guidance

Navigation From this screen, the LSM Workbench guides you through the individual steps of the data migration in the required order. You navigate from here to the individual steps and then return when you have completed the data migration. After each step, the radio button automatically jumps to the next required step. However, you should see this as a "non-binding recommendation". If necessary, you can return at any time to any step that you have already completed.

The following functions are available in this screen:

▶ **Execute**
This function executes the step where the radio button is currently set. Alternatively, you can also double-click on an item to execute it.

▶ **Personal menu**
This function lets you select your own set of steps from the ones displayed. This is advisable, for example, when you have already completed certain steps and no longer want them to appear in the list. You can also display steps that you've chosen to hide at any

time. When you click on the **Main steps** button, all the processing steps that are mandatory for a data conversion are automatically activated (see Figure 7.10).

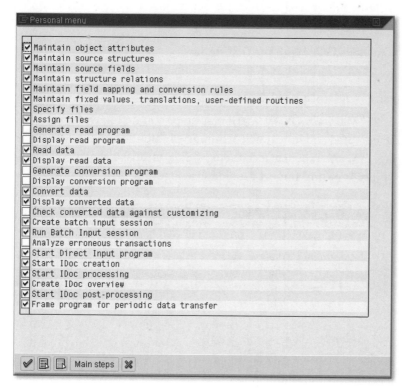

Figure 7.10 LSM Workbench — Personal Menu

▶ **Numbering on or Numbering off**
This function enables you to choose whether or not you want to number the selected steps sequentially.

▶ **Double Click = Display or Double Click = Change**
This function enables you to define the function of a double-click: Either display mode or edit mode. If you select **Double click=Edit**, you won't have to switch from display mode to edit mode in each step.

▶ **Object Overview**
This function displays all the information for the select object at a glance (see Section 7.2.18).

▶ **Action Log**
This function displays a detailed overview (date, time, user name) of all the steps performed so far. You can use menu path **Extras •Reset Action Log** to reset the action log. This action is recorded with a reference to the user and the date.

Now, let's begin with the first step.

7.2.3   Maintaining Object Attributes

In the **Maintain Object Attributes** step, you define which data will be migrated and how it will be imported into the SAP ERP system. In the LSM Workbench terminology, this means that you select the **Object Type and Import Method** (see Figure 7.11).

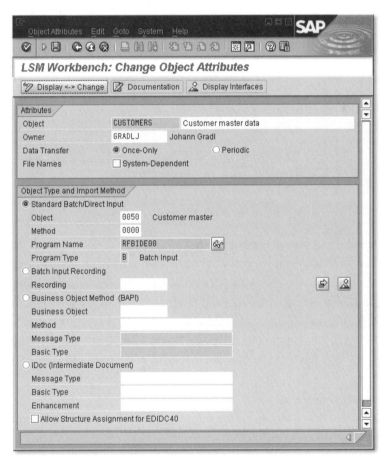

Figure 7.11 LSM Workbench — Maintaining Object Attributes

All the settings in the **Attributes** section are already preset. In the **Object Type and Import Method** section, choose **Batch Input** as the import method and use the **F4** input help to select the **Customer master** object (ID 0050). When you make your selection, you see that program RFBIDE00 is used, and that it is a standard batch input program.

Object type and import technique

When batch input and direct input are used, you can click on the **Display** button (eyeglasses icon) to display the documentation for the program and learn about its functions in detail.

The LSM Workbench also supports other import methods, or standard SAP interfaces. Therefore, we recommend using the following import methods for various data objects:

Other import techniques

▶ Customers and vendors: batch input

▶ Material master: direct input

▶ Purchase orders: IDoc

When choosing an import technique, you should consider the following aspects:

Criteria for choosing the import technique

▶ **Availability**
Not all data import techniques are available for every data object. You can click on the **Display Interfaces** button in the **Maintain Object Attributes** step to display all the available interfaces for a data object and adopt an appropriate value (see Figure 7.12).

▶ **Ease of use**
The batch input technique features easy-to-use functions for post-processing erroneous data.

▶ **Runtimes**
When very large data volumes are involved, direct input is preferable to batch input, because the batch input method may result in intolerably long runtimes. A general rule to approximate the time required is to use as a standard 3,000-5,000 transactions per hour, although this value can vary widely depending on the hardware used.

▶ **Complexity**
If the legacy system data is structured so simply that it can be saved in a single table, the recording technique may be preferable. The mapping for this technique (see Section 7.2.7) is usually not a

Recording only for data with simple structures

problem, because only a manageable number of fields have to be filled in SAP ERP.

▶ **Flexibility**

Use the recording technique only if the corresponding SAP transaction always uses the same screen sequence, regardless of the content of the data record. If your legacy data is structured such that a header record can have a variable number of item records, the recording technique is not applicable.

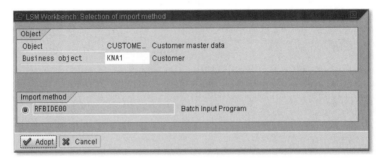

Figure 7.12 LSM Workbench — Display of Available Interfaces for a Business Object

Please note that if you apply import technique BAPI or IDoc, the program checks during the save operation whether a *partner agreement* is already available for the preset partner (see Section 7.7) and the selected message type. If not, the system attempts to create it. A partner agreement is a technical link between a sender or receiver of a message (partner) and a message type. Consequently, partner agreements define who may send or receive which types of messages.

Other object attributes

In addition to the main settings for object type and import technique, you can also maintain a number of other useful attributes in this step (see Figure 7.11); for example, enter a name for an object or change an existing name.

By entering data into the **Owner** field, you add the project to the list of all projects you created. You can display it afterwards in the initial screen under **My Objects**.

"Mini-Workflow"

You can use this field for a "mini-workflow" as described below:

▶ User 1 executes steps 1, 2, and 3 and changes the owner to user 2.

▶ User 2 executes steps 4, 5, and 6 and changes the owner to user 3, and so on.

Accordingly, you can see who is performing a step (or has to perform it) at any time.

You can also define whether the data transfer will be one-time or periodic; one-time data transfer is the normal case. In the event of periodic data transfer, you cannot read files from the frontend. In this case, the list of steps contains the additional step **Main program for periodic data transfer** (see Section 7.5).

Periodic data transfer

You can also choose whether or not you want the file names to be *system-dependent*. If you do, you can enter separate file names for each SAP ERP system later on. This is especially useful when you have to migrate data into several SAP ERP systems.

System-dependent file names

After you've defined that you want to migrate customer data using the batch input method, you can begin to define the legacy data.

7.2.4 Maintaining Source Structures

In the procedures described in the previous chapters, you were responsible for converting the data to SAP ERP format. The SAP ERP system didn't require any information on the format of the data exported from the legacy system. Because the LSM Workbench is responsible for converting the data here, it must know the structure of the data in the legacy system.

The legacy data for an application object usually consists of one or more *record types*. Typical record types are the header record and the item record. These record types are called *source structures* in the LSM Workbench. Two record types are involved in the example: The header record for each customer (see Figure 7.2) and the contact record for each contact person (see Figure 7.3), which, formally speaking, is an item record, because each customer can have any number of contact persons.

Two record types

In the **Maintain Source Structures** step of data migration, you must define the source structures of the object, with name, text, and hierarchical relationships. Therefore, in the navigation screen (see Figure 7.9), choose **Maintain Source Structures**, click on the **Create** button, and create a source structure with ID HEADER and text "Customer — header record." Then, position the cursor on the source structure you just created and click on **Create** again. The system asks whether the second source structure will be of *equal rank* or *subordinate*. Choose **Subordinate** and enter the ID CONTACT and the text "Customer — contact person record". The result is shown in Figure 7.13.

Equal ranking or subordinate? When should you choose *equal rank* or *subordinate*? Typically, record type 2 is "subordinate" to record type 1 when exactly one record with record type 1 exists for each record with record type 2. In the example, this means that each contact person record has exactly one corresponding header record; however, the reverse does not apply. Each header record can have one contact partner record, or several, or no contact partner records.

Other functions Furthermore, this step contains functions that can create new source structures, and change, move, and delete existing structures. Pushbuttons are provided for each of these functions.

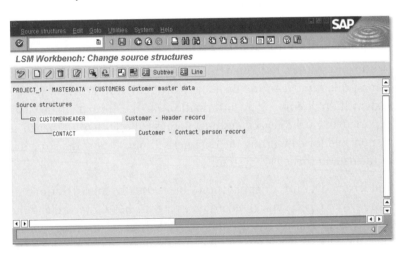

Figure 7.13 LSM Workbench — Maintaining Source Structures

7.2.5 Maintaining Source Fields

Typically, a source structure consists of several fields. These fields are called *source fields* in the LSM Workbench.

Defining source fields and attributes In the step — **Maintain Source Fields** — you create the source fields for the source structures you created in the previous step and set the necessary attributes (see Figure 7.9).

In the example, you have to define the fields **CUSTOMERNUMBER**, **NAME**, **STREET**, **CITY**, and so on for source structure **CUSTOMER-**

HEADER. This means you model the structure of your legacy data (see Figures 7.2 and 7.3) in the LSM Workbench.

A source field in the LSM Workbench is described by its field name, text, field length, and field type. You can enter this information individually, field by field.

Attributes of a source field

To do so, you must position the cursor on the source structure CUSTOMERHEADER, click the **Create Field** button, and enter the required attributes for the **CUSTOMERNUMBER** field. Then, position the cursor on source field **CUSTOMERNUMBER**, click the **Create Field** button again, and enter the required attributes for the **NAME** field, and so on, until you reach the results shown in Figure 7.14.

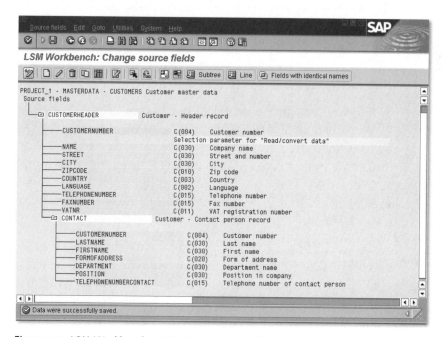

Figure 7.14 LSM Workbench — Maintaining Source Fields

The individual options for defining and maintaining the source fields are described in the sections below.

Creating Individual Source Fields

As we already mentioned, you must position the cursor on a source structure or existing source field and click on **Create Field**. The dialog box shown in Figure 7.15 opens.

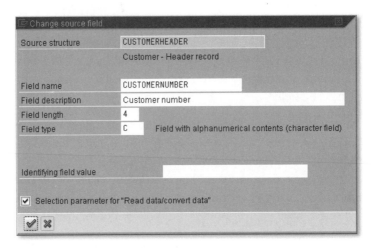

Figure 7.15 LSM Workbench — Creating Individual Source Fields

You can define the **Field length** as required. You can use the **F4** input help to select the **Field type** (see Figure 7.16).

Date fields, amount fields

If you define a field as a date field (field types DDMY, DMDY, or DYMD) or amount field (field types AMT1, AMT2, AMT3, or AMT4), you can choose later when you read the data (see Section 7.2.13) whether you want to convert date values to the internal date format (YYYYMMDD — four-digit date, followed by two-digit month, followed by two-digit day) and amount fields to the calculation format (1234.56 — no thousand separators, decimal point).

Identifying field value

If a file contains legacy data for multiple source structures, the LSM Workbench will need additional information on how to identify a record. To do so, you must enter a value in the **Identifying field value** field that can be used to determine which source structure belongs to that record. You can only specify an identifying field value for one field in each source structure.

Selection parameters

You can set a flag for the fields of structures in the top hierarchy level — the fields of source structure CUSTOMERHEADER in the example — in the **Selection parameter for "Read data/convert data"** field. If you set this flag, the corresponding field is made available as a selection parameter during steps **Read data** and **Convert data**. The flag is normally used to limit the scope of data during tests (see Figure 7.15).

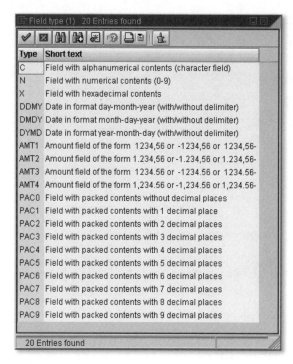

Figure 7.16 LSM Workbench — Possible Types of Source Fields

Maintaining Source Fields in Table Form

Instead of maintaining each source field individually, you can also maintain all the fields of a source structure at once. To do so, position the cursor on a source structure or existing source field in Figure 7.14 and click on **Table Maintenance**. A screen like the one shown in Figure 7.17 opens.

When you enter a field name and click on **Enter**, the following values are proposed:

Default values

- ▶ Field type: C
- ▶ Field length: 10
- ▶ Field text: If there is a domain (see Section 7.8.4) in the SAP ERP system whose name matches the field name, the name of this domain is proposed as the field text; otherwise, the field name is used.

Of course, you can always overwrite these default values if necessary.

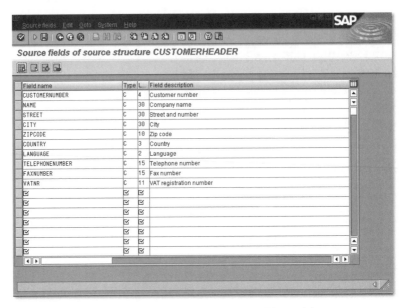

Figure 7.17 LSM Workbench — Maintaining Source Fields in Table Form

Copying Source Fields from Other Sources

To reduce the manual maintenance effort required, the LSM Workbench also supports options for copying descriptions of source fields from other sources. To copy source fields from other sources, position the cursor on a source structure or existing source field (see Figure 7.14) and click on **Copy Fields**. You are prompted to select a source in the dialog box shown in Figure 7.18.

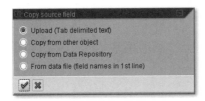

Figure 7.18 LSM Workbench — Copying Source Fields

Copying structure descriptions

The following sources are available:

▶ **Upload (Tab delimited text)**
In this case, the system expects the texts of the source fields in a text file whose columns are separated by tabs, like the one shown in Figure 7.19.

▶ **Copy from other object**
You can also copy source fields from the source structure of
another object in the LSM Workbench. If you choose this variant,
in the next step, you're prompted to select the corresponding
object (specifically, project, subproject, object).

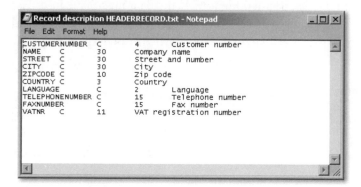

Figure 7.19 LSM Workbench — Copying Source Fields from Text File
(Tab Delimited Text)

▶ **Copy from Data Repository**
You can copy the source fields from a structure of the ABAP Dictionary in the SAP ERP system. If you choose this variant, in the
next step, you're prompted to select the required structure in the
ABAP Dictionary.

▶ **From data file (field names in 1st line)**
You can copy the source fields from a file that contains the corresponding legacy data. This file must be available on the PC in **Text
(Tab-Delimited) (*.txt)** format and contain the field names in the
first line. In the process, field type C is assigned as the field type
and the field name as the field text, while the field length is set to
the length of the longest field contents.

7.2.6 Maintaining Structure Relations

As we discussed in Section 7.2.4, data for an object in the legacy system consists of one or more record types, which are called *source
structures* in the LSM Workbench. Consequently, the record types of
the target format, ERP format, are called *target structures*.

Relationships between source and target structures

In the data migration step **Maintain Structure Relations**, you define the relationships between source and target structures. Here, you determine the possible target structures when you select the object type and the import method (see Figure 7.11).

In this case, this means your selection **Customers/Standard batch input** implicitly specified the format the data must have in order to enable processing by batch input program RFBIDE00. You can see the result when you call step **Maintain Structure Relations** (see Figure 7.20) in the navigation screen (see Figure 7.9).

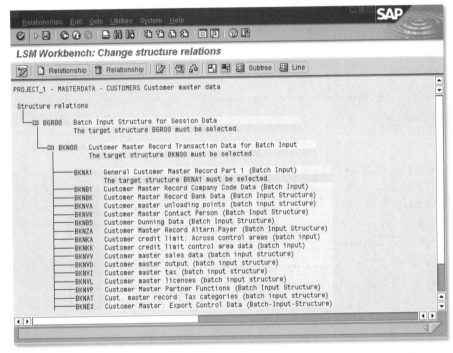

Figure 7.20 LSM Workbench — Maintaining Structure Relations — Initial State

Required target structures

Typically, there are target structures that have to be selected (**required target structures**). In this case, the following note is displayed: "The target structure must be selected" (see Figure 7.21).

To define structure relations, position the cursor on a target structure and click on the **Create Relationship** button. A dialog box opens, displaying the existing source structures for selection. If you want to change a relationship, first delete the existing relationship. A pushbutton is also provided for this purpose.

In addition, you can use **Check** to check the structural relationships for errors. The status bar then displays an error message or the message: "The structural relationships do not contain any errors."

Checking the structure relations

In the example, you will assign header structure CUSTOMER-HEADER to each of the target structures BGR00, BKN00, BKNA1, and BKNB1, and source structure CONTACT to target structure BKNVK. The result is shown in Figure 7.21.

Choose your target structures well

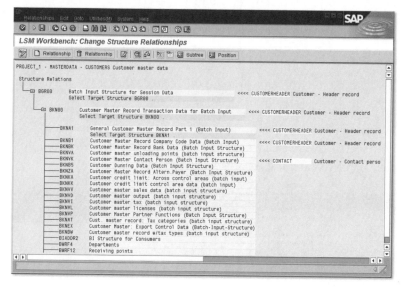

Figure 7.21 LSM Workbench — Maintaining Structure Relations

Conversely, your definitions mean that the customers you will create in the SAP ERP System will **not** contain a lot of information, namely, all the information contained the structures that you did *not* select — bank data, unloading points, dunning data, alternative payers, and so on.

In conclusion, we should add that many batch input and direct input programs use a control record named BGR00 or BI000. We highly recommend that you always assign the top-level source structure (header structure) to this control record.

Control records

7.2.7 Maintaining Field Mapping and Conversion Rules

You have now come to the data migration step that generally requires the most effort. Please note that so far, you have only modeled the structure of the legacy data in the LSM Workbench and described the relationships between the legacy system and the SAP ERP system at the structural level. You will now continue at the level of the individual fields.

Two steps in one Therefore, the specific activity in this step is to assign source fields to the target fields, and define how to convert the field contents. This step is also called **field mapping**. Strictly speaking, two steps are involved:

1. Assign the source fields to the target fields

2. Determine the conversion rules

Because these two steps are closely related, they have been combined in a single step in the LSM Workbench.

All target fields at a glance When you call this step from the navigation screen (see Figure 7.9), you see all the selected target structures, and their corresponding fields, in a hierarchical tree display (see Figure 7.22).

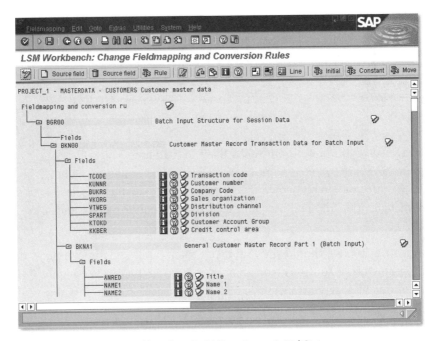

Figure 7.22 LSM Workbench — Field Mapping — Initial State

Because all the available target fields are now displayed, you can begin mapping the source fields to target fields and do this initially "on paper." This preparatory step is usually the user departments' responsibility, with the possible assistance of SAP consultants, as the necessary application skills are available there.

In the example, you arrive at the results listed in Table 7.2.

No.	Target Field	Source Field	Conversion Rule
1	BKN00-TCODE	–	Constant XD01
2	BKN00-KUNNR	CUSTOMERHEADER-CUSTOMERNUMBER	Prefix 9
3	BKN00-BUKRS	–	Fixed value FV_BUKRS
4	BKN00-KTOKD	–	Constant 0001
5	BKNA1-NAME1	CUSTOMERHEADER-NAME	Transfer (MOVE)
6	BKNA1-SORTL	CUSTOMERHEADER-NAME	Transfer (MOVE); cut off
7	BKNA1-STRAS	CUSTOMERHEADER-STREET	Transfer (MOVE)
8	BKNA1-ORT01	CUSTOMERHEADER-CITY	Transfer (MOVE)
9	BKNA1-PSTLZ	CUSTOMERHEADER-ZIPCODE	Transfer (MOVE)
10	BKNA1-LAND1	CUSTOMERHEADER-COUNTRY	Translation
11	BKNA1-SPRAS	CUSTOMERHEADER-LANGUAGE	Translation
12	BKNA1-TELF1	CUSTOMERHEADER-TELEPHONENUMBER	Transfer (MOVE)
13	BKNA1-TELFX	CUSTOMERHEADER-FAXNUMBER	Transfer (MOVE)
14	BKNA1-STCEG	CUSTOMERHEADER-VATNR	Transfer (MOVE)
15	BKNB1-AKONT	–	Constant 140000
16	BKNVK-NAME1	CONTACT-LASTNAME	Transfer (MOVE)
17	BKNVK-TELF1	CONTACT-TELEPHONE-NUMBER-CONTACT	Transfer (MOVE)
18	BKNVK-ABTNR	CONTACT-DEPARTMENT	Translation
19	BKNVK-NAMEV	CONTACT-FIRSTNAME	Transfer (MOVE)

Table 7.2 "Mapping on Paper" — Mapping and Conversion Rules for Customer Master Data

No.	Target Field	Source Field	Conversion Rule
20	BKNVK-ANRED	CONTACT-FORMOFADDRESS	Transfer (MOVE)
21	BKNVK-PAFKT	CONTACT-POSITION	Translation

Table 7.2 "Mapping on Paper" — Mapping and Conversion Rules for Customer Master Data (cont.)

Fields of control structure BGR00

Attentive readers will surely not have overlooked the fact that Table 7.2 does not contain a single field from control structure BGR00. This is because the LSM Workbench considers all the fields of structure BGR00 to be **technical** fields and presets them automatically. As a rule, no changes are required for these fields.

Once you have completed your "mapping on paper," the major part of your work is finished. Now, you only have to define this information in the LSM Workbench. The procedure is shown in Table 7.3. The sequence number in the first column refers to the sequence number in Table 7.2:

No.	Activity
1	Position the cursor on field BKN00-TCODE in Figure 7.22. Click on **Rule**. Select the **Constant** rule in the dialog box shown in Figure 7.23. Enter "XD01" in the next dialog box and confirm your entries.
2	Position the cursor on field BKN00-KUNNR in Figure 7.22. Click on **Assign Source Field**. Double-click to select CUSTOMERHEADER-CUSTOMERNUMBER from the list of possible source fields. Click on **Rule**. Then select the **Prefix** rule in the dialog box shown in Figure 7.23. Enter "9" in the next dialog box and confirm your entries.
3	Position the cursor on field BKN00-BUKRS in Figure 7.22. Click on **Rule**. Select the **Fixed Value (Reusable)**[1] rule in the dialog box shown in Figure 7.23. The LSM Workbench proposes BUKRS for the name. Adopt this proposal. You can enter the specific value in the next dialog box. Use this option and enter "0001".

Table 7.3 Implementing the "Mapping on Paper" in the LSM Workbench

---

1 These "reusable rules" are described in detail in Section 7.2.8.

No.	Activity
4	This step is analogous to Step 1.
5	Position the cursor on field BKNA1-NAME1 in Figure 7.22. Click on **Assign Source Field**. Double-click to select CUSTOMERHEADER-NAME from the list of possible source fields. Because the LSM Workbench automatically selects the **Transfer (MOVE)** rule, you don't have to configure any other settings.
6	This step is analogous to Step 5. In this case, however, the source field is longer than the target field. This means the content of the source field will be cut off during the migration.
7	This step is analogous to Step 5.
8	This step is analogous to Step 5.
9	This step is analogous to Step 5.
10	Position the cursor on field BKNA1-LAND1 in Figure 7.22. Click on **Assign Source Field**. Double-click to select CUSTOMERHEADER-COUNTRY from the list of possible source fields. Click on **Rule**. Select the **Translation (Reusable)** rule in the dialog box shown in Figure 7.23. The LSM Workbench proposes LAND1 for the name. Adopt this proposal.
11	This step is analogous to Step 10.
12	This step is analogous to Step 5.
13	This step is analogous to Step 5.
14	This step is analogous to Step 5.
15	This step is analogous to Step 1.
16	This step is analogous to Step 5.
17	This step is analogous to Step 5.
18	This step is analogous to Step 10.
19	This step is analogous to Step 5.
20	This step is analogous to Step 5.
21	This step is analogous to Step 10.

Table 7.3 Implementing the "Mapping on Paper" in the LSM Workbench (cont.)

When you follow the directions in Table 7.3, you'll see that the LSM Workbench translates your instructions into ABAP coding. It also lets you change or supplement this ABAP coding as needed. An example of this would be to replace the leading zero in telephone numbers with the country code. For instance, if you want to replace 06227 741117 with +49 6227 741117, you would have to replace the generated coding `BKNA-TELF1 = CUSTOMERHEADER-TELEPHONENUMBER` with the following coding:

```
Concatenate '+49' CUSTOMERHEADER-TELEPHONENUMBER+1 into BKNA1-
TELF1 separated by space
```

However, no such changes are required in our example.

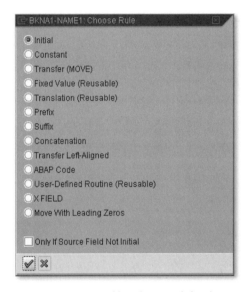

Figure 7.23 LSM Workbench — Predefined Conversion Rules

Summary Now you've processed all the instructions from Table 7.3. The result of your efforts is displayed in Figures 7.24 and 7.25. Here, we should point out that the initial fields are hidden in the figures. We were able to selectively display the fields using the **Display Variant** button, which is described in Section 7.8.1.

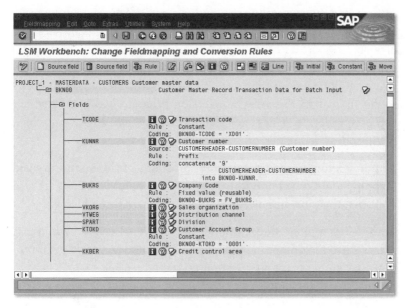

Figure 7.24 LSM Workbench — Field Mapping (Excerpt 1)

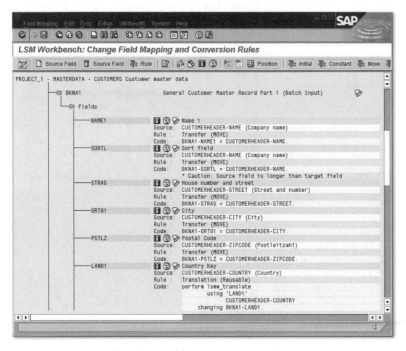

Figure 7.25 LSM Workbench — Field Mapping (Excerpt 2)

Syntax check At the same time, you can see whether your efforts have proven successful. To do so, click on **Check Syntax** (see Figure 7.25). This enables you to exit the LSM Workbench in order to generate the data conversion program and ensure that it has the correct syntax. When you have done everything correctly, the following message appears in the status bar: "The data conversion program was generated." If you use predefined rules exclusively and don't add any user-defined ABAP coding, syntax errors are unlikely.

You now know the most important functions of the **Maintain Field Mapping and Conversion Rules** step. Other useful functions are also available, the most important of which are introduced below.

Auto-fieldmapping **Auto-fieldmapping** is an extremely handy function. If you choose **Extras Auto-Fieldmapping** in Figure 7.22, the LSM Workbench proposes assignments for all your source and target fields.

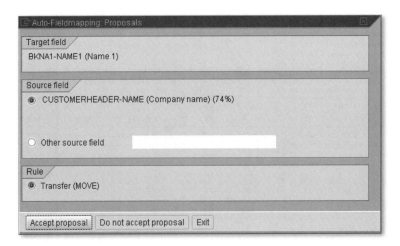

Figure 7.26 LSM Workbench — Auto-Fieldmapping

You can choose whether you want to search for fields with identical names or with similar names (with hit probability).[2] If you choose this function for target field BKNA1-NAME1 in the example, the proposal shown in Figure 7.26 appears.

---

2 The hit probability is the measure of similarity between two words. The greater the similarity between two words, the higher the hit probability. Therefore, the hit probability for two identical words would be 100%.

196

If you're working with many fields and the field names of the legacy system (specifically: the source fields) are identical or similar to the fields of the SAP ERP system (specifically: the target structures), auto-fieldmapping can help you to accelerate your work. Furthermore, you don't have to call the function individually for each field; instead, you can tab through all the fields using the cursor, or even navigate through all the fields of all target structures, with or without confirmation after every step.

Some target fields are preset by the system. These fields are called **technical fields** and are marked with rule type **Default setting**. The conversion rules for the fields are not displayed in the field mapping at first, but you can display them (see Figure 7.25) by clicking on the **Display Variant** pushbutton (see Section 7.8.1). Changing the default setting may seriously affect the flow of the data conversion. If you inadvertently change the default settings, you can restore them by choosing **Extras Restore default**.

Technical fields

The following information is displayed for each target field (see Figure 7.25):

▶ ERP field name

▶ Any assigned source fields

▶ Rule type (fixed value, translation, and so on)

▶ Coding

In addition, the following functions are available for each source and target field:

Functions in each source and target field

▶ **Field Documentation**
Short documentation is displayed for the target field on which the cursor is positioned. This documentation may contain links to additional information.

▶ **Possible Values**
A list of possible values for this target field is displayed. Whether this list is available depends on the definition of the target field in the Data Dictionary.

▶ **Documentation**
You can maintain the documentation for a field or other object, and explain the conversion rule in more detail, if necessary.

▸ **Source Fields Not Assigned**
When working with many fields, you can lose track of which source fields you have already assigned and which source fields you have not assigned. Choose **Extras Source Fields Not Assigned** (see Figure 7.25) to display the source fields that have not been assigned yet.

▸ **Remove the Assignment of a Source Field**
To remove a source field assigned, position the cursor on a target field in the tree structure and select **Remove Source Field**. If only one source field has been assigned, this field is removed. If several source fields have been assigned, a list of all source fields assigned is displayed. You can then select the corresponding source field by double-clicking on it.

Predefined conversion rules

Several of the predefined conversion rules for the step **Maintain Field Mapping and Conversion Rules** (see Figure 7.23) are described in detail below.

Initial

Resetting a field

This deletes the coding assigned to a target field, and all the source fields that are assigned to the target field. Lastly, the target field is set to an initial value, which can differ depending on the selected import technique:

▸ **Standard batch input/standard direct input**
The target field is set to the value of the character for "No data", called the "nodata character", which is usually defined in the control record (BGR00, BI000) and set to the default value "/".

▸ **Batch input recording**
The target field is filled with "/" as the nodata character.

▸ **BAPI, IDoc**
The ABAP command CLEAR is applied to the target field, filling character fields with blanks and numeric fields with zeros.

Constant

The target field is assigned a fixed value.

Transfer (MOVE)

You can transfer data from the source field to the target field using ABAP command `MOVE`. The command has the following function described in Table 7.4, dependent on the field type.

Assignment

Moreover, the conversion rules that apply to the ABAP command `MOVE` are also used. For more details, refer to the corresponding documentation in the SAP ERP system.

Field Type	Type of Transfer
C (character)	1:1 transfer
N (numeric)	1:1 transfer, including any leading zeros
Packed field	Unpack in target field using the ABAP statement `WRITE ... TO ...`
Date field	A dialog box opens, prompting you to transfer the date field: Internal format (YYYYMMDD) User format (such as 01/30/2003)
Amount field	If batch input or direct input is used, the amount value is formatted according to the settings in the user master. If BAPIs or IDocs are used, the amount value remains in the internal format.

Table 7.4 Type of Data Transfer Based on Field Type

Fixed Value (Reusable)

The target field is assigned a **fixed value object**, that is, a variable whose name begins with "FV_". This variable is set to a specific value in the step **Maintain Fixed Values, Translations, and User-Defined Routines**. Fixed values are reusable; therefore, you can use them in multiple objects in a project, which is in direct contrast to constants. You only have to define the specific value once.

In the example, you used a fixed value for the **Company Code** field. Assume that you want to migrate data for different company codes in sequence. You can use the corresponding fixed value in different objects; however, you must set the specific value only once, which is the primary advantage that fixed values have over constants. Therefore, a fixed value can be considered as a constant that is valid project-wide.

Constants valid project-wide

Translation (Reusable)

The target field is assigned coding, which converts the field contents of the source field based on a translation table. You can enter values of this translation table in the step **Maintain Fixed Values, Translations and User-Defined Routines** (see Figure 7.9 above). This procedure is described in detail in Section 7.2.8.

Prefix

You can specify any prefix to precede the contents of the source field.

Suffix

You can specify any suffix to follow the contents of the source field.

Concatenation

Joining two source fields

You can join two or more source fields and transfer the merged values to the target field.

Transfer Left Trim

The field contents are transferred left justified.

ABAP Coding

When you choose this option (or double-click on a target field), the ABAP editor starts. You can now edit generated ABAP coding or write and save your own coding. Most of the functions in the standard SAP editor are available here such as **Syntax Check**, **Pretty Printer**, and so on.

Click on the **Insert** button to add the following to your coding:

- **Source fields**: All available source fields are displayed for selection.
- **Global variable**: See Section 7.8.2.
- **Global functions**: See Section 7.8.3.

User-Defined Routine (Reusable)

The system creates the frame of a form routine (ABAP subroutine) with the name prefix "UR_". This routine is reusable, which means that you can also use it in other objects of the project. This represents the difference to ABAP coding, which you can define for a target field.

User-defined subroutine

For all kinds of reusable rules, the LSM Workbench proposes one to three possible names. One name is recommended by the system. We recommend using the proposed name. For detailed information on naming conventions, see Section 7.8.4.

When creating user-defined rules, observe the following:

▸ You must assign the correct number of source fields (according to the number of input parameters in the routine) prior to creating the routine.

▸ You must assign the source fields in the proper sequence (that is, in the sequence of the parameters).

X-Field

The **X-field** is a special function for processing IDocs. In some cases, a **checkbox structure** exists in addition to the data transfer structure (where the values to be transferred appear). This checkbox structure has the same field names as the data transfer structure, but all the fields in the structure have a length of 1 and are set to X or blank. These checkboxes determine whether the corresponding field is copied from the data transfer structure.

X-field in IDoc processing

The following coding is generated automatically for an X-field:

```
If not <field in the data transfer structure> is initial.
    <field in X-structure> = 'X'.
else.
    <field in X-structure> = ' '.
Endif.
```

You can use menu path **Extras Fill X-Structures** (see Figure 7.22) to insert this coding for entire target structures.

Filling X-structures

Only If Source Field Not Initial

The dialog box with the predefined rules (see Figure 7.23) contains a checkbox: **Only If Source Field Not Initial**. If you set this flag, the selected rule will be applied only if the source field in question contains a non-initial value.

7.2.8 Maintaining Fixed Values, Translations, and User-Defined Routines

You will now learn how to edit the reusable rules of a project.

Reusable rules   You used the following reusable rules in the example: Fixed value FV_BUKRS for the **Company Code** field and translations for the fields **Country**, **Language**, **Department**, and **Position**.

When you call the step **Maintain Fixed Values, Translations and User-Defined Routines** (see Figure 7.9 above), the screen template shown in Figure 7.27 opens.

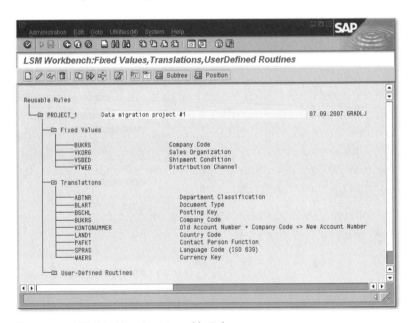

Figure 7.27 LSM Workbench — Reusable Rules

Alternatively, you can also double-click on a rule in step **Maintain Field Mapping and Conversion Rules** (see Figure 7.9) to maintain that rule.

Fixed Value

Here you can specify the length, type, flag for lowercase/uppercase, and value, in addition to the description of the fixed value.

In the example, you already assigned the value 0001 for fixed value FV_BUKRS in the previous step. If you have not done so yet, you can catch up now. To do so, position the cursor on entry "BUKRS" and click on **Edit entry** or, alternatively, double-click on the entry. The dialog box shown in Figure 7.28 opens.

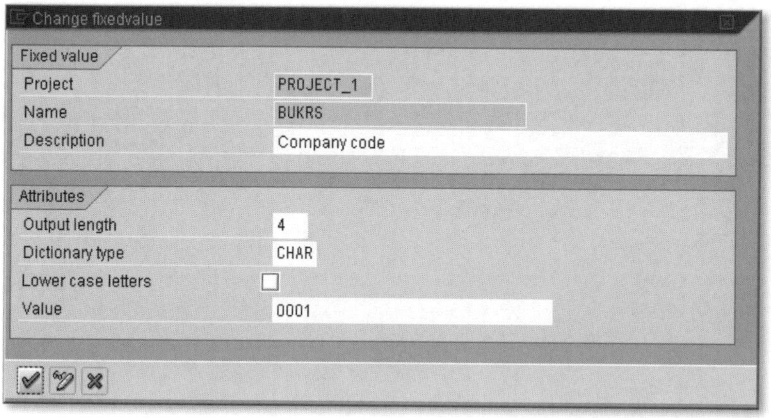

Figure 7.28 LSM Workbench — Fixed Value

We should also mention that the **F4** key is a very useful tool for getting help on any value field. Input help

Translation

The translation technique is used several times in our example, such as for the COUNTRY field. In the example, the legacy data contains the entries GER (Germany), GBR (Great Britain), ESP (Spain), and FRA (France). Because the SAP ERP system expects DE, GB, ES, and FR for these values, the following translation is required:

▶ GER → DE

▶ GBR → GB

▶ ESP → ES

▶ FRA → FR

This is exactly what the translation rule does. The following steps are required to define a translation rule (see Figures 7.29 to 7.31):

▶ **Source field, target fields**
You can enter information on the source field and target field here. If you want to create a new translation, you have to save your entries first before you can go to the next tab.

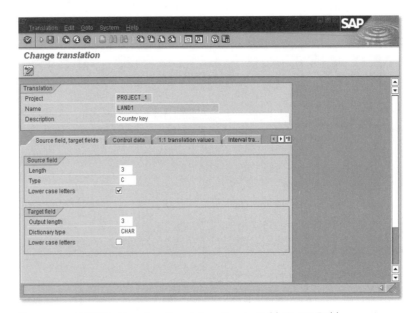

Figure 7.29 LSM Workbench —Translation: Source Field, Target Field

▶ **Control**
You can define the translation type here. You can specify which of the two translation tables will be searched for a value first and which alternative will be selected if no suitable entry is found (see Figure 7.30). In the example, the default settings are sufficient: If the search in the 1:1 translation table fails, the target field remains initial.

▶ **1:1 Translation Value**
Here you specify the value table to be used during translation. You can also upload the values from a PC file in **Text (Tab-Delimited) (*.txt)** format. To do so, click on **Upload**.

Input help
Another source of help is the fact that an **F4** input help function is available for the **New value** column.

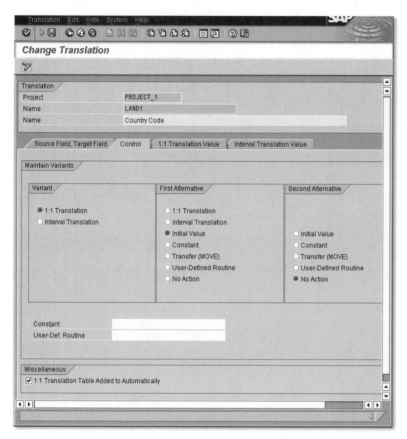

Figure 7.30 LSM Workbench — Translation: Control

Please note that only values for which the **OK** flag was set are included during translation.

An especially useful function is that the translation function collects the values automatically during data conversion. This means all the various values in the source fields are collected when you perform the **Convert Data** step (see Section 7.2.15). The benefits of this feature cannot be overemphasized. In most cases, you'll be surprised at how many entries have accumulated in your legacy data over time. To ensure a proper conversion, you must map all these values to values accepted by the SAP ERP system.

Automatic value collector

In the example, the conversion table has collected the entries ESP, FRA, GBR, and GER for COUNTRY in the left-hand column. Now, you only have to enter the proper values in the right-hand column, with the aid of input help, and check the **OK** flag. The result is shown in Figure 7.31.

You have to check the checkbox **1:1 Translation Table Added to Automatically** (see Figure 7.30) in order to activate the automatic value collector.

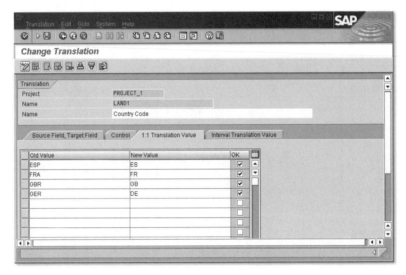

Figure 7.31 LSM Workbench — Translation — 1:1 Translation Values

▶ **Interval Translation Value**

Here you specify the value table to be used during translation by intervals. An upload option and **F4** input help are also available here. Furthermore, only values for which the **OK** flag was set are included here.

This translation feature is only rarely used. One possible application case is when you want to merge different groups of accounts from a number interval (old values) to new respective accounts (new value) when cleaning up a chart of accounts.

User-Defined Routine

As previously mentioned, you can add any ABAP coding to any target field. If your particular situation requires that you use such ABAP coding at various junctures within a project, you might want to employ a user-defined routine.

Let's assume that the phone numbers in your legacy data contain illegal characters that you must remove. Because phone numbers are used in different places in the SAP ERP system and can also be part of external correspondence, we recommend that you clean up these illegal characters.

In the overview of reusable rules (see Figure 7.27), position the cursor on the **User-Defined Routine** label and click on **Create**. In the dialog box that opens (see Figure 7.32), enter the name and description and click on **Enter** to confirm.

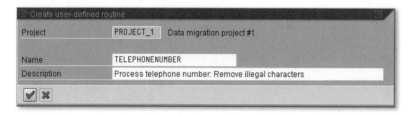

Figure 7.32 LSM Workbench — User-Defined Routine —Name and Description

Another dialog box opens (see Figure 7.33) in which you are prompted to enter the number of input and output parameters. In this example, you want to pass one phone number to the routine and get a "cleaned up" phone number back. Enter a "1" in both fields and click on **Enter** to confirm.

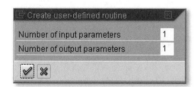

Figure 7.33 LSM Workbench — User-Defined Routine — Number of Parameters

You now see the ABAP editor, where the LSM Workbench has already provided a frame that you can fill with your own ABAP coding. All the familiar functions in the ABAP editor (Pretty Printer, syntax check, and so on) are available here (see Figure 7.34).

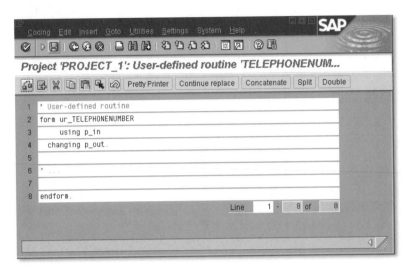

Figure 7.34 LSM Workbench — User-Defined Routine — Frame for ABAP Coding

The result is shown in Figure 7.35. You can now use this routine as part of the field mapping anywhere within the project.

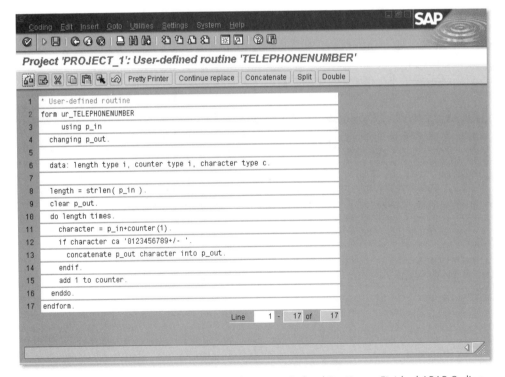

Figure 7.35 LSM Workbench — User-Defined Routine — Finished ABAP Coding

7.2.9   Addendum: Files

Before you continue with the steps that involve files in the LSM Workbench, read about the attributes that you can use to describe these files, as well as the types of files supported in the LSM Workbench.

Data can be saved in files in different ways. For a program to process these files correctly, the following file information has to be available:

▶ **End-of-record indicator or fixed record length**

There are different ways of indicating where one record ends and the next record begins within a file. The LSM Workbench supports the following three options:

▷ **End-of-record indicator**: Most common delimiter. It is used whenever the file is created with a text editor or exported from a spreadsheet program. Files with end-of-record indicators are also called text files.

▷ **Fixed record length**: Each record has the same length in bytes. This is frequently the case when the data has been exported from a mainframe application.

▷ **Hexadecimal length field (4 bytes) at start of record**: This delimiter is used in R/2-R/3 data migration.

Record delimiter

▶ **Table or sequential file**

There are two basic options for the contents of a file:

▷ **Table**: The file contents can have a table-like character. This occurs when all the records in the file have the same structure, that is, all the records in the file belong to the same source structure.

▷ **Sequential file**: If the file contains records for different source structures, you need to determine which records belong together. The only logical way to do so is by looking at the sequence. In this case, the file is called *sequential*.

Structure of the file contents

▶ **Separator**

Use the following options to determine when one field ends and the next field begins:

▷ **Separator**: A defined separator is inserted between two fields. Typical separators are tabs (tab-delimited), commas (comma-separated file), and semicolons. In practice, the use of commas

Field delimiter

or semicolons as separators often causes problems because these characters can appear in text fields, which produces undesired results.

▶ **No separator**: The LSM Workbench uses the defined source structure as a template; this information determines the field delimiters for the fields.

▶ **Field names at the start of the file**
The field names may appear at the start of the file. When table-like files are involved, this information can be used to assign the file content to the source fields. Consequently, the sequence of the source fields within the source structure doesn't necessarily have to match the sequence of the columns in the file. However, the system does expect to find separators between the individual fields.

Code page conversion when required

▶ **Character set (code page)**
If your legacy system runs in a different operating system environment than your SAP ERP system, the data in the legacy system may be encoded in a character set that the SAP ERP system cannot interpret. In this case, the code page must be converted, which the LSM Workbench does automatically. To enable this automatic conversion, you must specify the character set used to encode the data in the legacy system. Easy-to-use input help is also available.

Tip

When you work with files in the frontend, we recommend that you use the **Text (Tab-Delimited) (*.txt)** format. There are three advantages to using this type of file:

1. You can generate these files in all widely-used spreadsheet programs (such as Microsoft Excel).

2. Uploading the text files into the SAP ERP system is much faster than uploading files in the original format of the spreadsheet program (such as *.xls).

3. The tab character doesn't usually appear in the data. Alternatively, field values may contain commas and semicolons. Therefore, when you choose semicolons as your separator and your data contains a semicolon, this semicolon will be interpreted incorrectly as a separator, with the likely consequence that the data record in question cannot be processed properly.

7.2.10 Specifying Files

You have now come to the step where you describe the files that will be used in all the subsequent steps and specify them in the system.

Specifically, the following files are involved:

Files to specify

▸ The files on the PC and/or SAP application server that contain your legacy data
▸ Two internal work files from the LSM Workbench:
  ▹ The file for the read data
  ▹ The file for the converted data

In our example, the legacy data is available in two worksheets of an Excel file. Before you can specify them in the LSM Workbench, you must save each worksheet in **Text (Tab-Delimited) (*.txt)** format. Enter the names **Customers_Headerrecord.txt** and **Customers_Contact.txt** (see Figure 7.36).

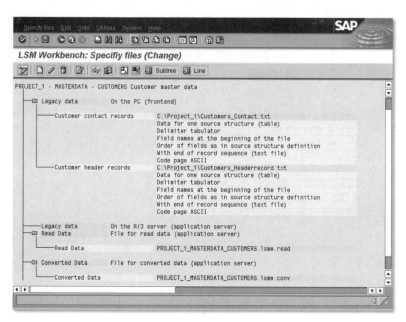

Figure 7.36 LSM Workbench — Specifying Files

Legacy Data in the Frontend (PC)

In this example, you assume that all the legacy data is available on your PC. Therefore, you should proceed as follows:

- In the navigation screen (see Figure 7.9), choose the step **Specify Files**.
- In edit mode, position the cursor on line **Legacy data – On the PC (frontend)** (see Figure 7.36).
- Choose **Add entry** to display the dialog box shown in Figure 7.37.
- You now enter the file path, the file name, the file description, and the other attributes as appropriate. Input help is available to assist you when selecting the file path.

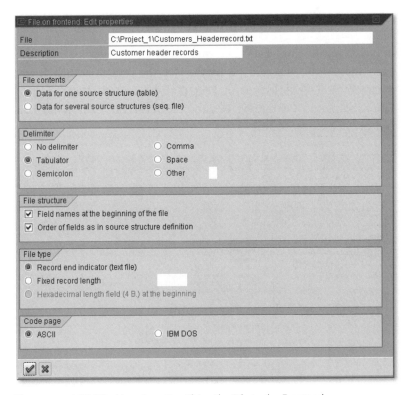

Figure 7.37 LSM Workbench — Specifying the File in the Frontend

Legacy Data on the SAP Application Server

The procedure is similar to the one used in the **Legacy Data on the PC** section if you want to use files saved on the application server:

- In edit mode, position the cursor on line **Legacy data – On the R/3 server (application server)** (see Figure 7.36).
- Choose **Add entry** to display the dialog box shown in Figure 7.38.

▶ Again, enter the file path, the file name, the file description, and the other attributes as appropriate.

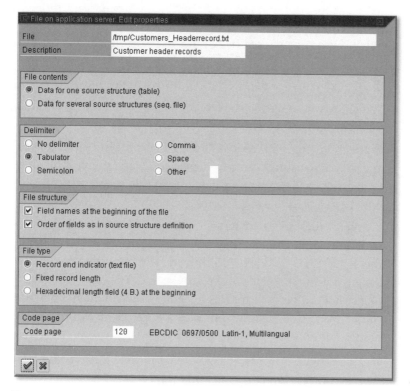

Figure 7.38 LSM Workbench — Specifying Files on the SAP Application Server

As far as the files with the legacy data are concerned, the LSM Workbench requires you to follow certain rules that, although they're not relevant for the example, may be important in your specific data migration situation. The most important rules are listed below:

Additional rules for files

▶ The SAP system registers with the operating system as user ID `<sid>adm` (`<sid>` stands for the three-character name of the SAP ERP system). Therefore, ensure that you have read/write authorization for the selected directory.

Required authorizations for the SAP System

▶ If a file contains data for multiple source structures, the field sequence in the file must match the sequence of the source fields defined in the LSM Workbench.

▶ If a file contains data for a single source structure, either the field sequence has to correspond to the source structure definition, or

Field sequence or field names

the field names have to be specified at the beginning of the file, which you can use to assign the columns in the file to the source fields.

▶ If a file contains end-of-line indicators (text file), packed fields are not allowed. In a packed field, not every digit is stored in a separate byte. Rather, the storage design is more compact.

▶ If a file contains separators, packed fields are not allowed.

Combination of frontend and application server allowed

▶ You can also use files in the frontend and on the SAP application server within an object.

▶ In the following step (**Assign Files**), a file containing data for several source structures can be assigned to several source structures. Conversely, a file containing data for a single source structure can only be assigned to a single source structure.

▶ If several files are used in an object, the corresponding source structures must contain fields of the same name. In the example, this is the CUSTOMERNUMBER field. The respective records are assigned using the fields of the same name. You can highlight the fields that can be used for this assignment when maintaining the source fields (see Figure 7.14): Click on the **Fields with identical names** button.

File for Read Data, File for Converted Data

Complete proposals

The LSM Workbench provides complete proposals for these two working files, **file for read data** and **file for converted data**, which you can usually adopt unchanged.

The **SAP home directory** of the SAP application server or the last directory you used in the LSM Workbench is selected as the file path.

Note

Transaction AL11 displays an overview of all SAP directories. The physical path of the SAP home directory is located under DIR_HOME.

The file name consists of the IDs for project, subproject, and object (separated by underscores), plus the file extension **lsmw.read** (for the file with the read data) or **lsmw.conv** (for the file with the converted data). The files in the example have the following names (see Figure 7.39):

▶ PROJECT_1_MASTERDATA_CUSTOMERS.lsmw.read for the file with the read data

▶ PROJECT_1_MASTERDATA_CUSTOMERS.lsmw.conv for the file with the converted data[3]

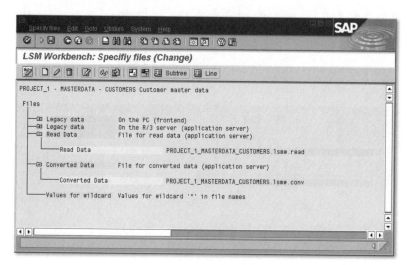

Figure 7.39 LSM Workbench — Specifying Files for the Read and Converted Data

The **Logical Path** and **Logical File Name** fields are only displayed when required by batch input/direct input programs called later. **F4** input help is available for both fields. Under no circumstances, should you use logical paths or file names that other applications can also use.

Logical path, logical file name

7.2.11   Using Wildcards in File Names

The use of wildcards is described based on an example: Assume that the legacy data is stored in the following four files:

Example

▶ File 1: C:\Project_1\Customers_Headerrecord_1.txt

▶ File 2: C:\Project_1\Customers_Contact_1.txt

▶ File 3: C:\Project_1\Customers_Headerrecord_2.txt

▶ File 4: C:\Project_1\Customers_Contact_2.txt

---

3 An undocumented feature is the **F4** input help for files on the application server. To activate this feature, you must use Transaction SE16 (Data Browser) to make an entry in the SAP ERP database table /SAPDMC/LSGCUST.

Two files each (***1.txt** and ***2.txt**) form a **set**; that is, file 2 contains the item data for the header records in file 1, while file 4 contains the item data for the header records in file 3.

When reading the data, you should process files 1 and 2 before files 3 and 4. You can achieve this with the appropriate settings in the **Specify Files** step, shown in Figure 7.40.

Wildcards in all file names — Note that you can also use wildcards in the names of the files of read data and converted data.

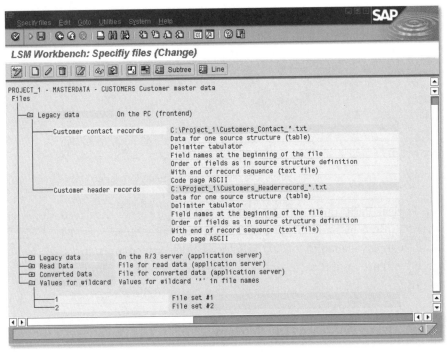

Figure 7.40 LSM Workbench — Using Wildcards in File Names

7.2.12 Assigning Files

In this step, you take the files you defined in the previous step and assign them to the source structures (see Figure 7.41).

In the example, you call the step **Assign Files** from within the navigation screen (see Figure 7.9), position the cursor on header structure, and click on **Assign file**. From the list of defined files, select the file that contains the header records. Proceed accordingly with source structure CONTACT.

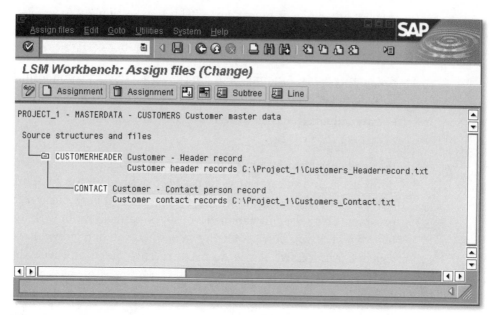

Figure 7.41 LSM Workbench — Assigning Files

Tip

Please note that if you change file names or properties subsequently, the file assignment is kept.

7.2.13   Reading Data

When you read the data, the files with the data from your legacy system are transformed to a technically homogeneous format. In the next step, the data is converted to SAP format.

From the navigation screen (see Figure 7.9), call the step **Read Data** to display the screen shown in Figure 7.42. The system first checks whether the data read program is still up-to-date. If not, it is regenerated automatically.

Program generated if necessary

If you want to process all data belonging to an object, click **Execute**. The process is started. If you want to migrate only a part of the data, you can limit the amount of data to be migrated in the **General selection parameters** section. Select the data in the **Transaction number** fields. We don't recommend using this selection option for your production migration, however, as you run the risk of skipping important data during the data migration.

Selection parameters

If you marked one or more source fields (see Section 7.2.5) as selection parameters when defining the source fields, these fields are also offered as selection parameters. There are also two checkboxes:

▶ **Amount fields**: Amount fields are converted to calculation format (with decimal point).

▶ **Date values**: Date fields are converted into the internal SAP format (YYYYMMDD).

Wildcards   If you use a wildcard (*) in the file names for the legacy data (see Section 7.2.11), and at least one value has been defined for the wildcard, a selection parameter for the wildcard is generated in the data read program. This selection parameter behaves normally in the following context. If you don't enter any values here, all defined wildcard values are processed. If you do make an entry here, however, the corresponding values are processed.

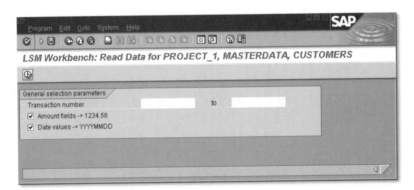

Figure 7.42 LSM Workbench — Reading Data — Selection Screen

In the example, adopt the proposed values and click on **Execute**.

Log   When the transaction is complete, a brief summary log appears (see Figure 7.43), indicating whether all the records were processed correctly.

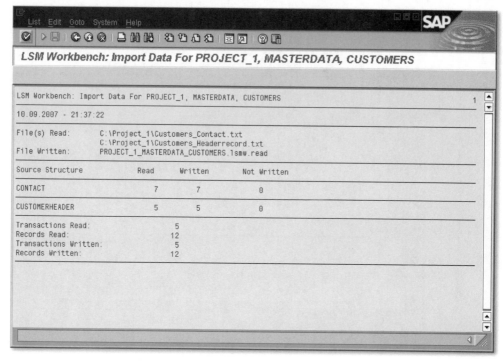

Figure 7.43 LSM Workbench — Reading Data — Log

7.2.14 Displaying Read Data

After you have read the data, you will want to view the results. You can display all or a part of the read data in table form. To help you better distinguish the results, the individual record types (source structure) are assigned different colors (see Figure 7.44).

Color codes

Click on **Change display** to toggle between a one line and multiline view. When you click on **Display color legend**, the colors for the individual hierarchy levels are displayed.

When you click on a specific line, all the information is highlighted. When you click on the **Field contents** button, you can achieve this same result (see Figure 7.45).

Now, you can also see any errors that occurred during the conversion of character sets or the processing of separators. Before you continue with the next step, you should correct any such errors.

Recognizing errors

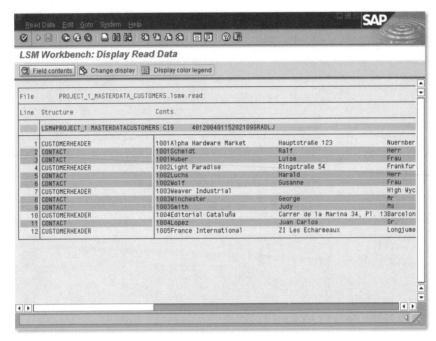

Figure 7.44 LSM Workbench — Displaying Read Data

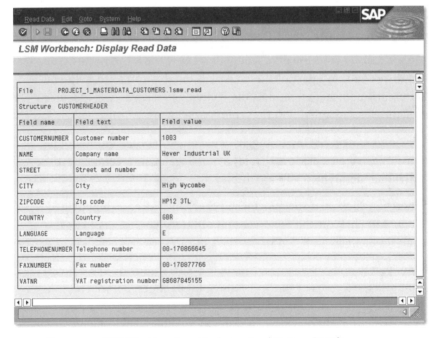

Figure 7.45 LSM Workbench — Displaying Read Data — Details

7.2.15 Converting Data

Once you have transformed the data from your legacy system to a technically homogeneous format with the read transaction, the data will now be converted to SAP ERP format, based on the field mappings and conversion rules you have defined.

Conversion according to mappings and conversion rules

From the navigation screen (see Figure 7.9), call the **Convert Data** step to display the screen shown in Figure 7.42. Once again, the system checks whether the data conversion program is still up-to-date. If not, it is regenerated automatically.

If you don't want to carry out a data selection, click **Execute** to start the process. Otherwise, enter a range in the **Transaction number** field.

If you marked one or several source fields as selection parameters when defining the source fields, these fields are also offered as selection parameters. If you use a wildcard in the file names for the legacy data and defined at least one value for the wildcard, a selection parameter for the wildcard is also provided. If you don't enter a wildcard or value here, all defined wildcard values are processed.

Selection parameters and wildcards

Figure 7.46 LSM Workbench — Converting Data — Selection Screen

If you selected BAPI or IDoc as the import technique under **Maintain Object Attributes** (see Section 7.2.1), additional selection parameters appear in the selection screen for the data conversion program (see Figure 7.47).

Additional function for BAPI/IDoc

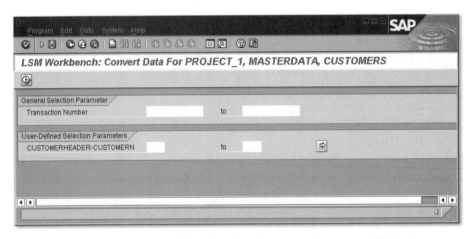

Figure 7.47 LSM Workbench — Data Conversion Program — Selection Screen — Additional Selection Parameters for BAPI/IDoc

If you select **Create file**, a file is created during data conversion. If you select **Create IDocs directly**, IDocs are collected during data conversion and submitted for IDoc creation in packages. You can determine the package size with parameter **Number of IDocs per package**. The default value is 50.

Log   In the example, you would click on **Execute** and then see a log like the one shown in Figure 7.48.

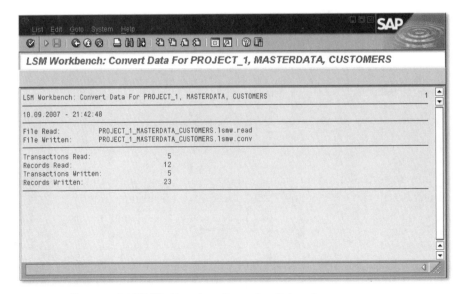

Figure 7.48 LSM Workbench — Converting Data — Log

7.2.16 Displaying Converted Data

Once you have triggered the data conversion, you can check the results. In this step, you have the same options as those described in the **Display Read Data** step (see Section 7.2.14). You should note, however, that the number of records here generally differs from the number of records in the legacy data, due to the different structures between legacy data and SAP format. However, the number of data units (here: five customers) should be identical.

Different number of records

In the example, a single BGR00 record is created, and for each customer a BKN00 record, a BKNA1 record, and a BKNB1 record. One BKNVK record is created for each contact person record (23 records, see Figure 7.49). Once again, you can double-click on a line to display the details for that line (see Figure 7.50).

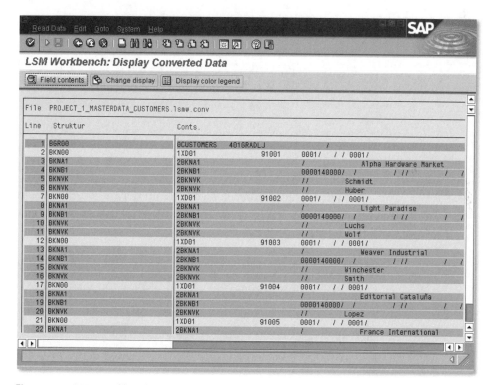

Figure 7.49 LSM Workbench — Displaying Converted Data

Figure 7.50 shows several fields with value /. The batch input program that is called next interprets this value as "Not specified" as opposed to the entry /.

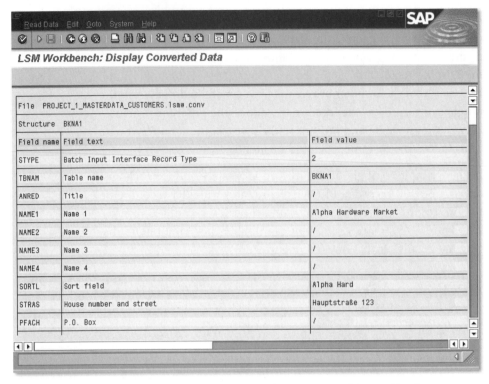

Figure 7.50 LSM Workbench — Displaying Converted Data — Details

7.2.17 Importing Data

Dependent on the import technique

The activities displayed after data conversion depend on the import technique you selected in the **Maintain Object Attributes** step (see Section 7.2.1):

Import technique	Data import step
Standard batch input or recording	Create batch input session
	Run batch input session
Standard direct input	Start direct input session
BAPI or Idoc	Start IDoc creation
	Start IDoc processing
	Create IDoc overview
	Start IDoc postprocessing

Table 7.5 Data Import Steps Dependent on the Import Technique

Therefore, in the example (standard batch input), you first have to perform the step **Create Batch Input Session** (see Figure 7.9). The name of the file with the converted data is already proposed. Therefore, you can click on **Execute** directly.

The further course of this step very much depends on which batch input program is used. In the example, the program reports several messages and then returns to the starting point. The batch input sessions that you create here have the same name as the object in the LSM Workbench, in this case, CUSTOMERS. Note that any number of batch input sessions with the same name could exist.

You're almost finished. Now, the only step left to perform is the **Run Batch Input Session** step (see Figure 7.9). The program starts SAP standard Transaction SM35. However, only the batch input sessions for the selected object are displayed. Note that if you used the name of the object in other projects or subprojects as well, batch input sessions from these objects can also be displayed. Because we already discussed how to process batch input sessions in Chapter 4, we won't repeat that same information here.

If you selected the direct input import technique (see Table 7.5), either call the standard direct input program for the object or choose between the direct input program and direct input transaction, depending on the object type, in the **Start Direct Input Session** step.

When you select BAPI or IDoc as the import technique, the import takes place in three main steps:

1. **Start IDoc creation**
   First, the file of the converted data is read. The "information packages" contained are stored in the SAP database in IDoc format; however, they're not stored in the database of the corresponding application. The system assigns a number to every IDoc and then deletes the file of the converted data.

2. **Start IDoc processing**
   The IDocs created in the first step are submitted to the corresponding application program. This application program checks the data and, if appropriate, posts it in the application's database.

3. **Create IDoc overview**
   A status overview appears, in which you can drill down to the individual IDoc level.

Importing data with batch input

Final Step: Processing the batch input session

Importing data with direct input

Importing data with BAPI or IDoc

Shortcut: "Create
IDocs directly" Note that if you choose the **Create IDocs directly** option during data conversion, the **Create IDocs** step is skipped (see Figure 7.47).

Whether the second step (**Start IDoc processing**) is initiated automatically depends on the settings in ALE-EDI Customizing. One essential setting is made in the partner agreement (for a partner and a message type, see Section 7.2.3). This agreement specifies whether the IDocs are to be processed immediately or via a background program.

> **Note**
>
> Please also note the following:
>
> ▶ Partner agreements automatically created by the LSM Workbench are set to **Initiation by background program**. You can change this setting manually at any time.
>
> ▶ When inbound IDocs are processed, *work items* are created in the standard system. Work items are elements of the SAP workflow that are usually not required during data migration. To learn how you can prevent the creation of work items — and the consequences of doing so — see SAP Note 149368.

Your example, which introduced you to the most important functions in the LSM Workbench, is now complete.

7.2.18 Object Overview

Before you exit the example completely, however, you should learn about one more function, which creates an overview of all the definitions you entered for the CUSTOMERS object.

Return to the navigation screen (see Figure 7.9) and click on the **Object Overview** button. The result is shown in Figures 7.51 to 7.53.

In addition to the list-based overview, you can display the overview in table form (**Overview in Table Format** button). You can use this overview as a template for your "mapping on paper" (see Section 7.2.7).

You can also list all the reusable rules that are actually used in the object (**Overview of Reusable Rules** button). This function is especially useful, because the contents of the conversion table are displayed for conversions as well.

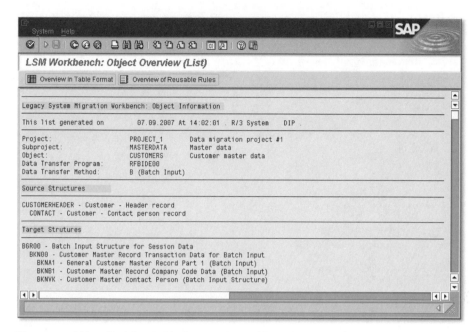

Figure 7.51 Object Overview in List Form — General Data, Source Structure, Target Structures

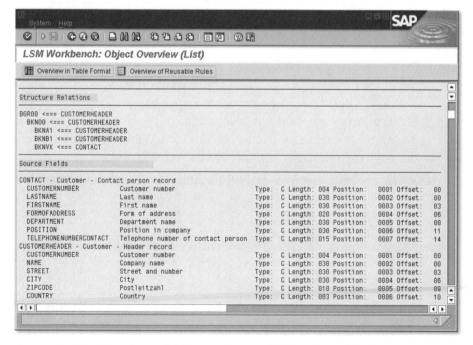

Figure 7.52 Object Overview in List Form — Structure Relations, Source Fields

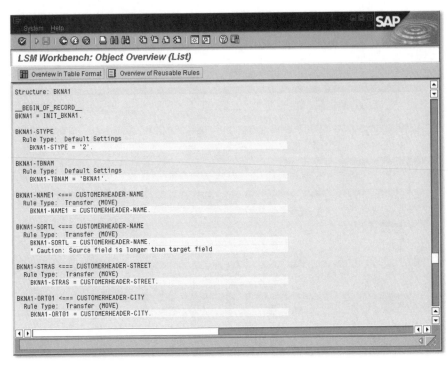

Figure 7.53 Object Overview in List Form — Conversion Rules (Excerpt)

7.3 Recordings

In the previous section, you learned about the main functions of the LSM Workbench based on the example **Migrate customer master data using standard batch input**. In this section, you'll work on another example to learn how the LSM Workbench is integrated with the recording function of the SAP ERP system. You already learned about the transaction recorder in Chapter 4. In the second example, we won't go into in as much detail as we did with the first example. Instead, we'll focus on those areas in the example where the procedure differs.

Example: creating a G/L Account

We have called our example **Create G/L Account**. You may ask why you shouldn't use the standard batch input program, RFBISA00, to migrate the G/L accounts. This is entirely possible. Because the legacy data here has only a few fields, however, it should be apparent to you by the end of this section that the recording function is the faster alternative.

Assume that your task is to create G/L accounts in the SAP ERP system based on the legacy data shown in Figure 7.54.

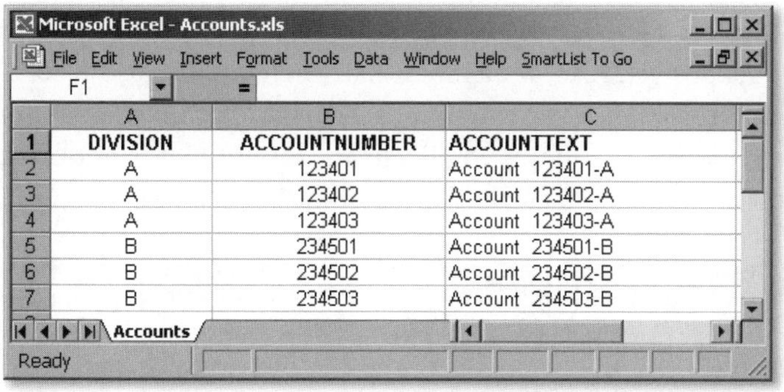

	A	B	C
1	DIVISION	ACCOUNTNUMBER	ACCOUNTTEXT
2	A	123401	Account 123401-A
3	A	123402	Account 123402-A
4	A	123403	Account 123403-A
5	B	234501	Account 234501-B
6	B	234502	Account 234502-B
7	B	234503	Account 234503-B

Figure 7.54 Example "Migration of G/L Account Master Data" (Excerpt)

Furthermore, it is assumed that you're already familiar with the corresponding transaction (Transaction FS01) and therefore know which data you must enter and where you must enter it (see Table 7.6):

Field from Transaction FS01	Input
Account number	**Account number** field from legacy data
Company code	Derive through translation of **controlling area** field from the legacy data A → 0001 B → 1000
Short text	**Account text** field from legacy data
Balance sheet account	X
Account group	SAKO
Group account number	110100
Balances in local currency	X
Field status group	G001

Table 7.6 Creating a G/L Account — "Mapping on Paper"

Your preparations are now complete and you can start working with the LSM Workbench.[4]

4 The group account number was set to a constant here in order to keep the example as simple as possible.

7.3.1 Creating and Editing Recordings

No simulation From the initial screen (see Figure 7.5), choose **Goto • Recordings**. An overview screen is displayed that lists all the recordings for the current project (see Figure 7.55). Note that a recording always belongs to a project. Also, remember that when you create a recording, the corresponding transaction is actually executed, and not merely simulated. Therefore, you'll use an account that is not listed among the legacy data to create the recording.

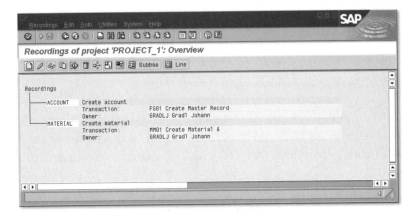

Figure 7.55 LSM Workbench — Recordings

> **Note**
>
> Unfortunately, you cannot use recordings that were created directly in Transaction SM35, because the LSM Workbench requires additional information that isn't contained in SM35 recordings.

In the overview screen of the recordings, click on the **Create recording** button. In the dialog box that opens (see Figure 7.56), enter the ID ACCOUNT and the description "Create account".

Figure 7.56 LSM Workbench — Creating a Recording

When you click on **Continue**, you are prompted to enter the Transaction code, FS01 (see Figure 7.57).

Figure 7.57 LSM Workbench — Entering the Transaction Code for the Recording

Enter the transaction code and confirm your entry. Transaction FS01 now appears, which you process with account 123499 (see Figures 7.58 through 7.60).

Figure 7.58 LSM Workbench — Recording — Transaction FS01 (Screen 1)

Figure 7.59 LSM Workbench — Recording — Transaction FS01 (Screen 2)

231

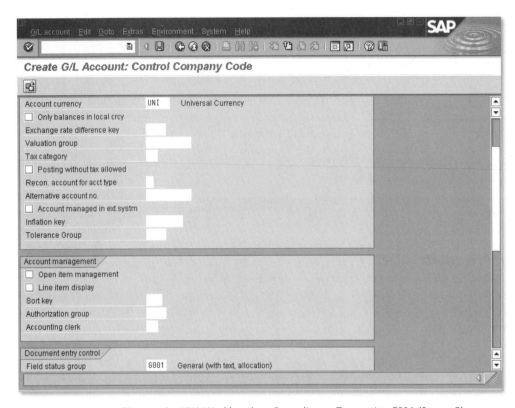

Figure 7.60 LSM Workbench — Recording — Transaction FS01 (Screen 3)

When you save the new account, the recording ends and the LSM Workbench assumes control again.

Tree display of recording – three columns A screen opens in which the recording is displayed with its technical components (see Figure 7.61). The display corresponds to the structure that you learned about in Chapter 4. The tree structure is arranged by transaction (FS01), screen (SAPMF02H 0402, and so on), and field (RF02H-SAKNR, and so on). The highlighted fields in the middle column[5] contain the values that you used when you created the recording or that were proposed by the SAP ERP system. The right column is blank, which indicates that postprocessing is required.

---

5 When you test this in the system, you will see the three columns clearly in different colors. The right column is highlighted insufficiently in a black-and-white screenshot.

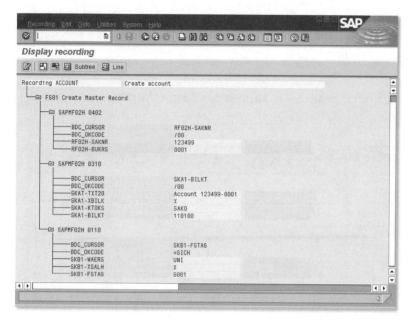

Figure 7.61 LSM Workbench — Result of Recording with Transaction FS01

As you learned in Section 7.2, the LSM Workbench requires a target structure to map the legacy data during the course of data migration. A structure requires field names, and you must assign these field names now. To do so, position the cursor on the first input field in the list — screen field **RF02H-SAKNR** with value **123499** — and double-click. A dialog box opens (see Figure 7.62), prompting you to enter a name and a description for the field. This information will appear later in the target structure. Enter "ACCOUNTNUMBER" as the name and "Account number" as the description and click on **Continue**.

Defining the field names of the target structure

Display recording	
Field name	RF02H-SAKNR
Name	ACCOUNTNUMBER
Description	Account number
Default value	123499

Figure 7.62 LSM Workbench — Recording — Assigning Field Names

Proceed accordingly with all the input fields that you want to supply with field values from the legacy data. Leave the names and descrip-

Naming the fields to be supplied

233

tions for the other fields blank. If the name and description of a field are blank, the LSM Workbench automatically uses the defined default value.

Therefore, you only need to enter the names and descriptions for three fields: **ACCOUNTNUMBER**, **COMPANYCODE**, and **ACCOUNT-TEXT** (see Figure 7.63).

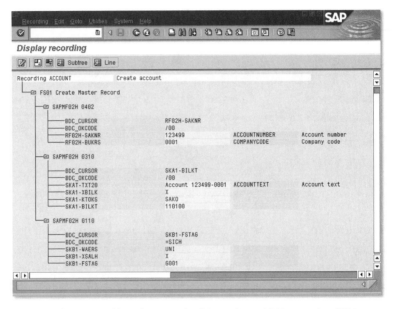

Figure 7.63 LSM Workbench — Result of Recording with Transaction FS01

For technical reasons, you must assign a name and a description to at least one field. Save the results and return to the overview screen with all the recordings in the project (see Figure 7.55).

Shortcut "Default"

Before you continue, you might want to learn about a useful shortcut for the last step. The screen in Figure 7.61, where you just postprocessed the recording, also contains the buttons **Default** and **All default**. If you use these buttons, the LSM Workbench automatically assigns the names and descriptions derived from the underlying screen fields, either to the field with the current cursor position or to all fields. The advantage of this function is its speed; the disadvantage is that the field names involved are not always mnemonic.[6]

---

6 In addition, two fields can be assigned the same name. Consequently, only one field with this name is available in the field mapping.

7.3.2   Using a Recording

You can now use the recording as usual in the LSM Workbench. In project PROJECT_1 and subproject MASTERDATA, create an object with ID ACCOUNTS and the text "Account master data". In step **Maintain Object Attributes**, under **Object Type and Import Technique**, select **Batch Input Recording** and, using the input help, the recording named ACCOUNT (see Figure 7.64).[7]

Define the source structure and source fields, using the procedure described in Section 7.2. In this case, this is not especially difficult, because you're only using one source structure and three source fields.[8] Therefore, define a source structure called ACCOUNTRECORD with the fields DIVISION, ACCOUNTNUMBER, and ACCOUNTTEXT. The result is shown in Figure 7.65.

Defining the source structure and source fields

The structure relations are nearly trivial, because you're only dealing with one source structure and one target structure. When you start the step **Maintain Structure Relations**, you see that the LSM Workbench is intelligent enough to define the sole possible allocation automatically.

Structure relations

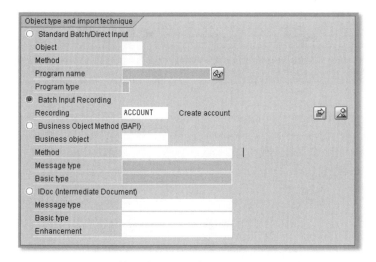

Figure 7.64 LSM Workbench — Recording — Maintaining Object Attributes

---

7   The LSM Workbench also allows you to chain several recordings, that is, to run two or more transactions in sequence for the same data record; however, this feature is rarely used.

8   In general, you can define only one source structure when you use the recording technique.

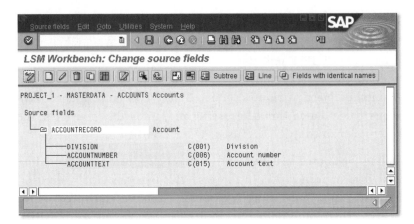

Figure 7.65 LSM Workbench — Recording — Source Fields

Field mapping and conversion rules

It is now time to maintain the field mapping and conversion rules. Once again, this usually complicated step is quite simple in this case, as you only need to supply three target fields with data. You already defined the strategy in Table 7.5. The result is shown in Figure 7.66. Once again, all the fields in the recording are automatically set to the default values defined in the recording.

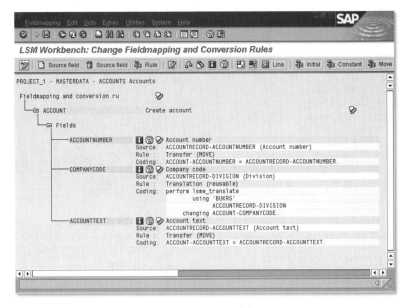

Figure 7.66 LSM Workbench — Recording — Field Mapping

You can perform the last steps quickly:

▸ Specify the file with the legacy data (not the Excel file, but instead the copy in **Text (Tab-Delimited (*.txt))** format) and assign it.

▸ Read the data and display it on screen for verification.

▸ Convert the data and display it on screen for verification.

▸ Generate and process a batch input session.

As this example illustrates, the recording technique in the LSM Workbench can help you attain your goals quickly, provided it is applicable to your situation.

What requirements must be met to enable use of the recording technique?

▸ The legacy data must be displayable in a single table, such that one row in the table corresponds to one transaction. Think of the first example from Section 7.2. In this example, each customer had a variable number of contact persons, therefore, the recording technique is not applicable here.

▸ The transaction must run through the same screen sequence for each data record.

7.4   Long Texts

You will now learn about long texts, a subject that is frequently neglected but one that can cause a lot of aggravation when not handled properly. **Long texts** are multiline texts. Usually, long texts for an object have to be migrated separately, because the SAP ERP system has a central repository for long texts in the database.

The LSM Workbench provides an object type with ID 0001 to migrate long texts. To make this object available, you must run the program `/SAPDMC/SAP_LSMW_SXDA_TEXTS` in the system in question.

Before you can begin to migrate the long texts, however, you must first learn how long texts are stored in the SAP ERP system.

7.4.1 Long Texts in the SAP ERP System

Long texts are stored in a text pool in the SAP system. The key of a long text is composed of four parts:

Key Field	Meaning	Example	Length	Check Table
OBJECT	Application object	MVKE = Material sales texts	10	TTXOB, TTXOT
ID	Text ID	0001	4	TTXID, TTXIT
NAME	Actual text key	Material number (18-place) + sales organization (4-place) + distribution channel (2-place)	70	(none)
SPRAS	Language	EN	1–2	T002

Table 7.7 Components of a Long Text Key

Text key: no standard rules

There is no uniform rule for the structure of the actual text key NAME. To determine the values for OBJECT and ID for a specific text type and the structure of NAME, proceed as follows:

1. Display the requested text type (material sales text, for example) and open the editor.

2. You can now choose **Goto • Header** to display the required information.

7.4.2 Target Structures and Field Mapping

Two target structures

You will now learn how you can use object type 0001 to migrate long texts. This object has the following two target structures:

▸ **/SAPDMC/LTXTH: Long text header**

- ▹ STYPE: Record type (technical field, value = 1)
- ▹ OBJECT: Application object
- ▹ NAME: Text name
- ▹ ID: Text ID
- ▹ SPRAS: Language

▶ **/SAPDMC/LTXTL: Long text line**

> ▷ STYPE: Record type (technical field, value = 2)

> ▷ TEXTFORMAT: Format field (two places)

> ▷ TEXTLINE: Text line

The **TEXTFORMAT** field contains text-formatting information. To map the field 1:1, enter character * in all fields.

An object in the LSM Workbench could then resemble the screens in Figures 7.67 to 7.70, which use the material sales texts as an example.

Specifically, perform the following steps:

1. **Define an object**

   In project PROJECT_1 and subproject MASTERDATA, create an object with ID MATSLSTXT and the text "Material sales texts."

2. **Maintain object attributes**

   In screen section **Object Type and Import Technique**, choose **Standard Batch/Direct Input**, **Object 0001**, and **Method 0001**.

3. **Maintain source structures**

   Define a source structure with the ID TEXTLINE and the text "Text line."

4. **Maintain source fields**

   Three fields are required: **MATERIALNUMBER** (length 18), **LANGUAGE** (length 2), and **TEXTCONTENTS** (length 72). All fields have type C

Long text
step by step

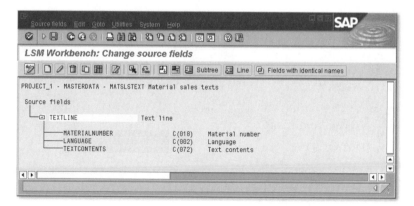

Figure 7.67 LSM Workbench — Long Texts — Source Fields

5. **Maintain structure relations**

Assign the only source structure, **TEXTLINE**, to the two target structures **/SAPDMC/LTXTH** and **/SAPDMC/LTXTL**.

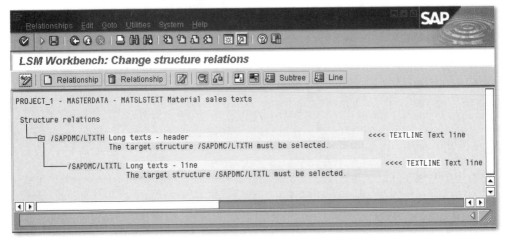

Figure 7.68 LSM Workbench — Long Texts — Structure Relations

6. **Maintain field mapping and conversion rules**

Perform the following activities (see Table 7.8):

Target Field	Activity
/SAPDMC/LTXTH-OBJECT	Assign constant MVKE
/SAPDMC/LTXTH-NAME	Assign source field TEXTLINE-MATERIALNUMBER Double-click on /SAPDMC/LTXTH-NAME
	Enter ABAP coding: /SAPDMC/LTXTH-NAME = TEXTLINE-MATERIALNUM-BER. /SAPDMC/LTXTH-NAME+18 = '0001'. /SAPDMC/LTXTH-NAME+22 = '01'.
/SAPDMC/LTXTH-ID	Assign constant 0001
/SAPDMC/LTXTH-SPRAS	Assign source field TEXTLINE-LANGUAGE
/SAPDMC/LTXTL-TEXTFORMAT	Assign constant *
/SAPDMC/LTXTL-TEXTLINE	Assign source field TEXTLINE-TEXTCONTENTS

Table 7.8 Overview of the Activities Performed on the Target Fields

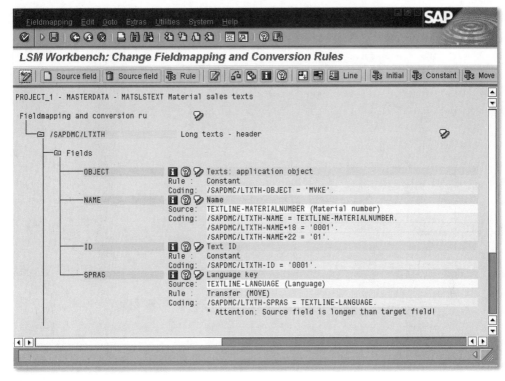

Figure 7.69 LSM Workbench — Long Texts — Field Mapping (Part 1)

If you use the default settings, you'll get an unwanted side effect, namely, a text header will be created for every text line, making each text line a separate text. To avoid this problem, you will have to reach into the "bag of tricks" in the LSM Workbench (see Section 7.8.3):

▸ Click on the **Display Variant** button and set the **Processing Times** checkbox.

▸ Various labels appear, including __END_OF_RECORD__ at the end of every target structure. Click this label at the end of target structure /SAPDMC/LTXTH. The ABAP editor appears, where you enter on_ change_transfer_record.

This statement means that the text header will be transferred only when it has changed, which is exactly what you want. This is the exact opposite of what occurred with the previous record.

Refer to Section 7.8 for more detailed information.

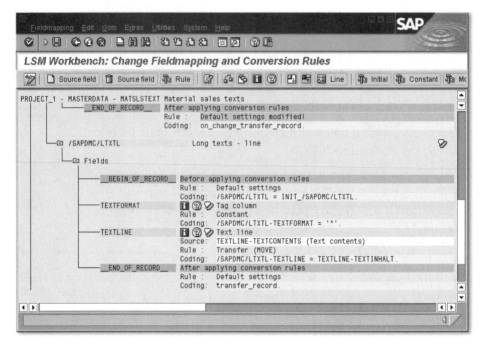

Figure 7.70 LSM Workbench — Long Texts — Field Mapping (Part 2)

7.4.3 Importing Long Texts

Import with direct input

You use the direct input technique to import the texts in to the SAP ERP system. You can call the relevant direct input program, /SAPDMC/ SAP_LSMW_IMPORT_TEXTS, from the LSM Workbench with **Start Direct Input Session**.

Postprocessing

After you have imported the long texts, the corresponding application may not always be able to read them, although they have been saved properly in the database. This is because some applications have a field in the master data that indicates whether a long text exists. The direct input programs don't fill this field, because these programs apply to all applications, and at runtime, they cannot determine to which application a text belongs.

There are two possible solutions:

1. Use a user-defined report to set the field and run it after you import the long texts.

2. Set the field when you define the conversion rules for the corresponding object (see Section 7.2.7).

7.5   Periodic Data Transfer

The LSM Workbench also supports periodic data transfers. In this case, we use the term **source system** instead of **legacy system**, because the system is not being replaced. The following requirements have to be met to enable periodic data transfer:

Source system, not legacy system

▶ The corresponding object in the LSM Workbench must be completely defined and tested.

▶ The application in the source system periodically makes one or more files available on the SAP application server.

▶ The object in the LSM Workbench doesn't access files on the frontend, because files on the frontend cannot be read during background processing.

When all these requirements are met, you can set the **Periodic** radio button in step **Maintain Object Attributes** (see Figure 7.11). The navigation screen (see Figure 7.9) displays the **Main Program for Periodic Data Transfer** step. This program performs the steps **Read Data**, **Convert Data**, and **Import Data** in the listed order.

Main program for periodic data transfer

You can schedule program /SAPDMC/SAP_LSMW_INTERFACE as needed. The numerous selection parameters for the program are illustrated in Figures 7.71 to 7.73.

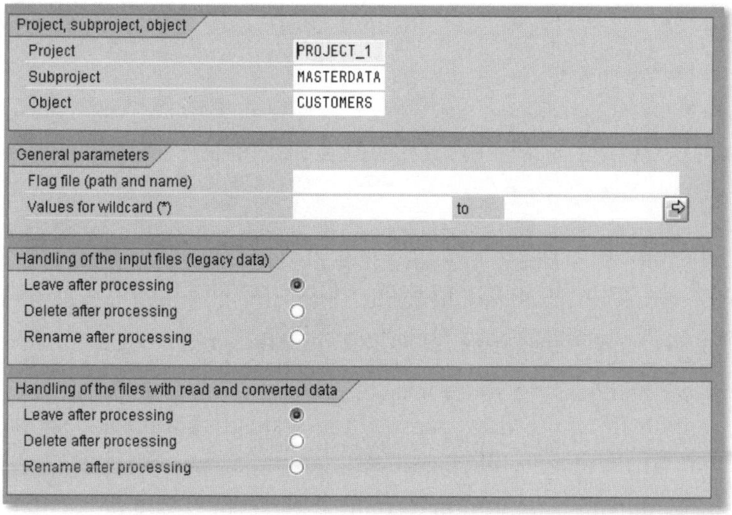

Figure 7.71 Main Program for Periodic Data Transfer — Selection Parameters (Part 1)

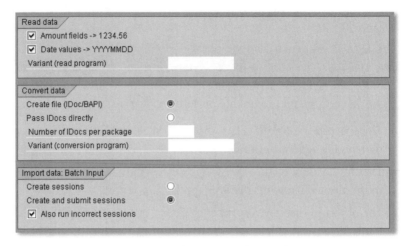

Figure 7.72 Main Program for Periodic Data Transfer — Selection Parameters (Part 2)

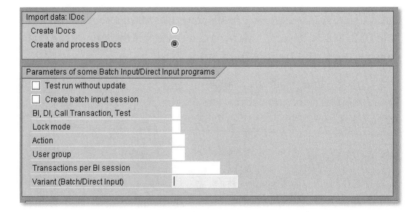

Figure 7.73 Main Program for Periodic Data Transfer — Selection Parameters (Part 3)

Flag file   Specification of a **flag file** is optional. A flag file serves to create a **handshake** with the source system, which provides the input files:

▶ The main program for periodic data transfer is only executed if the specified flag file exists.

▶ After finishing the data transfer, the main program for periodic data transfer deletes the flag file.

▶ The supplying application should behave in a complementary way: It checks whether the flag file exists before it creates new files.[9] If the flag file does exist, the program terminates. Otherwise, the files are generated, and the flag file is created.

The interaction between the source system and the SAP ERP system — with regard to the flag file — is illustrated in Figure 7.74.

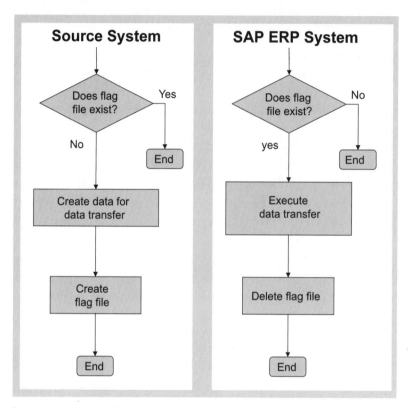

Figure 7.74 LSM Workbench — Periodic Data Transfer — Flag File Handling

You can specify variants for the read program, the conversion program and (in the batch input/direct input case) the batch input or direct input program. These variants must be defined beforehand. If you don't specify a variant, the default settings of main program /SAPDMC/SAP_LSMW_INTERFACE are used.

Variants

Some of the batch input and direct input programs provided by SAP use additional parameters, and some of these parameters are also used in other programs (see Table 7.9).

Additional parameters

---

9   The flag file can be blank. The system checks only whether the flag file exists.

Program	Parameters					
	Test run without update	Create batch input session	BI, DI, Call Trans-action, Test	Lock mode	Action	User group
RAALTD01 RAALTD11 (assets)	X					
RCCLBI01 RCCLBI02 RCCLBI03 (classes) RCCTBI01 (attributes)		X				
RCSBI010 RCSBI020 RCSBI030 RCSBI040 (BOMs)		X				
RCVBI010 (document info records	X					
RFBIBL00 (financial documents)			X			
RHALTD00 (personnel planning data)			X			
RLBEST00 (balances) RLPLAT00 (storage bins)		X				
RMDATIND (material masters)				X		
RPUSTD00 (personnel master data)					X	X

Table 7.9 Parameters of the Batch Input and Direct Input Programs

7.6   Transporting Projects

The LSM Workbench supports data transport for a project through both the SAP transport system and download/upload between two SAP ERP systems. In the process, the programs generated by the LSM Workbench are not actually transported; instead, new versions of the programs are generated in the target system.

7.6.1   Creating a Change Request

When you create a change request, this function creates an SAP change request that contains all the relevant information about an LSM Workbench project.

You can export and import this SAP change request with the usual tools in the SAP Change and Transport System (CTS). This function is located in the initial screen (see Figure 7.5) under **Extras • Create Change Request**.

When you transport project data in this way, you can trace the transports any time in the SAP CTS.

SAP Change and Transport System

Please also note the following:

▸ When you import a change request, the complete project is deleted from the target system first and then created again.

▸ When you export the transport request, the current version is exported (not the version that existed when you created the transport request).

▸ Because the entire project is exported, ensure that the project is "clean" when you export it.

7.6.2   Exporting Projects

In the initial screen (see Figure 7.5), choose **Extras • Export Project**. This first displays the structure tree of the selected project (see Figure 7.75). You can click on the **Select/Deselect** button to select whether you want to export the entire project or only parts of it. Then, select **Export (F8)**. A text file is created.

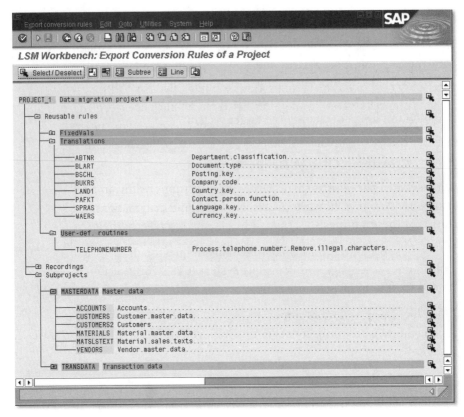

Figure 7.75 LSM Workbench — Exporting a Project

The selected elements are exported together with their documentation.

7.6.3 Importing Projects

You can then take the exported project and import it into a different SAP ERP system. Choose **Extras • Import Project** in the initial screen of the other SAP ERP system. The system prompts you to enter the name of the text file. The file is imported and its contents are analyzed. After the analysis, a list of the subprojects and objects found is displayed.

Existing elements are overwritten — Now, select the objects to be imported. Project data that already exists is check marked and will be overwritten by the import. To prevent an existing project in the target system from being overwritten, use the function **Import under different name**.

248

7.7 Preparations for Using IDoc Inbound Processing

IDocs (**Intermediate Documents**) were developed to exchange messages between different systems (for example, two SAP ERP systems). Comprehensive coverage of this topic would far exceed the scope of this book. Therefore, we simply want to make you aware that the procedure involves a standard interface, which makes the technique suitable for data migration as well.

As mentioned previously, the LSM Workbench supports this import technique. To use it, however, several settings and preparations are required. These settings are grouped in the initial screen of the LSM Workbench (see Figure 7.5) under **Settings • IDoc Inbound Processing** (see Figure 7.76). You must maintain these settings for each client and project.

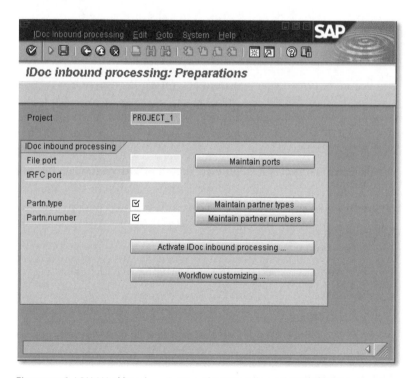

Figure 7.76 LSM Workbench — Settings for IDoc Inbound Processing

Perform the following steps:

1. The first requirement is a **File port** for the file transfer. If necessary, create a port with the required **file** type via **Maintain ports**. To do this, position the cursor on **File** and click on **Create** (you must be in Edit mode). The following settings are recommended:

   ▶ Port: LSMW

   ▶ Name: Legacy System Migration Workbench

   ▶ Version: IDoc record types SAP Release 4.x

   ▶ Output file: Enter any directory path and file name (such as *filelsmw*)

2. As an addition, you can specify a **tRFC port**. This port is required if you don't want to create a file during data conversion, but instead submit the data directly to IDoc inbound processing in packages. The following settings are recommended:

   ▶ Port: Can be assigned by the system as of Release 6.20

   ▶ Version: IDoc record types SAP Release 4.x

   ▶ RFC destination: Name of the SAP system

   ▶ Name of port: Legacy System Migration Workbench

3. Define a partner type or choose an existing one. The following settings are recommended:

   ▶ Partner type: US

   This partner type is available in the standard system in Release 4.5A and later. The partner type is not available in the standard system in Release 4.0B and earlier, and must be added. The following settings are recommended:

   ▶ Partner type: Create US

   ▶ Report name: /SAPDMC/SAP_LSMW_PARTNERTYPES

   ▶ Form routine: READ_USER

   ▶ Short text: any

4. Define a partner number or choose an existing one. The following settings are recommended:

   ▶ Partner number: LSMW

   ▶ Partner type: US

   ▶ Partner status: A

▶ Type: US

▶ Language: EN or DE

▶ Processed by: Your user ID

5. Activate IDoc inbound processing. Confirm the prompt with **Yes**. You have to do this once in each system.

6. Verify the workflow customizing. You also have to do this once in each system.

> Workflow customizing

The following entries of the workflow runtime system should be marked with a green checkmark (see Figure 7.77):

▶ Configure RFC destination

▶ Maintain system administrator for workflow

▶ Classify decision task as general

▶ Activate sending to objects and to HR objects

To do this, you can start automatic Customizing. After this, set item **Monitoring job for work items with errors** to **not scheduled**. If you don't do this, the SAP system will repeatedly try to post incorrect IDocs created during data migration.

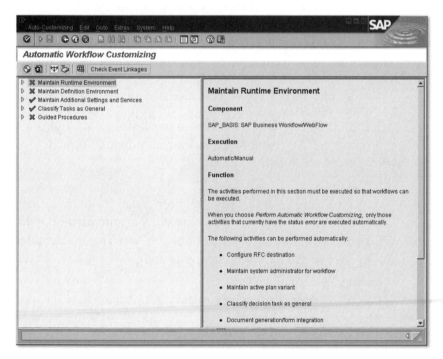

Figure 7.77 Workflow Customizing

7.8   Advanced LSM Workbench Features

This section deals with several topics that you will only find relevant if you want to work with the LSM Workbench intensively.

7.8.1   Display Variant and Processing Times

Click on the **Display variant** button in step **Maintain Field Mapping and Conversion Rules** (see Figure 7.22). The dialog box **Determine display variant** opens (see Figure 7.78).

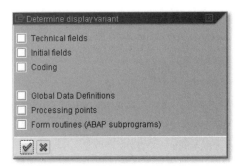

Figure 7.78 LSM Workbench — Determining a Display Variant

This function is useful mainly for experienced users who want to modify their field mappings. You can specify which information is displayed.

▸ **Technical fields**
Technical fields are target fields for which the LSM Workbench proposes a conversion rule (such as a constant). Typically, no changes are required.

▸ **Initial fields**
Initial fields are fields that have not been assigned a source field or conversion rule. This selection can help you summarize the display, but you should not use it until you have already identified the target fields relevant for your migration.

▸ **Coding**
When you check **Coding**, any existing ABAP coding is displayed, whether generated implicitly by the LSM Workbench or user-defined.

► **Global Data Definitions**

If **Global Data Definitions** is set, the label __GLOBAL_DATA__ is displayed. There, you can define variables, structures, tables, and so on to use in the field mapping of your own coding. Consequently, all the data definitions are consolidated at a central point, which helps to improve manageability.

► **Processing points**

Processing times make it possible for you to insert your own coding at specific processing times. The following processing times are available (see Table 7.10):

Processing Time	Default Setting
__BEGIN_OF_PROCESSING__	Before the beginning of data processing
__BEGIN_OF_TRANSACTION__	Before the beginning of transaction data processing
__BEGIN_OF_RECORD__	Before applying the conversion rules for a source structure
__END_OF_RECORD__	After applying the conversion rules for a source structure Default setting: Transfer_record.
__END_OF_TRANSACTION__	After finishing transaction processing Transfer_transaction.
__END_OF_PROCESSING__	After finishing transaction processing

Table 7.10 Processing Times

► **Form routines (ABAP subprograms)**

You can also display the label __FORM_ROUTINES__ for form routines (ABAP subroutines). This enables you to define ABAP subroutines in your own coding in the field mapping, as well as use include programs with form routines.

7.8.2 Global Variables

The LSM Workbench uses a number of global variables internally. You can use these variables in your own ABAP coding within the LSM Workbench. Choose **Maintain Field Mapping and Conversion Rules** in the list of steps (see Figure 7.9). Double-click on a target field to display the coding and choose **Insert • Global Variable**.

You can use the following variables in your ABAP coding (see Table 7.11).

Global variable	Name
g_project	Current project
g_subproj	Current subproject
g_object	Current object
g_record	Current target structure
g_cnt_records_read	Number of records read
g_cnt_records_skipped	Number of records skipped
g_cnt_records_transferred	Number of records transferred to output file
g_cnt_transactions_read	Number of transactions read
g_cnt_transactions_skipped	Number of transactions skipped
g_cnt_transactions_transferred	Number of transactions transferred to output file
g_cnt_transactions_group	Number of transactions contained in the current batch input session
g_userid	User ID
g_groupname	Name of the current batch input session
g_groupnr	Sequence number of the current batch input session

Table 7.11 Global Variables in the LSM Workbench

7.8.3 Global Functions

The LSM Workbench provides a series of functions that you can use anywhere within ABAP coding. These functions allow you to influence the flow of the data conversion program considerably. Therefore, use them with extreme caution.

Choose **Maintain Field Mapping and Conversion Rules** from the list of steps (see Figure 7.9) and double-click on a target field to display its coding. Then select **Insert • Global Functions**. The following functions are available (see Table 7.12):

Global Function	Description
transfer_record.	Transfers current record (for the current target structure) to the output buffer.
transfer_this_record '...'.	Transfers a record of another target structure to the output buffer. The name of the target structure must be specified as an argument in single quotes.
at_first_transfer_record.	Transfers the current record to the output buffer, if it is the first transaction.
on_change_transfer_record.	Transfers the current record to the output buffer, if it has changed to the last record.
transfer_transaction.	Writes the current transaction to the output file. This transfers all the records in the output buffer to the output file.
skip_record.	The current record is not transferred to the output buffer.
skip_transaction.	The current transaction is not written to the output file.

Table 7.12 Global Functions in the LSM Workbench

7.8.4 Reusable Rules – Naming Conventions

As you have learned, reusable rules are rules that can be used project-wide, that is, in all the objects of a project. Reusable rules are fixed values, translations, and user-defined routines.

If you assign a reusable rule to a target field, the system proposes up to three different names. To understand the naming conventions, see the definition of data objects in the SAP ERP system.

Up to three name proposals

Data object definition in the SAP system is performed on three levels:

Data objects in the SAP system

1. **Domain**
   At the lowest level, technical attributes are defined, such as field type, field length, value table, and fixed values.

2. **Data element**
   At the second level, you define "semantic" characteristics, such as language-dependent texts and documentation, based on a domain and its characteristics.

3. **Field**

At the top level, you define attributes of the field, such as foreign key dependencies, search helps, and so on, in the context of a structure or table.

In particular, this means that there are usually several data elements that refer to a given domain. Typically, a data element has multiple fields that refer to a specific element that is being highlighted.

Recommendation: use the proposal

We generally recommend that you accept the names proposed by the system. Exceptions apply only when the domain is extremely general in nature, such as CHAR1 or XFELD. If you used the name of the domain in this case, the reusable rule might not be usable for another field, since this field may have a completely different meaning.

This naming procedure keeps the number of conversion rules small and maintains the consistency in data conversion.

Table 7.13 contains an example.

No.	Field	Data Element	Domain	Name
1	BUKRS	BUKRS	BUKRS	Company code
2	CO_CODE	CO_CODE	BUKRS	Company code

Table 7.13 Naming Convention

Both fields are named **Company code**. The field names are different, but the domain is the same. Therefore, both fields should be filled with the same fixed value, the same translation, or the same user-defined routine.

7.9 Tips and Tricks

This section describes several techniques that may come in handy when you need to use them, which is, hopefully, not too often. If you encounter similar situations (as those discussed here) in your migration project, however, the described solutions can save you a considerable amount of work.

7.9.1 Determining the Transaction Code at Runtime

Let's assume that you want to transfer a set of data records, some of which already exist in the system. If a given data record already exists, you want to call the change transaction instead of the entry transaction. The following solution is explained based on the example of the customer master.

You first have to determine which case is involved. In the example with the customer master, this involves checking whether Table KNA1 already contains an entry with the customer number in question.

Create or change

Perform the following steps:

1. Insert the following under __GLOBAL_DATA__ (see Section 7.8.2):

   ```
   TABLES: KNA1.
   ```

2. Insert the following ABAP coding in field BKN00-TCODE:

   ```
   SELECT count(*) FROM kna1 WHERE kunnr = <old_customernum-
   ber>.
   IF sy-dbcnt = 0.
     bkn00-tcode = 'XD01'.
   ELSE.
     bkn00-tcode = 'XD02'.
   ENDIF.
   ```

   Consequently, Transaction XD01 is called for new records (which must be created) and Transaction XD02 is called for existing records (which must be changed).

7.9.2 Skipping a Record

You may want to exclude certain data records in your legacy system from the migration to SAP ERP. You can filter these values beforehand, when you export the data from the legacy system. The LSM Workbench provides a simple feature for performing this task. In this case, you want to skip a record, that is, you don't want to convert it or transfer it to the output file.

The solution is simple. You formulate the corresponding condition in ABAP and implement it in the following ABAP statements:

```
if <bedingung>.
  skip_record.
endif.
```

You can insert these ABAP statements in the coding of any field in the involved target structure.

Please note that only one record (such as one contact person for a customer) is skipped, and not the entire data object (such as the customer).

7.9.3 Skipping All Records of a Transaction

If you want to skip all the records of a data object (that is, a transaction) dependent on a specific condition, insert the following ABAP statements anywhere within the field mapping:

```
if <bedingung>.
  skip_transaction.
endif.
```

7.9.4 Duplicating a Record

Example Assume that you want, or must, create two or more target records from a single source record. For example, the customer master consists of a record that contains the fields FIRSTNAME, LASTNAME, and TELEPHONE for two contact persons (see Figure 7.79). Alternatively, the BKNVK record must be filled for each contact person in the SAP ERP system.

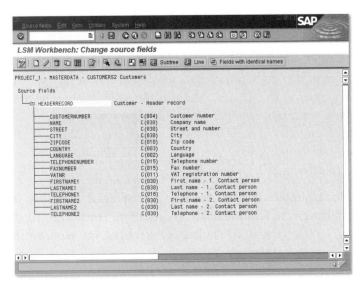

Figure 7.79 LSM Workbench — All Fields in a Source Structure

To solve this problem, you can define the rules shown in Figure 7.80 for target structure BKNVK.

The critical point in the coding is at processing time __End_of_ Record__. The first transfer_record statement transfers the BKNVK record with the data of the first contact person. The BKNVK record is then initialized, filled with the data of the second contact person, and written with the second transfer_record statement. This creates two BKNVK records.

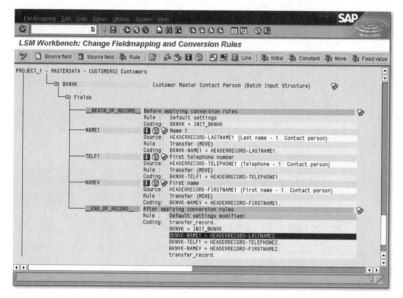

Figure 7.80 LSM Workbench — Duplicating a Record

7.9.5 Assigning Multiple Source Structures to a Target Structure

You may want to assign multiple source structures to a target structure. In this case, you should proceed as follows. Create the source structures as you would normally. Then, assign the subordinate source structure to the target structure. Consequently, the fields of both source structures will be available for the fields of the target structure. Figure 7.81 illustrates this constellation. The lower part of the diagram shows the ABAP coding, which the LSM Workbench generates from the structure relations.

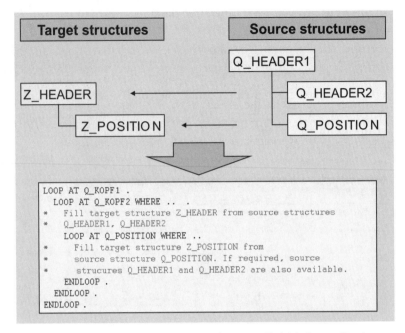

```
LOOP AT Q_KOPF1 .
  LOOP AT Q_KOPF2 WHERE .. .
*    Fill target structure Z_HEADER from source structures
*    Q_HEADER1, Q_HEADER2
    LOOP AT Q_POSITION WHERE ..
*      Fill target structure Z_POSITION from
*      source structure Q_POSITION. If required, source
*      strucures Q_HEADER1 and Q_HEADER2 are also available.
    ENDLOOP .
  ENDLOOP .
ENDLOOP .
```

Figure 7.81 LSM Workbench — Structure Relations — Multiple Source Structures for One Target Structure

7.9.6 Error Messages in the Conversion Log

You will usually want to be informed about errors that occur during conversion. To do so, you can output your own error messages to the conversion log. Two options are available:

1. Use the ABAP statement WRITE in the coding, for example, WRITE: 'Error during conversion of field ....'.

2. In the field mapping, go to the ABAP editor and choose **Insert Message**. You can also output existing messages in the SAP ERP system, for example:

```
WA_ERRORTAB-ID = '/SAPDMC/LSMW'.
WA_ERRORTAB-MSGNO = 012.
WA_ERRORTAB-PAR1 = 'A'.
WA_ERRORTAB-PAR2 = 'B'.
WA_ERRORTAB-PAR3 = 'C'.
WA_ERRORTAB-PAR4 = 'D'.
INSERT WA_ERRORTAB INTO TABLE G_ERROR_TAB.
```

The corresponding error message then appears in the conversion log.

7.10 Summary

You now know that the LSM Workbench is a tool that offers comprehensive support for your data migration requirements. Moreover, while you may not know every single detail about this tool, as you continue to work with the LSM Workbench, you will learn just how invaluable a tool it is. For more information and the latest news, visit the SAP Service Marketplace at *https://service.sap.com/lsmw*.

This chapter describes a tool which is currently provided by SAP only in conjunction with consulting services. For this reason, we'll limit the descriptions of this tool to its functional scope, without going into detail on how to operate it.

8   SAP Accelerated Data Migration

In order to select the optimal data migration techniques for a data migration project, you need to know all the techniques that are available. For this reason, it is worth describing the functionality of *SAP Accelerated Data Migration* (SAP ADM).

8.1   Availability

SAP Accelerated Data Migration was developed within SAP's *Custom Development* area; that is, the area that specializes in customer-specific developments. Therefore, SAP ADM is not part of the standard version of SAP ERP.

Available only as a "package:" software plus consulting services

Usually, end users of SAP systems can obtain SAP ADM only in combination with consulting services, which are provided by SAP or specifically trained partners.

The reason for this "bundling" is that SAP ADM has been designed for processing very large quantities of data. Consequently, SAP ADM cannot perform any complex checks of the data to be migrated, as you will see later on in this chapter. Therefore, for reasons of security, SAP permits only specifically-trained personnel to use SAP ADM.

Speed versus security

Consequently, the SAP ADM solution is not provided free of charge. At the time that this book was printed, SAP provided SAP ADM at no cost only to customers who had a "Safe Passage"[1] contract.

---

1   "Safe Passage" refers to a program that offers Oracle clients a *safe passage* to SAP.

To use the SAP ADM software, you must first install it on the target system (i.e., on the system to which you want to migrate the data). The full functional scope of SAP ADM has been available from SAP ERP 2004 onwards, which is also known as SAP ECC 5.0. A downsized version of SAP ADM can already be used with SAP R/3 Enterprise (Release 4.7).

8.2 Overview of SAP ADM

Migration tool with contents

SAP ADM is a migration tool that is based on the *Migration Workbench* (MWB).

While the MWB is a pure tool, SAP ADM actually contains data, namely, structured migration objects taken from the application areas of SAP ERP and SAP CRM, such as the "Employee," "Customer," "Vendor," or "Purchase Order" objects. Furthermore, SAP ADM has an interface called SII, which enables you to download data from non-SAP systems.

Very high throughput and wide area of usage

Contrary to all other data migration techniques described in the preceding chapters, SAP ADM writes the data directly into the tables of the SAP ERP database. This method allows for a high, even a very high, throughput (usually at least 20 times higher than the throughput that's possible with the batch-input technique). However, the general risk involved in this method is that if you don't know exactly how to use the SAP ADM, you might migrate data that is inconsistent or, worse, even unusable. To reduce this risk to a manageable extent, the migration objects have comprehensive checks.

Because SAP ADM doesn't need to use any existing data import interface, it can be used in a wide variety of scenarios, which includes virtually all types of data:

► Master data

► Transaction data, irrespective of its processing status

► Historical data

Migration objects and Guided Procedures

Similar to the LSMW, SAP ADM summarizes the migration tasks into migration objects and projects. From a technical point of view, a migration object consists of the following elements:

- Sender definition
- Receiver definition
- Mapping rules at structure and field levels
- Conversion rules for converting the field contents

The system uses *Guided Procedures* to guide you through predefined steps in each migration project.

In this context, it is essential that you define rules for converting the field contents. To do that, you can draw on a set of predefined rules, as is the case with the LSMW as well. These rules include the following:

Predefined rules

- Translation tables
- Fixed values
- Control parameters

The conversion logic also enables you to enter your own specific rules. Moreover, you can extend and modify the predefined rules via the conversion logic of the migration tool.

Furthermore, SAP ADM allows you to define different variants of a rule and to control the selection of the required variant via a *migration customizing* process.

You can define rules for converting field contents at different levels:

Area of validity of rules

- **At project level**
  This enables you to use rules in other migration objects of the same project.
- **At object level**
  This allows you to use rules in other locations of the same migration object, but not in other migration objects.

8.3 Specific Features

SAP ADM contains a migration cockpit, which allows you to monitor and control the entire migration process across all migration objects. The status of the individual processing steps is indicated by traffic light colors.

Migration cockpit

SAP ADM knows and takes into consideration existing dependencies between migration objects in different situations:

Dependencies between migration objects

► If you want to import data for a migration object, SAP ADM first checks whether the data of the "predecessor objects" has already been loaded successfully. If it has, the tool notifies the user that this has occurred.

► If you want to delete a migration object, SAP ADM determines the list of depending migration objects and notifies the user that these migration objects will be deleted as well.

► SAP ADM has a job monitor that enables you to define a network of background jobs, which factors the dependencies between the migration objects.

Testing support

In data migration projects, you often encounter the following problem. You want to test the data migration process under "real" conditions (i.e., in the production system); however, at the same time, you don't want to have any test data in your production system. To resolve this problem, SAP ADM provides two very efficient features:

► **Simulation run**
SAP ADM allows you to simulate the data import. During this process, the system runs through all processing steps, except that it doesn't write the data to the database. Even the logbook is updated and can be analyzed afterwards.

► **Delete function**
This function enables you to delete all table entries of a migration object, which were generated during a specific import run. You can repeat the data import process with the same data, without having to reset the entire system.

Migrating historical data, open documents, and documents in process

Due to the import technique used, SAP ADM can also migrate historical data, such as bill of materials (BOM) containing components that are no longer valid. In addition, SAP ADM enables you to migrate documents in nearly any processing state. This means you no longer have to resort to the following two makeshift solutions:

► You no longer need to split up the documents into a closed and an open part.

► You no longer need to use two different systems – a "live" system and a legacy system to search for closed documents.

Another advantage is that due to the data import technique, documents don't need to be renumbered.

8.4 Overview of the Typical Process

The following sections describe the typical process employed by SAP ADM, as shown in Figure 8.1.

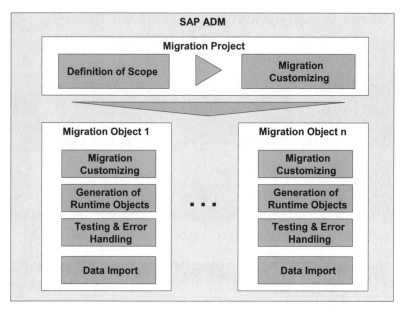

Figure 8.1 SAP ADM — Typical Process

Scope of the migration project

You only need to choose the migration objects you require for your migration projects from the pool of migration objects contained in the standard delivery. Each of these migration objects is associated with sender structures, receiver structures, mapping rules at structure and field levels, as well as conversion rules for the field contents.

Choosing among predefined migration objects

Migration Customizing at Project Level

Now you have to make the necessary settings for the conversion rules, which apply to the entire project.

267

Work Steps per Migration Object

Then, you must carry out several work steps for each of the selected migration objects.

1. First you must perform migration customizing at object level, which is similar to that at project level.

2. Then you must generate the runtime objects, that is, the programs required for data conversion and data import.

3. Next, you must test the migration object by using, among other things, the simulation function described above.

4. Finally, you must import the data (live run).

The following sections illustrate this process in greater detail.

8.5 Typical Process in Detail: Process Cockpit

8.5.1 Start

Transaction MWBSP

Once you have installed SAP ADM successfully, you must call Transaction MWBSP to start the tool. The initial screen provides an overview of the status of all defined projects (see Figure 8.2).

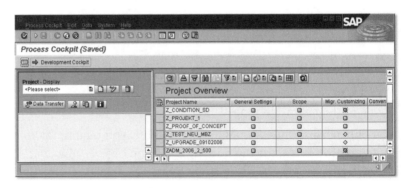

Figure 8.2 SAP ADM — Initial Screen — Project Overview

Process cockpit and development cockpit

This overview is part of the *process cockpit*. SAP ADM groups the entire functionality into a *development cockpit* and a process cockpit. Migration objects are defined (i.e., developed) in the development cockpit. The process cockpit processes the defined migration objects for the data migration.

The particular advantage of SAP ADM is that you don't have to develop migration objects from scratch. The standard delivery contains numerous migration objects that you can customize according to your specific requirements using the functions of the development cockpit. This means that only in exceptional cases do you have to develop entirely new migration objects in the migration project. Therefore, you typically use only the process cockpit.

8.5.2 Defining the Scope

First, you must create a new project, Z_PROJECT_1 (see Figure 8.3).

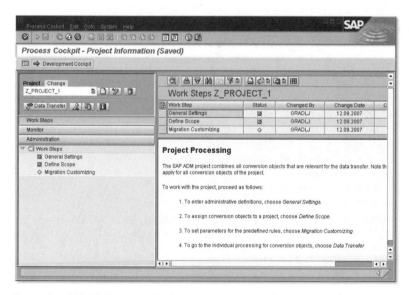

Figure 8.3 SAP ADM Process Cockpit — Creating a Project

The system then displays an overview of the project status (see Figure 8.4).

Figure 8.4 SAP ADM Process Cockpit — Project — Work Steps

Then you must enter some *general settings* (see Figure 8.5).

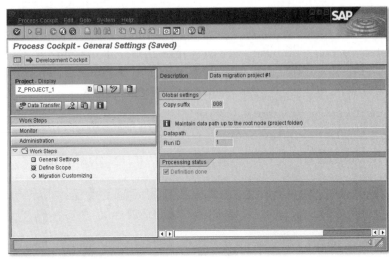

Figure 8.5 SAP ADM Process Cockpit — Project — Work Steps — General Settings

Defining the scope of the migration project

The most important work step consists of defining the *scope* of the project. To do that, you must select the required migration objects from a list of available migration objects provided by SAP (see Figure 8.6).

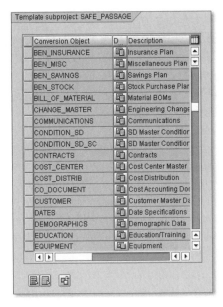

Figure 8.6 SAP ADM Process Cockpit — Project — Work Steps — Defining the Scope — Migration Objects Provided by SAP (Excerpt)

For this example, you should select the CUSTOMER migration object. SAP ADM copies the migration object and complements its name with a prefix and a suffix for technical reasons (see Figure 8.7).

In a "real" migration project, you would select more migration objects; however, for our purposes, this single migration object should suffice.

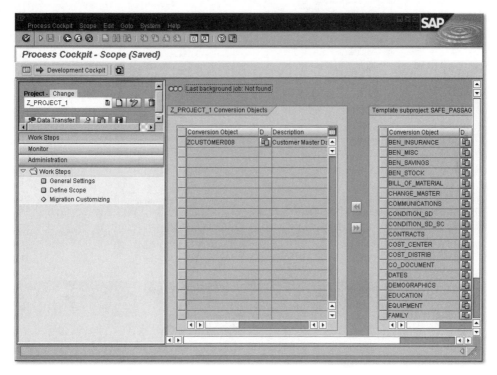

Figure 8.7 SAP ADM Process Cockpit — Project — Work Steps — Defining the Scope

8.5.3 Migration Customizing at Project Level

Once you have defined the scope, you must carry out the migration customizing process at project level. This task consists of making the necessary settings for all rules that apply to all migration objects of the project (see Figure 8.8).

Rules at project level

In doing so, you must first determine which of the available variants should be used. The following variants are available: simple migration with check (using the ABAP command MOVE), translation, fixed value, or custom ABAP coding (see Figure 8.9).

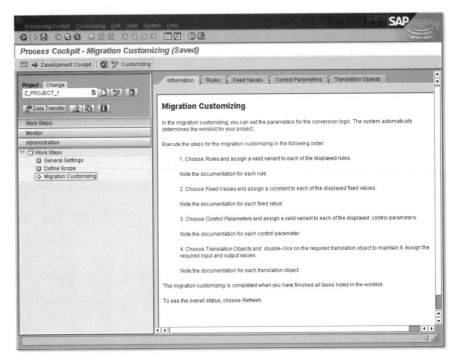

Figure 8.8 SAP ADM Process Cockpit — Project — Work Steps — Migration Customizing

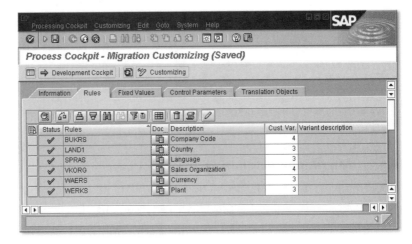

Figure 8.9 SAP ADM Process Cockpit — Project — Work Steps — Migration Customizing — Rules

After that, you must make the necessary settings for fixed values and translation objects (see Figures 8.10 and 8.11).

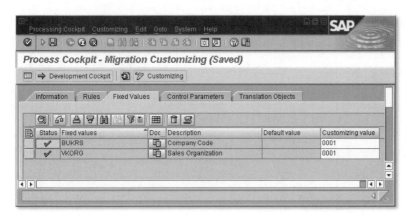

Figure 8.10 SAP ADM Process Cockpit — Project — Work Steps — Migration Customizing — Fixed Values

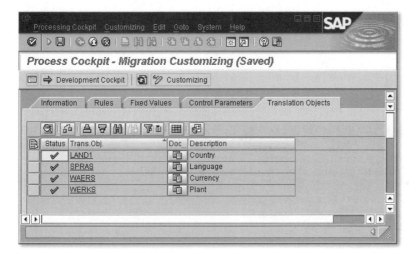

Figure 8.11 SAP ADM Process Cockpit — Project — Work Steps — Migration Customizing — Translation Objects

Moreover, you must specify the relevant value pairs for translations. For this purpose, you can use a value help and a check function on the receiver's side (see Figure 8.12).

Value pairs for translations

This step completes the work to be done at project level. You can now start customizing the individual migration objects.

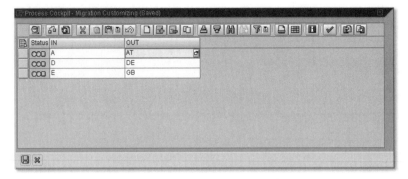

Figure 8.12 SAP ADM Process Cockpit — Project — Work Steps — Migration Customizing — Translation Table

8.5.4 Work Steps per Migration Object

The following sections describe the most important steps to be carried out with regard to a migration object.

Again, migration customizing comes first. You must now enter the same settings as the ones described in Section 8.5.3 for each migration object (see Figure 8.13).

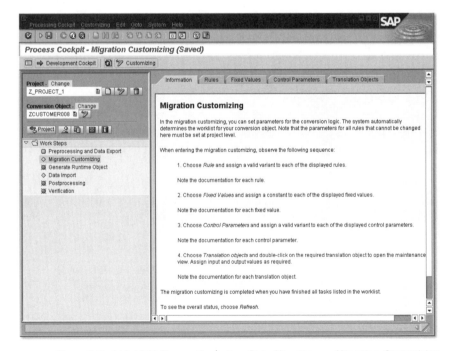

Figure 8.13 SAP ADM Process Cockpit — Data Migration — Migration Customizing

Once you have done that, you can generate the runtime objects required for the data migration at the push of a button; these runtime objects are responsible for translating and importing the data (see Figure 8.14).

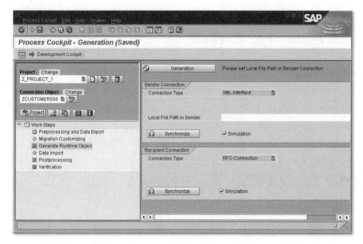

Figure 8.14 SAP ADM Process Cockpit — Data Migration — Generating Runtime Objects

After generating the runtime objects, you can start importing the data (first in test mode, of course). SAP ADM provides comprehensive support here (see Figure 8.15).

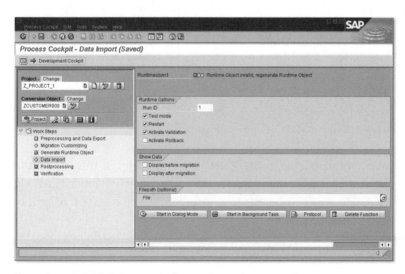

Figure 8.15 SAP ADM Process Cockpit — Data Migration — Data Import

Finally, if the results obtained in test mode are acceptable for you, the big moment has come: the live run. Again, SAP ADM can support you here. If you see that something's wrong after importing the data, you can delete the imported data again.

8.6   Development Cockpit

As mentioned earlier, the great strength of SAP ADM is based on the fact that it can draw on a large number of migration objects. However, if you still need to develop your own migration objects, the development cockpit SAP ADM provides numerous functions to do so (see Figure 8.16).

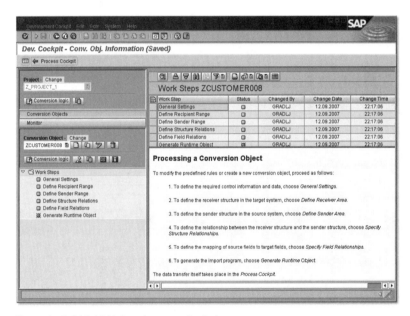

Figure 8.16 SAP ADM Development Cockpit

Defining custom receiver structures

When you create an entirely new migration object, this means that you also have to compile the receiver structures by yourself (see Figure 8.17). This is different from using the Legacy System Migration Workbench (LSMW).

When doing so, SAP ADM allows you to reference the structures of the Data Dictionary (see Figure 8.18).

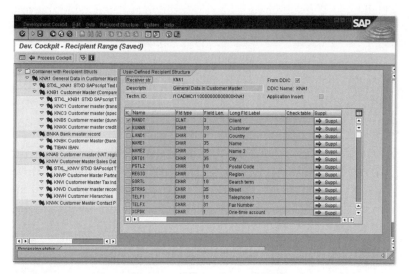

Figure 8.17 SAP ADM Development Cockpit — Receiver Structures

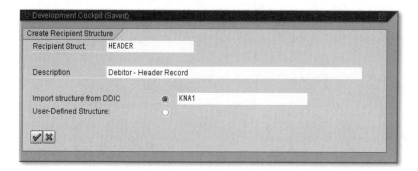

Figure 8.18 SAP ADM Development Cockpit — Defining Receiver Structures

In contrast to the LSMW, SAP ADM also allows you to modify or customize the receiver structures according to your requirements. Apart from that, the sequence of work steps to be carried out when developing a migration object is defined in the same manner as in the LSMW.

You can edit sender structures in the same way as receiver structures (see Figure 8.19).

Once you have defined the receiver and sender structures, you can establish relationships between them in the *Structure Relations* work step (see Figure 8.20).

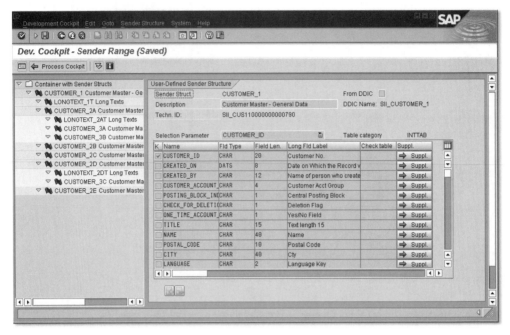

Figure 8.19 SAP ADM Development Cockpit — Sender Structures

Figure 8.20 SAP ADM Development Cockpit — Structure Relations

After defining the relations at structure level, you can define the relations at field level (see Figure 8.21). The following mappings were made in our example: sender structure CUSTOMER_1 was mapped to receiver structure KNA1; sender structure LONGTEXT_1T was mapped to STXL_KNA1, and so on.

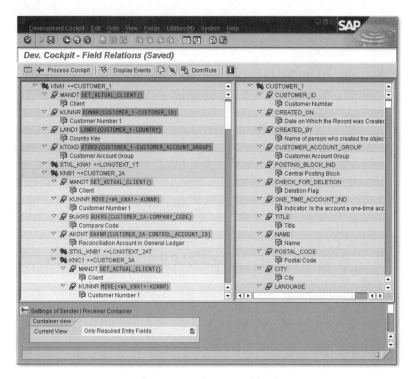

Figure 8.21 SAP ADM Development Cockpit — Field Relations

In the next step, you must define the field relations as well as the respective migration rules. As you have already learned in the context of the LSMW, this is one of the most complex parts of the entire process. This step concludes the development of a migration object.

Finally, you should note that you need to proceed in a similar manner if you want to customize an existing migration object to meet your requirements.

8.7 Checklist for SAP ADM

To make it easier for you to determine whether SAP ADM is the right tool for your requirements, we recommend that you look at the checklist below. The more that the following statements apply to your specific situation, the more likely it is that SAP ADM is the right solution for you.

▶ You have to migrate a large number of business objects.

▶ You have to migrate a large quantity of data.

▶ You have to migrate more than just open items and an opening balance sheet.

▶ You have to migrate historical data as well.

▶ The data migration process is supposed to be carried out within the current fiscal year.

▶ Your company acts in a strongly regulated environment.

8.8 Additional Information on SAP ADM

For additional information, please visit the SAP Service Marketplace at *http://service.sap.com*. There, you will find comprehensive materials about SAP ADM in the SAP Support Portal under **Knowledge Exchange • Ramp-up Knowledge Transfer • SAP Services**.

This chapter introduces several simple yet effective techniques for avoiding programming during data migration projects, thereby saving you time and money.

9 Techniques for Avoiding Programming

9.1 Problem Area: Data Conversion

When programming is required in a data migration project, it is usually needed for the following two activities:

▶ **Exporting the legacy data from the legacy system**
If the legacy system doesn't provide any functions for exporting the data, you'll have to develop appropriate programs yourself or hire someone to do so. This step is usually not critical from a cost perspective, because the legacy system experts generally work at your company, which means costly external support is not needed.

Exporting data

▶ **Converting the legacy data to the SAP data format**
The situation is much different when you convert the legacy data into the SAP data format. This activity requires knowledge of both the structure of the SAP ERP data format and of ABAP, SAP's programming language, because the data conversion (data transformation) takes place in the SAP ERP system. These two skills are not always available in sufficient quantities during an SAP ERP implementation.

Converting data

Consequently, this chapter will focus on the problems associated with converting the legacy data to the SAP data format.

9.2   Techniques for Converting Data

The techniques described here for avoiding programming during data conversion will show you how to use the *Extended Computer Aided Test Tool* (eCATT) and the *Legacy System Migration Workbench* (LSM Workbench or LMSW) to migrate your legacy data to the SAP ERP system with a minimum of programming — hopefully none at all.

80 % automation in the LSM Workbench

How is this possible? You learned in Chapter 7 that many conversion functions are available in the LSM Workbench at the touch of a button — without any programming. The predefined rules — assignment, translation, fixed value, prefix, constant, and so on — usually cover around 80 % of all required conversion tasks. Therefore, this chapter is dedicated to the remaining 20 %. To eliminate most of this remaining 20 %, you will learn how to use programming-free techniques in Microsoft Excel and/or Microsoft Access to format your legacy data, thus enabling you to perform the entire conversion without programming, using the LSM Workbench, for example.

Modifying structures and field contents

There are two basic problem areas, or situations that the standard conversion functions in the LSM Workbench cannot deal with (or at least not gracefully). The following areas are affected:

▶ Modifying structures

▶ Modifying field contents

We will describe these problem areas in detail in the following sections.

9.2.1   Modifying Structures

You have to modify structures when the fields are distributed to tables differently in the legacy system and the SAP ERP system.

Flat structures in the legacy system are no problem

If the structure from the legacy system is "flatter" than the structure in the SAP ERP system, that is, if certain data is stored in a single table in the legacy system, but distributed among several tables in the SAP ERP system, the solution is simple. The LSM Workbench enables you to assign several structures from the SAP ERP system (target structures) to the same structure in the legacy system (source structure). This was illustrated in the example involving customers in Chapter 7. The corresponding structure relations are shown again in Figure 9.1.

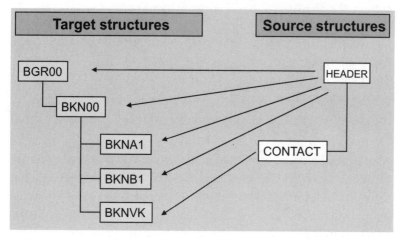

Figure 9.1 Source Structures Flatter Than Target Structures — Example "Customers"

The opposite case, where the structures in the legacy system are "deeper" than those in the SAP ERP system, is more complex. Based on the example of the customers, for example, this is the case when the data in the customer header is distributed between two structures in the legacy system. This situation is illustrated in Figure 9.2. As described in Chapter 7, you can only assign a single source structure to a target structure.[1] How can you solve this problem? Microsoft Access offers a simple solution.

The basic idea is to group the two structures HEADER1 and HEADER2 together to form a single structure. In database terminology, this is referred to as a *join*.

Join with MS Access

Assume, for example, that the fields in the HEADER structure from the customer example are distributed between structures HEADER1 and HEADER2 as follows:

- **HEADER1**
  CUSTOMERNUMBER, NAME, STREET, CITY, ZIPCODE, COUNTRY

- **HEADER2**
  CUSTOMERNUMBER, LANGUAGE, PHONENUMBER, FAXNUMBER, VATRN (VAT registration number)

---

1 One way to assign multiple source structures to a target structure was described in Section 7.9.5; however, it cannot always be applied.

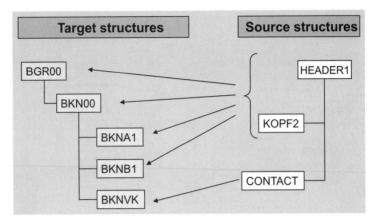

Figure 9.2 Source Structures Deeper Than Target Structures —
Example "Customers"

With Microsoft Access, you can use the drag-and-drop technique —
without any programming — to effortlessly create a structure that
contains all fields of both structures.

To do so, you should proceed as follows:

1. Import tables HEADER1 and HEADER2 into Microsoft Access.[2]

2. Define a *select query* for these two tables.

3. Define the key relationships by dragging the corresponding fields,
   that is, drag the CUSTOMERNUMBER field from HEADER1 to the
   CUSTOMERNUMBER field of HEADER2.

4. Use drag-and-drop to select all the table fields from HEADER1 and
   HEADER2 for the results table.

5. Save the query under the name HEADER1_HEADER2.

6. Run the query.

7. Export the results in format **Text (Tab-Delimited) (*.txt)**.

8. Process this file with the LSM Workbench.

The select query described above is shown (in draft view) in Figure 9.3.

---

2 Access can read worksheets from Excel files directly, without requiring them to be
   saved in format **Text (Tab-Delimited) (*.txt)**. You can also establish a *link* between
   Access and an Excel file. In this case, Access retrieves the information directly
   from the original file.

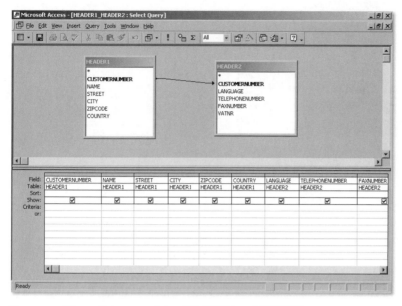

Figure 9.3 Microsoft Access — Join of HEADER1 and HEADER2

The structure relations are now simplified as shown in Figure 9.4. Therefore, you can take the case that the LSM Workbench could not solve initially (see Figure 9.2) and transform it to a situation whose structure relations correspond to those shown in Figure 9.1, which the LSM Workbench can now process.

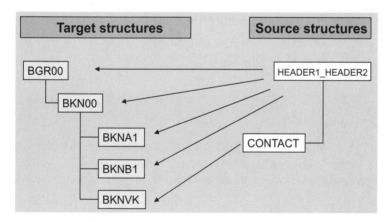

Figure 9.4 Simplified Structure Relations After Join of HEADER1 and HEADER2

This simple yet effective join technique can be applied in multiple areas, as the more abstract example shown in Figure 9.5 illustrates.

Generalizing the technique

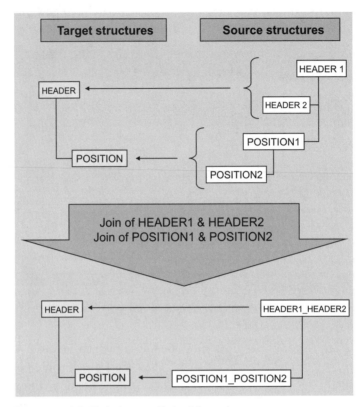

Figure 9.5 Join Technique — Abstract Example

9.2.2 Modifying Field Contents

This section shows you how you can use Microsoft Excel to perform frequently required modifications to field contents, again avoiding programming.

Date Formats

Date values appear in practically every data object. The SAP ERP system expects these values in a specific format, depending on the selected import technique:

Batch input
▶ Under the batch input technique, the system generally expects date values to have the same format as the one defined in the settings for the SAP ERP user ID, such as MM/DD/YYYY. Reminder: when you choose menu path **System • User Profile • Own Data** in the SAP ERP initial screen, and then select the **Defaults** tab, you

see the screen shown in Figure 9.6. You can specify here how you want date values to be displayed (among other things).

▶ The BAPI and IDoc import techniques generally require date values to be in the internal format YYYYMMDD.   **BAPI and IDoc**

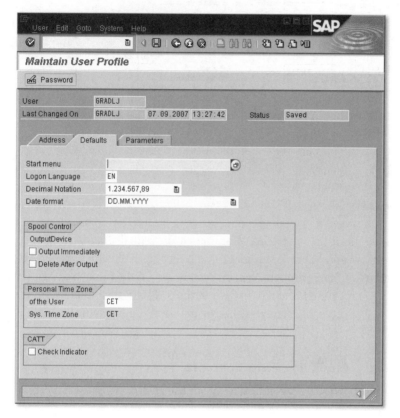

Figure 9.6 SAP ERP System — Maintaining the User Profile

How can you convert date values from MM/DD/YYYY to YYYYM-MDD, for example? To do so, proceed as follows:

1. Select the appropriate table column in Microsoft Excel, right-click to open the context menu, and choose **Format Cells...**
   and then select the **Numbers** tab.

2. Click the category **Custom** and enter the value "YYYYMMDD" in the **Type** field, as shown in Figure 9.7.

3. When you now save the file in format **Text (Tab-Delimited) (*.txt)**, the date values will be output in the format YYYYMMDD.

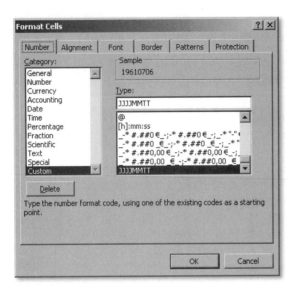

Figure 9.7 Selecting Date Format YYYYMMDD

Please note that the LSM Workbench described in Chapter 7 provides comprehensive support for converting date values. When you declare a field from the legacy system as a date value (see Section 7.2.5) and assign it to a date field in the SAP ERP system later on, the LSM Workbench calculates the correct format automatically.

Support by the LSM Workbench

Number Formats

Like date values, number values appear in practically every data object. The SAP ERP system also expects a specific format here, depending on the selected import technique:

Batch input
▶ The batch input import technique generally expects number values to have the format configured in the settings for the SAP ERP user ID — analogous to date values — for example, 1,234,567.89 with a comma as the thousand separator and period as the decimal point (see Figure 9.6 above).

BAPI and IDoc
▶ The BAPI and IDoc import techniques normally expect number values in the internal format 123456.78, that is, without thousand separators and with a period as the decimal point.

How do you convert a number format, for example, from 123,456.78 to 123456.78? Once again, the procedure is simple:

1. Select the appropriate table column in Microsoft Excel, right-click to open the context menu, and choose **Format Cells...** . The dialog box shown in Figure 9.8 appears.

Converting
number formats

2. Select the **Number** tab.

3. Click on the **Number** category and deactivate the checkbox. **Use 1000 Separator (.).).**

4. When you now save the file in format **Text (Tab-Delimited) (*.txt)**, the number values will be output in the format 123456.78.

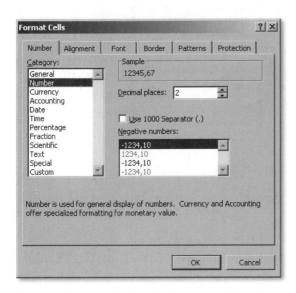

Figure 9.8 Selecting the Number Format — Without Thousand Separator

If your locale uses the decimal comma, you now have to convert the decimal comma to a decimal point. To do so, while Excel is open, select the **Regional Options** from the Windows system settings and make the appropriate changes there (see Figure 9.9). The data in Excel is updated instantly.

Once again, note that the LSM Workbench described in Chapter 7 provides support for converting number formats: when you declare a field from the legacy system as an amount field (see Section 7.2.5) and assign it to an amount field in the SAP ERP system later on, the LSM Workbench calculates the correct format automatically.

LSM Workbench
provides support

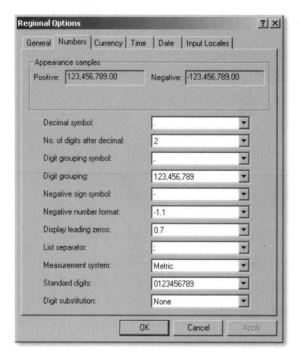

Figure 9.9 Regional Options — Selecting the Decimal Point

Modifying Currency Formats

Based on a currency field as an example, you will now learn how you can split data from a single field in the legacy system into two or more fields.

Splitting field contents Assume the legacy system contains both an amount and a currency unit in a single field; for example, 123456.78 EUR. You have to provide the amount and currency unit separately in the SAP ERP system. To do so, proceed as follows:

1. Select the appropriate table column(s) in Microsoft Excel and choose **Data • Text to Columns...** The first step of the **Convert Text to Columns Wizard** appears (see Figure 9.10).

2. Select the **Delimited** option and click on **Next**. Step 2 of the Convert wizard now opens (see Figure 9.11).

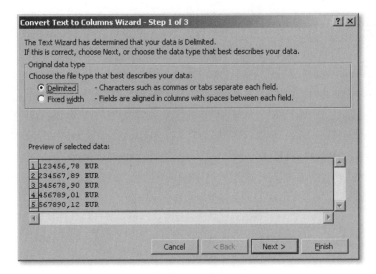

Figure 9.10 Convert Text to Columns Wizard — Step 1

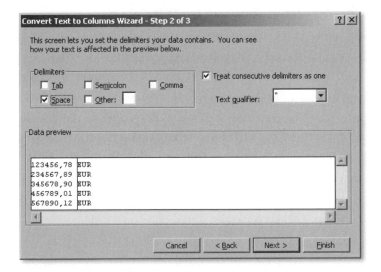

Figure 9.11 Convert Text to Columns Wizard — Step 2

3. Select **Space** as the delimiter. You can check the results immediately in the preview.

4. Click **Next** to continue to Step 3 (see Figure 9.12). You can now adopt the default settings and click **Finish** to end the transaction.

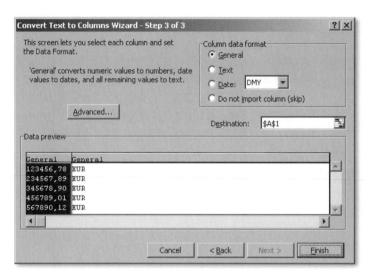

Figure 9.12 Convert Text to Columns Wizard — Step 3

5. Save the file in format **Text (Tab-Delimited) (*.txt)**.

Converting Numbers with Plus/Minus Signs to Absolute Amounts

Eliminating plus/minus signs

In this example, assume that your legacy system exports an amount field, which you must import into the SAP ERP system without plus/minus signs, because SAP ERP saves these signs in the posting key (e.g., in Financial Accounting). Therefore, you need the absolute amount of the field. How can you eliminate the plus/minus sign?

1. Select the appropriate table column in Microsoft Excel, right-click to open the context menu, and choose **Format Cells...** (see Figure 9.13).

2. Select the **Number** tab.

3. Click on the **Custom** category and select type **####,##;[Red] ####,##**. This means negative numbers are displayed in red, but without plus/minus signs.

4. When you now save the file in format **Text (Tab-Delimited) (*.txt)**, the number values will be saved in the format 123456.78, without the plus/minus signs.

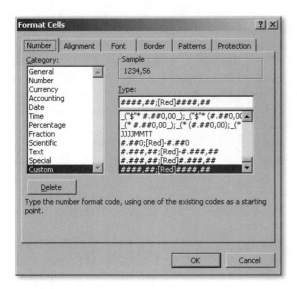

Figure 9.13 Selecting the Number Format — Negative Numbers in Red, but Without Plus/Minus Signs

Leading Zeros in Bank Sort Codes

In some countries, such as Spain, banks have sort codes that can begin with zeros. If the Customizing in your SAP ERP system is configured such that sort codes must have a specific length, you will have to provide these leading zeros. Otherwise, the SAP ERP system will reject the input with an error message.

If you open a file in Excel that has a column with bank sort codes, the leading zeros are removed because Excel interprets these values as numbers.

Saving leading zeros

To suppress this Excel feature, proceed as follows:

1. Open the text file with Excel. The first step of the **Text Import Wizard** opens.

2. Choose the **Delimited** option as shown in Figure 9.14 and proceed with the second step.

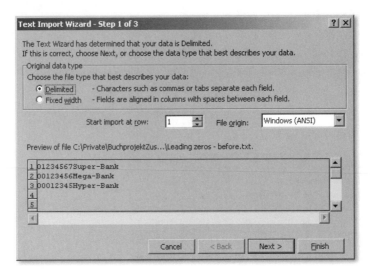

Figure 9.14 Text Import Wizard — Step 1

3. Select **Tab** as the delimiter (see Figure 9.15). Again, you can check the results immediately in the preview.

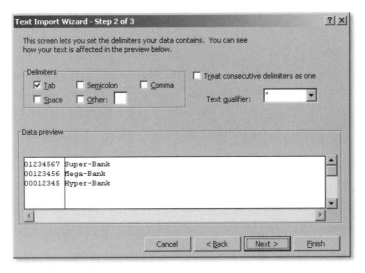

Figure 9.15 Text Import Wizard — Step 2

4. In the third step, select the column with the sort codes, and activate the column data format **Text** (see Figure 9.16). The leading zeros will now be retained. Click **Finish** to exit the transaction.

5. Save the file as usual in format **Text (Tab-Delimited) (*.txt)**.

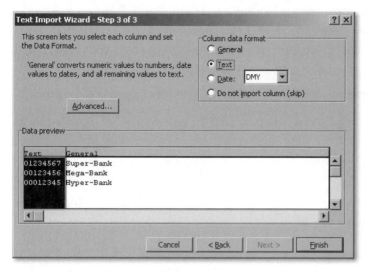

Figure 9.16 Text Import Wizard — Step 3

Joint Translation of Two Fields

Chapter 7 described how you could use a table to translate a field from the legacy system to a field of the SAP ERP system at the touch of a button. In some cases, however, the value of a specific field from the SAP ERP system can be determined only by analyzing two (or more) fields in the legacy system at the same time.

Assume, for example, that you want to renumber your accounts in the course of replacing your legacy system. You want to determine a new account number dependent on the legacy account number and company code. Therefore, the challenge is to use a table like the one below to convert the data (see Table 9.1):

Renumbering accounts

Source fields			Target field
OldAccount	Company code	NewAccount	
4000	1000	400001	
5000	1000	500001	
4000	2000	400002	
5000	2000	500002, and so on	

Table 9.1 Deriving the New Account Number from Company Code and Old Account Number

Merging two source fields in a single field

How can you take care of the translation in this case? To solve this problem, you can merge the two source fields in a single field, transforming the situation to a 1:1 translation, which you already dealt with above. Therefore, your solution strategy is as follows:

1. Concatenate the two source fields to form a single source field.
2. Perform a 1:1 translation from the new source field (created by the concatenation) to the target field.
3. You can easily perform the first step, the concatenation, in Microsoft Excel:
4. Add a new column to your account file and name it **OldAccount_CompanyCode**.

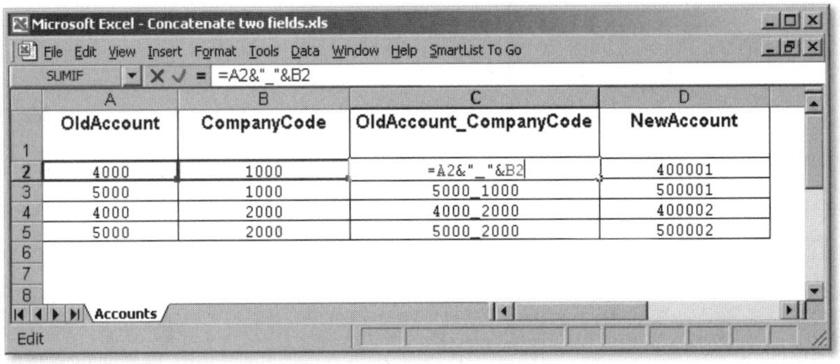

Figure 9.17 Concatenating Two Fields

5. Enter the following formula in cell C2: =A2&"_"&B2.
6. This example assumes that the **OldAccount** field is located in column A and the **CompanyCode** field is located in column B (see Figure 9.17).
7. Copy this formula to all the other rows. This concatenates the field contents of **OldAccount** and **CompanyCode** and separates them with an underscore (_) to improve readability.
8. When you now save the file in format **Text (Tab-Delimited) (*.txt)**, you have merged the two fields **OldAccount** and **CompanyCode** to form a single field and can now start the 1:1 translation.

You could perform the translation in the LSM Workbench as shown in Figure 9.18.

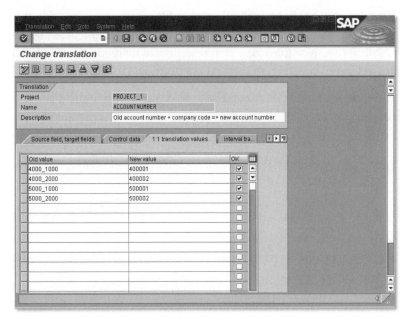

Figure 9.18 LSM Workbench — Translation of Concatenated Fields to the New Account Number

If you delete columns A and B from the Excel file and merely save columns C and D in format **Text (Tab-Delimited) (*.txt)**, you can use the upload function of the translation in the LSM Workbench. This saves you from having to enter the values manually.

Upload function in the LSM Workbench

9.2.3 Accessing Data in the SAP ERP System

During the data conversion, you may have to access data in the SAP ERP system.

Assume that customer numbers in your legacy system have evolved over time and that you want to reorganize them as part of your migration to SAP ERP. Accordingly, you decide to have the SAP ERP system assign new customer numbers during the data migration. Therefore, you will choose *internal number assignment*. To avoid losing the reference between the old and new customer numbers, you will save the old customer number in a special table field in the SAP ERP system that you define for this specific purpose.

Customer numbers evolved over time

If you also want to migrate open debit items, however, which usually support only the old customer number, you will have to replace the old customer number with the new number in these open items, because the old number is used only for information purposes in the SAP ERP system and does not represent an account that can be posted to.

The reference between the old and new customer numbers is available only in the SAP ERP system, specifically in SAP ERP table KNB1. To establish this reference when converting the data from the documents, you can either program a custom solution or use the following procedure:

▶ Download the excerpt of the SAP ERP table that creates the reference between the old and new customer numbers to your local PC.

▶ Use Microsoft Access to replace the old customer number with the new customer number in the document data.

Specifically, proceed as follows:

1. Migrate your customer master data to the SAP ERP system using internal number assignment. In the process, store the old customer number in field **KNB1-ALTKN**.

2. Start Transaction SE16 (Data Browser) in the SAP ERP system and enter "KNB1" in the **Table Name** field.

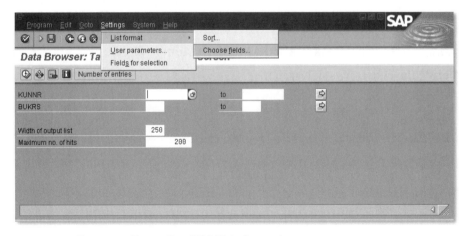

Figure 9.19 Transaction SE16 (Data Browser)

3. Use fields **KUNNR** and **BUKRS** to select all the relevant data records.

4. Enter a sufficiently large number in field **Maximum no. of hits**.

5. Choose menu path **Settings · List format · Choose fields...** and select the fields **MANDT**, **KUNNR**, and **ALTKN** in the subsequent dialog box (see Figure 9.20). Click on **Transfer** to confirm your selection.

Figure 9.20 Transaction SE16 (Data Browser) — Field Selection

6. When you press **Execute (F8)**, the screen shown in Figure 9.21 opens.

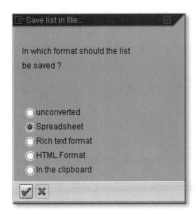

Figure 9.21 Transaction SE16 (Data Browser) — Saving the File

7. Now choose menu path **System · List · Save · Local File**.

8. In the dialog box that opens, select the **Spreadsheet** format and select **Continue**.

9. Enter a file name with extension .*xls* and click on **Generate**

10. When the data has been transferred to your local PC, open the file in Excel. You will have to make several corrections — delete blank rows and columns, for example — so your file looks similar to the one in Figure 9.22.

	A	B	C	
1	MANDT	KUNNR	ALTKN	
2	100	1000000040	3697	
3	100	1000000041	1865	
4	100	1000000042	1347	
5	100	1000000043	4547	
6	100	1000000044	4588	
7	100	1000000045	4566	
8	100	1000000046	4533	
9	100	1000000047	4500	
10	100	1000000048	2640	
11	100	1000000049	3697	
12	100	1000000050	1865	
13	100	1000000051	4098	
14	100	1000000052	1347	

Figure 9.22 Table with Old and New Customer Numbers

You can now use Microsoft Access and this table to replace the old customer number, ALTKN with the new SAP ERP customer number, KUNNR, in the document data.

Replacing the old customer number with the new one

To do so, define a select query in which you use the old customer number to establish a relationship between the table containing the document data and the table containing the relationship between the old and new customer numbers. Then select the new customer number as well (see Figure 9.23).

Alternatively, you can upload the generated table (see Figure 9.22) without the **Client** column to a translation table in the LSM Workbench and use it there.

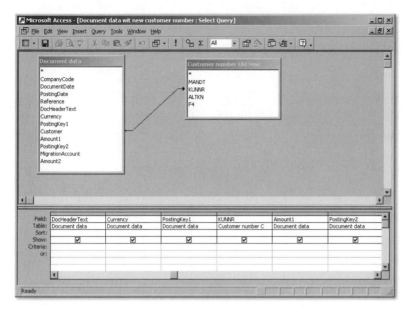

Figure 9.23 Select Query in Microsoft Access for Replacing the Old Customer Number with the New One

9.3 Summary

Make sure that the use of these techniques is documented in detail, as this is the only way to ensure that no essential steps have been omitted during the migration of your production data.

Documentation required

In addition, note that the techniques described here cannot be integrated directly in automated processes, such as periodic data migration.

Problems with automatic process flows

Nonetheless, you are now aware of several situations that seem to require programming at first glance, but where the clever use of Microsoft Office applications can help you to avoid more cost-intensive programming.

Now that you've been introduced to the individual data migration techniques, you can critically assess them. In this chapter, you'll learn about the advantages and disadvantages of each procedure, and the main criteria necessary to select a procedure for a specific situation.

10   Assessment of Data Migration Techniques

10.1   Advantages and Disadvantages of the Procedures

10.1.1   Batch Input

With the batch input procedure, comprehensive checks are performed when importing the data to the SAP ERP system, that is, when processing the batch input session. These checks correspond to the checks performed during dialog processing. This minimizes the risk of incorrectly entering data; however, these additional checks have a negative impact on system performance. Depending on the system hardware and configuration, the batch input interface transfers between 10 and 40 data records per minute to the database server of the SAP ERP system.

Safe, but slow

Incorrect transactions that the SAP ERP system could not process during the batch input session remain in the batch input session (*error session*), while successfully executed transactions are removed from the batch input session. Consequently, during error handling — the repeated, visible processing of the batch input session — you see only the incorrect transactions that require manual postprocessing. You can either process the full error session right away, or divide it into smaller sessions to be processed later on, possibly by several different individuals.

Easy-to-use error correction

The delivery scope of the SAP ERP system contains standard batch input programs for a wide variety of applications, which you can use

Standard batch input programs

303

for your data migration, possibly in combination with the LSM Workbench (see Section 7.2). Consequently, not only can you take advantage of the batch input technique features described above, but you can also benefit from the clear user guidance in the LSM Workbench.

Standard batch input programs are usually capable of generating the suitable screen sequence for a given set of input data, enabling it to be processed without errors.

Call transaction versus batch input

As described in Section 4.4, two basic options for processing the supplied data are available when executing a batch input program:[1]

▶ **Processing with call transaction**
The call transaction technique usually always processes the data faster than is possible with batch input sessions. Contrary to the batch input sessions, however, the call transaction procedure doesn't support any automatic, interactive correction or log functions.

This technique also enables synchronous processing of the data. The user can choose between synchronous and asynchronous database updates in the selection screen when executing the program. The latter option is preferable for achieving a consistent system load.

▶ **Combined processing with batch input and call transaction**
The general benefits of the batch input procedure, such as data security and error correction options, have already been mentioned. If you want to combine these benefits with improved performance during the data transfer, you should consider the combined use of the batch input and call transaction procedures. To do so, you have to use the call transaction procedure to execute the data migration program and also name an error session where all the incorrect transactions that the call transaction procedure cannot process will be placed. Manual postprocessing of the error session can begin as soon as the initial program is complete. This procedure enables you to achieve two seemingly irreconcilable objectives: speed and data security.

---

1   Some standard batch input programs also support this option.

If you need to migrate data for which no standard batch input programs are available, however (see Section 4.3), custom programming is unavoidable given the conventional approach. Even though the SAP ERP system generates these programs almost automatically, based on an underlying recording, you still have to enhance the coding, which requires at least rudimentary ABAP skills. You must equip the program with additional functionality, for example, to enable it to read more than just one data record (i.e., a full migration file) into the SAP ERP system and process it there (see Section 4.4).

Programming required

A program generated from a recording maps the process flow of that recording precisely; however, SAP transactions can react differently to different input data. This means the sequence of the screen templates is not always identical; it is frequently dependent on the specific input data.

Special features of a recording

A generated batch input program supports only the screen sequence from the recording, however. Therefore, you will have to define alternate screen sequences in the program logic that will be processed dependent on specific conditions, in order to react to the possibility of changing screen templates. This, in turn, means that you will have to create different recordings for the same transaction to generate the appropriate source code to deal with every eventuality, which can become an extremely complex task.

You can avoid custom programming altogether by exporting your recording and using it as the foundation for mail merge processing. Specifically, this means you have to transform all the data records for migration into the recording format in order to import them back into the SAP ERP system, generate a batch input session from them, and process that session (see Section 4.5).

Combined with Word Mail Merge processing

You cannot assume that recording an SAP ERP transaction will always result in a data migration tool for producing the required batch input sessions. Accordingly, you should always reject recordings in which the number of line items per data record can vary. This is the case, for example, in the migration of purchase orders. In the extremes, purchase orders can consist of only one purchase order item or of several hundred.

Problem case

Even though programming tricks can help you deal with such situations, this is not the objective of this book. Instead, we highly recommend that you use the LSM Workbench for such situations, as it lets you solve such problems quickly, elegantly, and, most importantly, without programming.

The transfer of customer master data, including contact persons, described in Section 7.2 can also be attributed to this area.

10.1.2   eCATT

Relatively simple procedure

The preparation involved in data migration using the eCATT is extremely simple. You merely have to know which transaction you want to use to migrate the data. If you know this transaction, you can record a sample data record with all the relevant information for the data migration (test script), which you can then parameterize to determine the format of the data to be migrated. You can then export the result of the parameterization, namely, the *variant,* to your PC (test data) to process it further there. In other words, you can arrange all the data records for migration according to the format of the variant and import it back to the SAP ERP system (test configuration).

Shortest preparation time and no programming involved

If you need to perform a data migration that all the described procedures support, your preparation time will be the shortest if you use the eCATT for data migration. *Preparation time* is defined as the time required to create an environment (batch input, eCATT, LSM Workbench) where the data migration can take place.

Because the eCATT doesn't require programming for data migration, it's also suitable for less technically oriented individuals.

Because the same input checks are performed when you execute a test case as in dialog or batch input processing, the speed with which the data can be imported is nearly identical in both procedures.

Special features of a recording

Like a batch input recording, the test script records the exact sequence of the transaction to be processed and its corresponding screen sequences. Once again, this means that the procedure is not flexible enough to react to differing screen sequences that can result from different data constellations.

Limited error correction functions

Unlike the batch input procedure, the eCATT is not capable of collecting incorrect transactions from the data migration and presenting them for subsequent manual processing. When a test case is executed *in the background* and there is no opportunity for interaction, all error-free transactions are posted as expected. Incorrect transactions are skipped and, at most, highlighted in the log. Should you neglect to analyze the log subsequently, some data records that have to be migrated may be left out, permanently falsifying the results of the migration.

If you consider the original reason for creating the eCATT, however — the automatic generation of test data to test business processes in the SAP ERP system — there is no reason to expect sophisticated functions for error correction like the ones that are available in batch input processing.

If you use the eCATT for data migration, as we have done in this book, you can avoid this problem by running all the test cases in **Display errors only** mode. This enables you to correct problems interactively as soon as errors in the dataset are detected. Once the error is corrected, the system automatically switches to background processing and continues in this mode until another error occurs. This switching between dialog and background processing continues until the session is complete.

Display errors only

If you assume that approximately 3,000 data records can be processed each hour (this assumption itself is highly dependent on the deployed hardware), it is apparent that this procedure can be extremely time-consuming when large data volumes are involved. Moreover, a constant user presence is required to correct any detected errors. If you can presume that the data is of high quality, however, with only a few or no errors, this issue is not as critical.

Problems with large data volumes

10.1.3 LSM Workbench

The undisputed strength of the LSM Workbench is its intuitive user guidance, which directs the user through the complex data migration process. The user is led through a logical sequence of work steps, while the thread is flexible enough to allow variances that have proven useful in practice.

Clear user guidance and organization

The clear outline, with its organizational units *Project* and *Subproject*, is very useful for keeping organized. The more complex your data migration project is, the more you will appreciate the outline. The project structure also supports the consistent distribution of the components relevant for the data migration — from the development system through the consolidation system to the production system.

If you use different import techniques within a migration project (e.g., standard batch input, batch input recording, direct input, BAPI, IDoc), the LSM Workbench ensures that the procedure is still largely uniform from the user perspective, because all the work steps can be called from a single user interface.

The greatest strength of the LSM Workbench probably lies in its data conversion functions. Therefore, using the LSM Workbench is recommended whenever the structure and format of the data vary widely between the legacy system and the SAP ERP system.

The LSM Workbench offers a high degree of flexibility at many different levels. Because it supports all the major import techniques, the range of data objects that can be migrated is very wide. The combination of predefined conversion rules, which can be implemented at the touch of a button, and the option to implement your own ABAP coding at any juncture makes the possibilities nearly infinite.

However, a high degree of flexibility will inevitably lead to a certain amount of complexity. Although the LSM Workbench succeeds in hiding this complexity in a great many places, you should not underestimate the initial effort involved in learning how to use it. One indicator of this is the fact that Chapter 7 is by far the longest chapter in this book.

10.2   Reasons for Favoring a Certain Procedure

Once you have familiarized yourself with the strengths and weaknesses of each procedure, the next step is to select an adequate procedure for your specific migration task. Generally, you should always use the procedure that just provides the minimum of functions that you need for your particular situation. This means that the complexity of the procedure increases exponentially with the complexity of the migration task, with custom programming being the last resort.

10.2.1 Complexity of the Migration Task

If the migration task is not very complex (i.e., if it involves a uniform dataset with standardized transactions and screen sequences), you can use a recording. This can involve a batch input recording that you can combine with Word mail merge processing or the LSM Workbench. Alternatively, you could record a test script as it is used by the eCATT.

Minor complexity versus increased complexity

If the dataset is not homogeneous, as expressed in changing screen sequences, it is difficult to model such situations in recordings. Instead, you need a procedure that can process different screen sequences without requiring manual intervention. The solution is therefore a combination of the LSM Workbench and a standard batch input program. If the standard batch input program that you need is not available, look for suitable BAPIs or IDocs, which you can also integrate with the LSM Workbench.

10.2.2 Quality of the Legacy Data

If you can assume a high degree of data quality, there is only a low or even negligible risk that incorrect data records will be created. Because error handling plays only a minor role in such situations, you can use procedures with limited support for error processing, such as the eCATT and batch input procedures combined with call transaction.

High data quality versus low data quality

However, if the data quality is low or unknown, the probability of errors is correspondingly high. In such cases, you will appreciate the benefits of the batch input procedure, especially the error sessions and their easy-to-use correction options.

10.2.3 Data Volume

If you have to migrate relatively few data records (less than 10,000 transactions), the throughput of the batch input technique or the eCATT should be sufficient.

Small data volume versus high data volume

If you have to deal with 100,000 or more data records, the time factor is the central focus of your migration task. In such situations, the decision-making factors are reduced to a single question: how can you transfer the data to SAP ERP as quickly as possible? The answer here is the direct input procedure, provided the SAP ERP system supports it for the specific application. If this is the case, you can combine it with the LSM Workbench.

If a BAPI exists for the application, you can also use it for the data migration along with the *Data Transfer Workbench* (DX Workbench) (see Section 12.1).

10.2.4 The Importance of Data Security

Security before speed

If you require an extremely high degree of data security, you will have to rule out all data migration procedures that write data directly to the database. Even though the direct input procedure supports controlled writing to the database, the checks in such situations are insufficient. Instead, we highly recommend using the batch input procedure, with its sophisticated error detection and handling functions.

Speed before security

If you're certain that your data is of high quality and can therefore skip the time-consuming input checks that reduce throughput, you can consider the direct input procedure for large data volumes.

10.2.5 Reusability

Given the constant need for higher efficiency and lower costs, your goal should be to always reuse existing procedures for similar situations. Under no circumstances should an insignificant change to the task at hand require you to start over from scratch.

eCATT

If you want to take a test script that you recorded with the eCATT and use it for similar future migrations, you can do so by extensively parameterizing the fields. Moreover, if you link the eCATT to Change and Transport Management (CTS), you can distribute test scripts, test data, and the test configuration to several different SAP ERP systems.

LSM Workbench

The LSM Workbench enables you to modify existing data migration objects at any time. Various scenarios are imaginable here. On the one hand, there are several ways to copy a project (in the context of the LSM Workbench) from one system to another and to modify it in the new system. On the other hand, you can also copy and alter a project within a single system.

310

In general, you can always edit recordings to make them reusable, either directly in the recording editor or in a file where you saved the recording. This procedure is not recommended, however, because it requires numerous manual changes to the recorded information.

Batch input recording

10.2.6 Restrictions

Because all test cases are based on recordings, the general restrictions associated with recordings (see Section 10.1.1) also apply here. For information on dealing with incorrect data records, see Section 10.1.2; notes on performance appear in Section 10.2.3.

eCATT

As described in detail in Chapter 7, the LSM Workbench provides powerful tools for processing various file formats and converting structures and field contents. Chapter 9 discusses its limitations. If the structures in the legacy system have a greater hierarchy depth than the structures in the SAP ERP system, for example, the LSM Workbench will not be able to deal with them (at least not without additional tricks). Complex conversions, such as the case of converting two source fields to a single target field as described in Chapter 9, also require additional effort.

LSM Workbench

Two primary restrictions apply to the batch input procedure: custom-recorded functions are incapable of dealing with transactions that have variable screen sequences, and the procedure does not have sufficient throughput to support large data volumes.

Batch input

10.2.7 User-Friendliness

If you define user-friendliness as the degree to which the requirements of a migration procedure are fulfilled, the LSM Workbench with its numerous design options is clearly superior to the other procedures. Nonetheless, the complexity associated with this flexibility may frighten potential users at first. Still, we hope that this book has reduced, if not eliminated, such uncertainties, enabling you to apply the full spectrum of options supported by the LSM Workbench to your specific migration task.

LSM Workbench

The attraction of the eCATT is that the procedure is identical for all data migration tasks. Another advantage is that only a relatively small number of steps are required for a given migration task. If you

eCATT

define user-friendliness as ease of learning, then these two factors speak clearly in favor of the eCATT.

Mail merge processing

Although combining batch input recording with Word mail merge processing requires more steps than the eCATT, the procedure is the same for every migration task here as well. Your additional preparation work is rewarded with an easy-to-use option for handling incorrect error messages: the batch input error session.

10.2.8 Summary

Ranking in terms of functionality

The migration techniques can be clearly ranked according to their functional scope:

1. LSM Workbench

2. Batch input recording/call transaction

3. eCATT

This ranking means that everything you can do with the eCATT is also possible with the batch input recording or call transaction methods. In turn, the latter two techniques represent only a fraction of the options available in the LSM Workbench.

Complexity and functionality

Because you should always select the simplest possible procedure for a data migration project, first examine whether the eCATT can help you to achieve your migration objectives. If not, examine a more complex procedure such as batch input recording or call transaction method. If these methods don't achieve the desired results either, you will have to use the most powerful procedure, namely, the LSM Workbench.

Table 10.1 shows a decision matrix that takes the various decision-making factors into account.

Example

Let's assume that you have to deal with the following situation. The *complexity* of your migration task is relatively low, and you have a medium-sized *data volume*. Because you don't have any information about the *data quality*, you will have to assume that a high probability of errors exists. As far as efficiency is concerned, you are highly interested in *reusing* the procedure to deal with similar situations in future.

		Complexity		Data Quality		Data Volume	
		High	Low	High	Low	High	Low
Data Quality	**High**	LSM	eCATT, CT				
	Low	LSM	BI				
Data Volume	**High**	LSM	LSM + DX	LSM + DX	LSM		
	Low	LSM	eCATT, BI, CT	eCATT, CT	BI		
Reusability	**Important**	LSM	eCATT	eCATT	LSM	LSM	eCATT
	Unimportant	LSM	BI, CT	CT	BI	LSM	BI, CT

Key:
BI = Batch input recording, possibly combined with mail merge processing in Microsoft Word
LSM = LSM Workbench (with standard batch input, batch input recording, direct input, BAPI, IDoc)
CT = Call transaction
DX = Data Transfer Workbench (see Section 12.1)

Table 10.1 Decision Matrix for Data Migration Procedures

By applying the above decision matrix to this set of factors, you can derive the following information:

- Reusability important → eCATT
- Low data volume → eCATT
- Low data quality → BI
- Low complexity → eCATT

Typically, you should always use the simplest available procedure to solve every partial problem. Because you have to solve the overall problem, however, and not just partial problems, you have to select the procedure that takes into account all the different aspects of the problem at hand. For the preceding situation, batch input recording is the choice, especially when combined with Word mail merge processing in order to avoid programming. However, note that in the above example, the objective of reusability is sacrificed in favor of the other objectives.

Always use the simplest procedure

If you apply the above decision matrix logically to your own migration projects, you will be able to identify the procedure that best meets your needs.

Decision matrix

In the previous chapters, you learned about migration techniques that can be used equally for all SAP applications. In this chapter, we'll compare the specific techniques for migrating fixed assets, before introducing you to a technique for migrating data with Microsoft Excel — a procedure that enables you to avoid having to use ABAP programming entirely.

11 Migrating Fixed Assets with Microsoft Excel

11.1 Assessment of Procedures for Migrating Fixed Assets

The migration of fixed assets is characterized by the fact that the data has to be transferred from an upstream system or from a manually managed fixed asset card file. This is usually the first activity after configuring Asset Accounting and classifying the assets. In this context, data migration refers to both migrating the asset master records and transferring the corresponding transactions, such as depreciation and acquisitions.

SAP ERP provides several options for migrating fixed assets:

▶ **Automatic migration using direct input**
This procedure is recommended for very large asset portfolios (more than 100,000 fixed assets) when you have to transfer the data to SAP ERP as quickly as possible. The speed of this method comes at the expense of the data quality, however, as only rudimentary checks are performed during the import process. Furthermore, this method doesn't support asset retirements that have already taken place, nor does it support group assets with asset subnumbers. The corresponding SAP ERP program is called RAALTD11 and can also be run with the LSM Workbench (see Chapter 7).

Migrating master and transaction data

Very large asset portfolio

Large asset portfolio

▶ **Automatic migration using batch input**

Batch input is generally safer than direct input. With the batch input procedure, comprehensive checks are performed during the data import, minimizing the risk of creating incorrect data records. However, these additional checks have a negative impact on system performance. This procedure is recommended for transferring large asset portfolios (between 50,000 and 100,000 fixed assets). Depending on the installed hardware and the system configuration, the batch input interface transfers between 10 and 40 asset master records (including transactions) to the subledger in Asset Accounting each minute. Conversely, the direct input procedure can process 10 times this number. Another advantage of the batch input procedure is that it supports asset retirements, as long as the legacy data transfer is performed at the end of the fiscal year. The corresponding SAP ERP program in this case is called RAALTD01, which you can integrate with the LSM Workbench similarly to RAALTD11.

Medium-Sized Asset Portfolio

▶ **Automatic transfer using Microsoft Excel**

You should use this procedure whenever you have a medium-sized number of legacy assets to transfer (less than 50,000 assets) and want to avoid having to use ABAP programming. Because an asset record usually requires at least five rows in Microsoft Excel, as you will see below, and an Excel worksheet contains only a limited number of rows, you may have to distribute the assets to be migrated among several Excel files and then import them into SAP ERP one after another. The Excel procedure offers similar performance to the batch input procedure. Please note, however, that you cannot use the Microsoft Excel method to migrate asset retirements, group assets, asset subnumbers, or investment support.

Medium-to-large asset portfolio

▶ **Automatic transfer using BAPI**

In contrast to the procedures described above, this procedure also supports the transfer of asset retirements when the legacy data transfer is performed in mid-year. We recommend using the BAPI method with the LSM Workbench whenever you have to migrate medium-to-large asset portfolios (between 50,000 and 100,000 assets). Please note, however, that this method doesn't support asset groups or investment support.

▶ **Manual transfer transaction/eCATT**

If only a few assets (less than 100) have to be migrated, you should consider whether automatic migration techniques are required at all, or whether it might be more efficient to use a specific data transfer transaction (AS91) to migrate the legacy data manually. None of the restrictions described for the other procedures apply to manual migration.

Small asset portfolio

▶ If you have to migrate more than 100 fixed assets, entering the data manually in Transaction AS91 can be arduous. Because this transaction offers useful support, however, you should consider integrating Transaction AS91 in an eCATT test script, which doesn't require any ABAP programming. In this context, Transaction AS91 is also suitable for migrating medium-to-large data volumes. You can read more about the eCATT in Chapter 5.

eCATT test script

This brief comparison shows the strengths and weaknesses of the individual methods. Therefore, before you choose a procedure, you should know exactly which data you want to migrate to SAP ERP and how important the factors of performance and data security are in your specific situation. Once you have clarified these criteria, you can choose the method you deem most appropriate to perform the legacy data transfer. It also shows, however, that the requirements of a data migration project can become so complex that they cannot all be satisfied by a single procedure. In such cases, look for a *combination of procedures*. Consider a situation, for example, in which the number of assets to be transferred is so large that only the direct input procedure and its high performance can be considered, but at the same time involves asset retirements, which direct input does not support. In such cases, you have to define which procedure you will use to migrate which assets.

Selecting the migration procedure

Regardless of which data transfer method you choose, your first step is to configure the SAP ERP system to enable the transfer of legacy data. To do so, choose **Financial Accounting · Asset Accounting · Asset Data Transfer · Set Company Code Status** in Customizing (Transaction SPRO, see Figure 11.1).

SAP ERP customizing

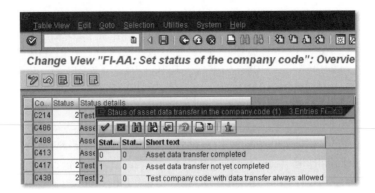

Figure 11.1 Setting the Status of the Company Code

We differentiate between three system statuses:

System statuses in
Asset Accounting

▶ **Test status = 2**
If this status is set, you can enter postings in Asset Management and migrate legacy data.

▶ **Transfer status = 1**
This status supports only the legacy data transfer, which means the postings to Asset Management are blocked in the SAP ERP system.

▶ **Production status = 0**
Set this status when you have completed the legacy data transfer successfully. No further transfers of legacy data are allowed. Postings are required to implement any future changes in values.

You must set the company code status to either **2** or **1** to transfer the legacy data.

No integration
between
general ledger
and subledger

At this time, we should mention that the G/L accounts in Financial Accounting are not updated in any of the preceding procedures; only the corresponding asset master data and line items in Asset Management are updated. Therefore, the legacy data transfer does not support automatic integration between the general ledger and the subledger, as is normally the case for subledger postings. You must reconcile the balances manually with the particular G/L accounts in an additional step.

If Financial Accounting is already live in your SAP ERP system before you implement Asset Accounting, however, the balance sheet accounts for the fixed assets and the corresponding depreciation accounts will already be up-to-date. This means that you don't have to transfer the balances from Asset Accounting to the general ledger (see Section 11.4).

11.2 Types of Legacy Data Transfer

Depending on when the assets are transferred to the SAP ERP system, you can choose between a legacy data transfer at the *end of a fiscal year* and a *mid-year* legacy data transfer. The data transfer date is the date on which the posting status of the legacy assets will be migrated from the legacy system to SAP ERP. Please note that the data transfer date is generally different from the time the data is physically recorded in SAP ERP. The physical recording of the legacy data often takes place after the data transfer date, because various closing activities are required in the legacy system.

End of fiscal year or mid-year

11.2.1 Legacy Data Transfer at End of Fiscal Year

If the legacy data transfer date is the *end of the last closed fiscal year* (usually December 31, YYYY), the master data, acquisition and production costs, and accumulated depreciation are transferred to the ERP system in their values from *end of the last closed fiscal year* (31.12.YYYY). In this case, no mid-year depreciation or transaction postings can be included in the legacy data transfer.

Master data, APC, and accumulated depreciation

To configure the necessary Customizing settings, select the following menu path: **Financial Accounting · Asset Accounting · Asset Data Transfer · Parameters for Data Transfer · Date Specifications · Specify Transfer Date/Last Closed Fiscal Year** (see Figure 11.2).

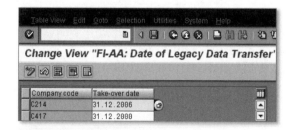

Figure 11.2 Legacy Data Transfer at End of Fiscal Year

Here you must specify the last fiscal year before the transfer.

11.2.2 Legacy Data Transfer in Mid-Year

In a mid-year legacy data transfer, the transfer date is after the end of the last closed fiscal year. Under these framework conditions, the master data and accumulated values are transferred at the beginning of the year (usually 01/01/YYYY + 1). Also, you must migrate all the depreciation and transaction postings that have occurred during the current year (that is, in YYYY + 1). Configure the Customizing settings required to transfer the assets — as of March 1, 2007, for example — analogous to the procedure described in Section 11.2.1 (see Figure 11.3).

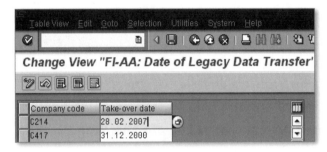

Figure 11.3 Mid-Year Legacy Data Transfer on March 1, 2007

In addition to the data transfer date, you have to record the period when the last depreciation was posted in the legacy system. You configure the necessary Customizing settings under **Financial Accounting • Asset Accounting • Asset Data Transfer • Parameters for Data Transfer • Date Specifications • Specify Last Period Posted in Prv. System (Transf.During FY)** (see Figure 11.4).

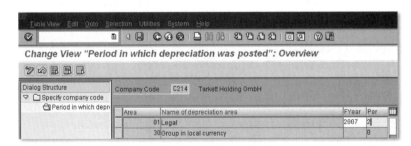

Figure 11.4 Specifying the Period of the Last Depreciation Posted in the Legacy System

You can differentiate your handling of depreciation postings in the current year (YYYY + 1):

▶ **Transfer of depreciation posted in the current year**
One alternative is to transfer all the depreciation posted in the legacy system up to the transfer date. With regard to the last example, this means transferring the depreciation posted in the legacy system up to 02/28/YYYY + 1. Accordingly, the new system — SAP ERP in this case — posts the first scheduled depreciation on 03/31/YYYY + 1.

▶ **No transfer of depreciation posted in the current year**
The other option is not to transfer the depreciation posted in the current year. The total depreciation from the current year that has accumulated up to the transfer date is duplicated as extraordinary depreciation, which occurs after the legacy data is transferred to SAP ERP. In our example, you also have to start an extraordinary depreciation posting run on 03/31/YYYY + 1. Therefore, all depreciation accumulated in YYYY+1 is posted in March. You can then start the scheduled depreciation posting runs in April.

11.2.3   Other Options for Transferring Asset Data

You can use the parameterizations described below (see Figure 11.5), but they are not required.

▶ **Recalculate depreciation for previous years**
If you want to define a new depreciation area in SAP ERP that did not exist in your legacy system, such as book valuation or tax-based valuation of the fixed assets, you can have the SAP ERP system recalculate the accumulated depreciation for this depreciation area up to the last closed fiscal year. For this purpose, you can use the depreciation parameters defined in SAP ERP. You can use this option only when the company code is set to test status **2**.

▶ **Recalculate replacement values and base insurable values**
If you activate this option, the system assumes that the acquisition value has been fully posted at the time of capitalization.

▶ **Specify sequence of depreciation areas**
This option has a direct impact on performance when you use the batch input method to migrate the legacy data. In this context, you must enter the independent depreciation areas first. Dependent

depreciation areas whose values are derived from the independent depreciation areas should be named last.

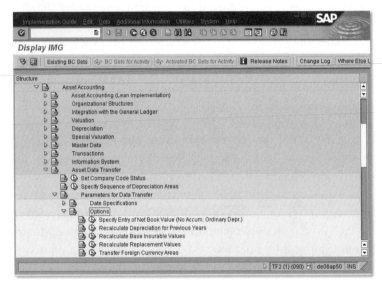

Figure 11.5 Other Options for Transferring Asset Data

Note that the order of the depreciation areas in the migration file can differ from the sequence defined in Customizing.

11.3 Case Example: Migrating Fixed Assets with Microsoft Excel

Now that you've learned about the Customizing settings that are required, regardless of which migration method you use, we'll describe the migration of asset data with Microsoft Excel in more detail.

Small and medium-sized asset portfolios

This method is useful particularly when you have to migrate only small or medium-sized data volumes. Because the number of rows is finite in Microsoft Excel worksheets, an Excel file can process only a limited number of fixed assets. If you run out of rows in a Microsoft Excel worksheet, you can simply split the data among several Excel files and then import the files into the SAP ERP system in sequence.

The next section describes how to use this method, based on a brief case example.

11.3.1 Which Data Should You Transfer?

As we mentioned in Chapter 2, "Which data should you transfer?" is the first question that you must address in any data migration project. Only after you answer this question can you consider the best migration method to use and compose the team necessary to support the data migration project.

In this example, you assume that the user department responsible for asset accounting already uses the correct SAP terminology. This means that translation of field texts in the legacy system to the corresponding field texts in the SAP ERP system — a process that may require a great deal of coordination and system demonstrations — is not necessary. Moreover, the user department must be able to provide an Excel file that contains the asset values to be migrated in table form (one complete data record in each row; see Figure 11.6). Extracting the data from the legacy system is also not always a simple task. You may have to refer to external consultants to accomplish this task, a fact that you will have to address when assembling your project team.

Assumptions

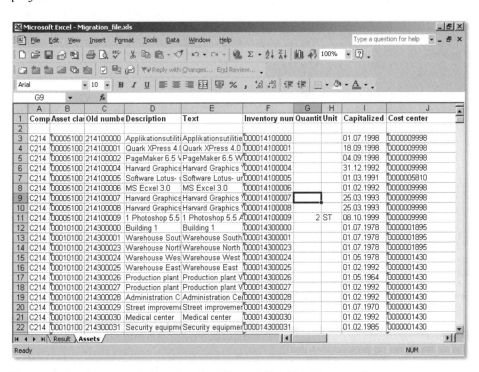

Figure 11.6 Fixed Assets to Be Transferred to Microsoft Excel (Not Formatted)

Master and transaction data The Excel file contains one complete data record in each row, consisting of master data information such as the company code, asset class, (legacy) asset number, and cost center, along with transaction data such as the accumulated Acquisition and Production Costs (APC) and accumulated depreciation for each depreciation area (the latter of which doesn't appear in Figure 11.6).

11.3.2 Data Format for the Transfer to SAP ERP

Data format The SAP ERP system expects the data to be transferred in a specific format. Consequently, even if the Excel file provided by the user department contains all the relevant information, the file still cannot be imported into SAP ERP in this format. To be transferred correctly, the structure of the Excel file must resemble the structure displayed in Figure 11.7.

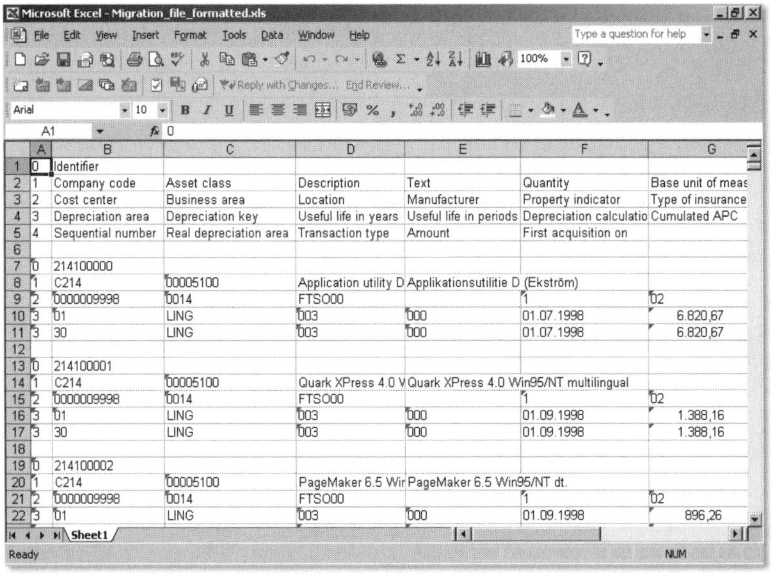

	A	B	C	D	E	F	G
1	0	Identifier					
2	1	Company code	Asset class	Description	Text	Quantity	Base unit of meas
3	2	Cost center	Business area	Location	Manufacturer	Property indicator	Type of insurance
4	3	Depreciation area	Depreciation key	Useful life in years	Useful life in periods	Depreciation calculatio	Cumulated APC
5	4	Sequential number	Real depreciation area	Transaction type	Amount	First acquisition on	
6							
7	0	214100000					
8	1	C214	00005100	Application utility D	Applikationsutilitie D	(Ekström)	
9	2	0000009998	0014	FTSO00		1	02
10	3	01	LING	003	000	01.07.1998	6.820,67
11	3	30	LING	003	000	01.07.1998	6.820,67
12							
13	0	214100001					
14	1	C214	00005100	Quark XPress 4.0 V	Quark XPress 4.0 Win95/NT multilingual		
15	2	0000009998	0014	FTSO00		1	02
16	3	01	LING	003	000	01.09.1998	1.388,16
17	3	30	LING	003	000	01.09.1998	1.388,16
18							
19	0	214100002					
20	1	C214	00005100	PageMaker 6.5 Wir	PageMaker 6.5 Win95/NT dt.		
21	2	0000009998	0014	FTSO00		1	02
22	3	01	LING	003	000	01.09.1998	896,26

Figure 11.7 Fixed Assets to Be Transferred to Microsoft Excel (Formatted)

Header section and asset section Rows 1 to 5 of the Excel file form the *header section*. You use them to determine which asset information (company code, asset class, cost center, accumulated APC, accumulated depreciation, and so on) you want to migrate. The remaining rows, starting from row 6, determine the *asset section*. The values for the individual assets to be migrated are entered here. Note that a blank row appears between the header section and the asset section. Furthermore, the individual assets in the asset section are each separated by a blank row.

At the minimum, the Excel file must provide placeholders (fields) in the header section for the identifier — that is, the asset number from the legacy system — the company code, the asset class, and the capitalization date of the asset. You have to supply these fields with values for every fixed asset in the lower asset section. If you have defined required entry fields for certain asset classes in Customizing for Asset Accounting, you will also have to reserve fields for these required entry fields in the header section, as they also have to be assigned values in the asset section.

Minimum data for transfer

Aside from the minimum requirements that you defined in the header section, you don't have to fill all the fields in the asset section with values. The header section merely represents the maximum set of fields that can be transferred. You can decide whether you want to use all the fields for each individual asset.

Relationship between header section and asset section

The asset values to be transferred are organized in *record types*. You enter the record type in the first column of the Excel file. The subsequent columns contain the fields that are assigned to each record type. A maximum of five record types is supported, but not all record types are required.

Data structured by record type

▶ **Record type 0**
Contains only the identifier, the number of the fixed asset in the legacy system. This identifier is required to assign any errors that occur during the data migration to a specific asset. The error log that is generated during the data migration is described in Section 11.3.5.

▶ **Record type 1**
The asset master data is entered here, along with general data and inventory data.

▶ **Record type 2**
Contains posting information and time-dependent data.

▶ **Record type 3**
The depreciation areas are defined here, along with accumulated and posted values. Please note that the depreciation area always has to be named first.

▶ **Record type 4**

Contains all asset transactions. The sequence number and depreciation area have to be entered in the first two columns. The sequence number differentiates the various postings in the current year. Therefore, you can use record type 4 whenever you want to transfer data in mid-year (see Table 11.1).

Record Type	Sequence Number	Area	Transaction Type	Amount	Posting Date
4	1	01	100	5000	01/01/2007
4	1	02	100	4900	01/01/2007
4	2	01	100	1000	01/01/2007

Table 11.1 Asset Transactions in a Mid-Year Data Transfer

If certain record types are not required to transfer the data — such as record type 4 in the previous example — you don't have to include them in the structure of the Excel file (in either the header or asset sections).

As mentioned above, the asset values are listed below the header section. You enter them in the Excel file according to the structure of the header section.

Assume, as shown in Figure 11.7, that you have defined the header section for record type 1 such that the company code appears in column B and the asset class appears in column C. In this case, the field contents of all record type 1 fields will be interpreted as the company code in column B and as the asset class in column C. Accordingly, you must ensure for every asset that all the rows that are identified as record type 1 have the company code in column B and the asset class in column C. The procedure is similar for the other record types.

Dealing with leading zeros Remember that fields that are displayed with *leading zeros* in the SAP ERP system must have this same format in the Excel file. Accordingly, the company code must always have four places and the asset class must have eight.

Using placeholders When you start preparing for the legacy data transfer, it is entirely possible that the enterprise structures have not all been defined yet. If the name of the company code has not been defined yet, for example, you can define a variable for it (e.g., CoCd = X). You can then use the Excel **Find and Replace** function to set the company code to the desired values prior to the data transfer.

Now that you're familiar with the data transfer format used by SAP ERP, the next step in the case example is to take the Excel file that was provided by the user department and format it according to the requirements of the SAP ERP system (see Figure 11.7). Because formatting the data manually is an onerous task, even if only a small number of assets have to be transferred, you can use the small macro described in the next section to format the Excel file automatically.

Formatting the migration file

11.3.3 Formatting Data with Visual Basic

Macros are useful whenever you have to perform an activity repeatedly in Microsoft Excel. Instead of performing this activity manually each time, you can automate the process. In this example, this means that you can automatically format the file provided by the user department in order to prepare it for the upload to SAP ERP. This automation involves a number of commands and functions that are saved in a Visual Basic module and can be performed at any time (e.g., to format the data).

Purpose of a macro

You have to use Visual Basic to write this macro, which represents a custom data formatting program in Microsoft Excel. Because the procedure is not complicated and can be used as a template for transferring all assets with the Excel procedure, it is described below.

The macro is based on the following assumptions:

▶ The assets to be transferred are available in table-like form in a worksheet of an *.xls* file (see Figure 11.6).

▶ Record types have been assigned to the asset values to be transferred.

▶ The macro adds an additional worksheet, which formats the asset values appropriately for the data transfer to SAP ERP, to the *.xls* file.

To create a macro, open the file that your user department provided in Excel and choose **Tools • Macro • Macros...** The dialog box shown in Figure 11.8 opens.

Creating the macro

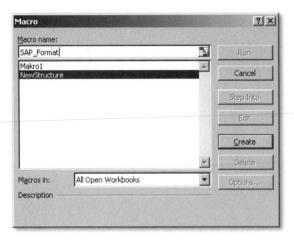

Figure 11.8 Creating a Macro in Microsoft Excel

Enter a name for your macro and click **Create**. An editor appears, in which you must enter the following program coding in Visual Basic:

Source code

```
1 Sub NewStructure()
2
3    Dim vRow As Variant, vResRow As Variant
4    Dim MaxRow As Integer
5    Const kOriginalSheet = "Assets"
6    Const kResultSheet = "Result"
7    vResRow = 1
8
9    MaxRow =
         Worksheets(kOriginalSheet).UsedRange.Rows.Count
11 With Sheets(kResultSheet)
12 For vRow = 3 To MaxRow
13        .Cells(vResRow, 1).Value = "0"
14        .Cells(vResRow, 2).Value =
          Sheets(kOriginalSheet).Cells(vRow, 3).Value
16     vResRow = vResRow + 1
17        .Cells(vResRow, 1).Value = "1"
18        .Cells(vResRow, 2).Value =
          Sheets(kOriginalSheet).Cells(vRow, 1).Value
20        .Cells(vResRow, 3).Value =
          Sheets(kOriginalSheet).Cells(vRow, 2).Value
22        .Cells(vResRow, 4).Value =
          Sheets(kOriginalSheet).Cells(vRow, 4).Value
24        .Cells(vResRow, 5).Value =
          Sheets(kOriginalSheet).Cells(vRow, 5).Value
26        .Cells(vResRow, 6).Value =
```

```
              Sheets(kOriginalSheet).Cells(vRow, 7).Value
28            .Cells(vResRow, 7).Value =
              Sheets(kOriginalSheet).Cells(vRow, 8).Value
30            .Cells(vResRow, 8).Value =
              Sheets(kOriginalSheet).Cells(vRow, 6).Value
32       vResRow = vResRow + 1
33            .Cells(vResRow, 1).Value = "2"
34            .Cells(vResRow, 2).Value =
              Sheets(kOriginalSheet).Cells(vRow, 10).Value
36            .Cells(vResRow, 3).Value =
              Sheets(kOriginalSheet).Cells(vRow, 12).Value
38            .Cells(vResRow, 4).Value =
              Sheets(kOriginalSheet).Cells(vRow, 13).Value
40            .Cells(vResRow, 5).Value =
              Sheets(kOriginalSheet).Cells(vRow, 14).Value
42            .Cells(vResRow, 6).Value =
              Sheets(kOriginalSheet).Cells(vRow, 15).Value
44            .Cells(vResRow, 7).Value =
              Sheets(kOriginalSheet).Cells(vRow, 16).Value
46            .Cells(vResRow, 8).Value =
              Sheets(kOriginalSheet).Cells(vRow, 9).Value
48            .Cells(vResRow, 9).Value =
              Sheets(kOriginalSheet).Cells(vRow, 17).Value
50            .Cells(vResRow, 10).Value =
              Sheets(kOriginalSheet).Cells(vRow, 18).Value
52            .Cells(vResRow, 11).Value =
              Sheets(kOriginalSheet).Cells(vRow, 19).Value
54            .Cells(vResRow, 12).Value =
              Sheets(kOriginalSheet).Cells(vRow, 20).Value
56       vResRow = vResRow + 1
57            .Cells(vResRow, 1).Value = "3"
58            .Cells(vResRow, 2).Value =
              Sheets(kOriginalSheet).Cells(vRow, 21).Value
60            .Cells(vResRow, 3).Value =
              Sheets(kOriginalSheet).Cells(vRow, 22).Value
62            .Cells(vResRow, 4).Value =
              Sheets(kOriginalSheet).Cells(vRow, 23).Value
64            .Cells(vResRow, 5).Value =
              Sheets(kOriginalSheet).Cells(vRow, 24).Value
66            .Cells(vResRow, 6).Value =
              Sheets(kOriginalSheet).Cells(vRow, 25).Value
68            .Cells(vResRow, 7).Value =
              Sheets(kOriginalSheet).Cells(vRow, 26).Value
70            .Cells(vResRow, 8).Value =
              Sheets(kOriginalSheet).Cells(vRow, 27).Value
```

```
72          vResRow = vResRow + 1
73          .Cells(vResRow, 1).Value = "3"
74          .Cells(vResRow, 2).Value =
            Sheets(kOriginalSheet).Cells(vRow, 28).Value
76          .Cells(vResRow, 3).Value =
            Sheets(kOriginalSheet).Cells(vRow, 29).Value
78          .Cells(vResRow, 4).Value =
            Sheets(kOriginalSheet).Cells(vRow, 30).Value
80          .Cells(vResRow, 5).Value =
            Sheets(kOriginalSheet).Cells(vRow, 31).Value
82          .Cells(vResRow, 6).Value =
            Sheets(kOriginalSheet).Cells(vRow, 32).Value
84          .Cells(vResRow, 7).Value =
            Sheets(kOriginalSheet).Cells(vRow, 33).Value
86          .Cells(vResRow, 8).Value =
            Sheets(kOriginalSheet).Cells(vRow, 34).Value
88 vResRow = vResRow + 2
89 Next vRow
90 End With
91 End Sub
```

Listing 11.1 Visual Basic Macro for Data Formatting in Excel

Remarks on programming

We don't intend to deal with the syntax of Visual Basic at this point. Not only would this exceed the scope of this book, it would detract from our main focus of this book, which is avoiding having to program wherever possible. You should consider programming only as a last resort, when your specific situation does not permit any other solution. We have provided an explanation of the coding in the text that follows, which should suffice to enable you to transfer the legacy data using the Excel procedure. This means that you can use the above macro as a template for your migration activities, making only minor changes to reflect your specific requirements. The program sections you have to modify are described in detail further below. If you would like to learn more about Visual Basic, please consult the specialized literature on this subject.

Sub/End Sub

Every macro created in Visual Basic starts with Sub <name>() — Sub NewStructure() in this case — and ends with End Sub (see program lines 1 and 91). Visual Basic creates this frame automatically as soon as you create a macro. The statements required for the formatting are specified in between them.

As with most programming languages, you must first declare your variables and constants (see program lines 3-6). You declare variables with `Dim <name> As <data_type>` and constants with `Const <name>`. Accordingly, the macro consists of the variables `vRow`, `vResRow`, and `MaxRow`, where `vRow` and `vResRow` have data type *variant*, which allows any characters. Conversely, `MaxRow` has data type *integer*, which means this variable can process only whole numbers.

Declaration of variables

You declare `kOriginalSheet`, the original worksheet provided by the user department (see Figure 11.6), and `kResultSheet`, the worksheet formatted by the macro, as constants. These constants are assigned the values `Assets` and `Result`. If you want to name your worksheets differently, you merely have to change the values assigned to the constants in the declaration section, without having to change the placeholders for the constants — `kOriginalSheet` and `kResultSheet` — in the program.

Declaration of constants

Once you have declared the variables and constants, you can initialize the variables, or set them to initial values (see program lines 5-10). `MaxRow` is set to the number of rows in the original worksheet. If you want to migrate 1,000 legacy assets, for example, and the data record of your first asset appears in line 3 of the original worksheet, as in the above example, `MaxRow` is set to 1002.

Initializing the variables and formatting

Once the variables and constants have been declared and initialized, you can begin formatting the worksheet for upload to SAP ERP, `kResultSheet`. This formatting begins at `With Sheets (kResultSheet)` and ends at `End With` (see program lines 11-90). In between is a loop (see program lines 12-89), which is increased incrementally from row 3 of the original worksheet, where the first data record is located, until its end. This is achieved with the `Next vRow` command, which is located in program line 89. This ensures that all the data records from the original worksheet can be processed and transformed to the correct format.

The first time you run the loop, cell A1 of the formatted worksheet, which is addressed in Visual Basic with `Cells(1,1)`, is set to the value 0 (see program line 13). This means record type 0 of the first data record appears in the upper-left corner of the worksheet, which corresponds to the required format. The cell to the right, `Cells(1,2)`, is set to the identifier of the original worksheet, which is located in

Simulating the loop

`Cells(3,3)`, in cell C3 (see program lines 14 and 15). All the information for record type 0 of the first asset has now been entered.

Addressing the cells
Note that you can address the cells of the formatted worksheet with `.Cells(x,y).Value`, while addressing the cells of the original worksheet requires preceding `Sheets(kOriginalSheet)`. This is due to the parameter of the `With Sheets` statement, `kResultSheet`. In all cases in which no `Sheets` (worksheet) appears before the cell address, the system assumes that the worksheet in the parameter of the `With Sheets` statement — `kResultSheet` in this case — is involved (see program line 11).

Formatting record types 1 and 2
The variable `vResRow` is now increased by 1, resulting in the new value 2 (see program line 16). This means the row changes, with the result that the next cell addressed in the formatted worksheet is `Cells(2,1)`, which is set to the value 1, which in turn identifies record type 1 (see program line 17). The next statements supply the cells of the formatted worksheet to the right of `Cells(2,1)` with the records for record type 1 from the original worksheet. These are contained in row 3 for the first asset to be migrated and are addressed accordingly with `Cells(3,1)`, `Cells(3,2)`, and so on (see program lines 18-31). Once all the information for record type 1 has been set, the next row change takes place in the formatted worksheet, which means the preparation for record type 2 can begin (see program lines 32-55).

Formatting record type 3
The procedure for record type 3 is different. Because two depreciation areas have to be transferred, two rows have to be provided for this record type. Accordingly, the information for the first depreciation area is saved in `Cells(4,x)` and the information for the second depreciation area in `Cells(5,x)`. In this example, x can assume values between 1 and 8 (see program lines 56–87).

Because the transactions from the current year are not relevant for the data transfer, the information for record type 4 is not needed. Formatting of the first data record is now complete.

Processing the subsequent records
As mentioned above, a blank row must be inserted between the individual assets to ensure an error-free data transfer. This is achieved with the `vResRow = vResRow + 2` statement, which is located in program line 88. After `vRow` has also been increased by 1 and is now set to 4 (see program line 89), the second asset from the original work-

sheet, which is contained in row 4, can be formatted in a similar fashion. This process continues until `vRow = MaxRow`, that is, until the last row of the original worksheet is reached and all the assets have been converted to the data transfer format. Figure 11.9 shows the result of the macro.

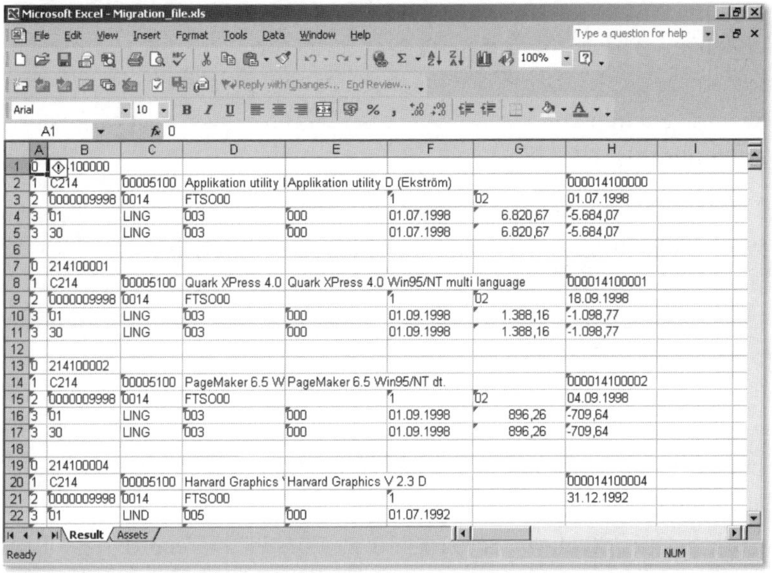

	A	B	C	D	E	F	G	H	I
1	0	100000							
2	1	C214	00005100	Applikation utility I	Applikation utility D (Ekström)			000014100000	
3	2	0000009998	0014	FTSO00		1	02	01.07.1998	
4	3	01	LING	003	000	01.07.1998	6.820,67	-5.684,07	
5	3	30	LING	003	000	01.07.1998	6.820,67	-5.684,07	
6									
7	0	214100001							
8	1	C214	00005100	Quark XPress 4.0	Quark XPress 4.0 Win95/NT multi language			000014100001	
9	2	0000009998	0014	FTSO00		1	02	18.09.1998	
10	3	01	LING	003	000	01.09.1998	1.388,16	-1.098,77	
11	3	30	LING	003	000	01.09.1998	1.388,16	-1.098,77	
12									
13	0	214100002							
14	1	C214	00005100	PageMaker 6.5 W	PageMaker 6.5 Win95/NT dt.			000014100002	
15	2	0000009998	0014	FTSO00		1	02	04.09.1998	
16	3	01	LING	003	000	01.09.1998	896,26	-709,64	
17	3	30	LING	003	000	01.09.1998	896,26	-709,64	
18									
19	0	214100004							
20	1	C214	00005100	Harvard Graphics '	Harvard Graphics V 2.3 D			000014100004	
21	2	0000009998	0014	FTSO00		1		31.12.1992	
22	3	01	LIND	005	000	01.07.1992			

Figure 11.9 Fixed Assets to Be Transferred to Microsoft Excel (Formatted, without Header Section)

Uploading the File

Just to ensure that we have clarified this information, please note that the macro does not yet provide the file that you can upload to SAP ERP. It merely formats the asset section. Therefore, to create a file that the SAP ERP system can read, you have to add the header section. To do so, copy the worksheet from Figure 11.9 that you just formatted to a new file called *Upload.xls*, and insert the header section accordingly (see Figure 11.7 above).

Structuring migration data in record types

If you want to use this macro to format your data, you don't have to worry about the correct assignment between the header and asset sections in advance. Instead, you simply let the macro generate the asset section and then append the header part later at the top of your final *Upload.xls*, in line with the result of the asset part. You should also understand the second assumption of the macro in this context. You merely have to take the data from the worksheet provided by the user department, assign it to record types in your mind, and note the corresponding columns. If you identify columns 1, 2, and 4 as columns that have to be assigned to record type 1, for example, you can leave program lines 18 to 23 unchanged. However, if the identifier, which belongs to record type 0, is located in column 1 instead of column 3, and column 3 contains information for record type 1, you must change the statement in program lines 14 and 15 from

```
.Cells(vResRow, 2).Value =
Sheets(kOriginalSheet).Cells(vRow, 3).Value
```

to

```
.Cells(vResRow, 2).Value =
Sheets(kOriginalSheet).Cells(vRow, 1).Value
```

Program lines 18 and 19 would change accordingly from

```
.Cells(vResRow, 2).Value =
Sheets(kOriginalSheet).Cells(vRow, 1).Value
```

to

```
.Cells(vResRow, 2).Value =
Sheets(kOriginalSheet).Cells(vRow, 3).Value
```

Modifying the program
Additional changes are needed, for example, when your original worksheet contains more data transfer fields for record type 1. In these circumstances, you have to add these additional data transfer fields in program lines 18 to 31. It is sufficient in this case to make a copy of an existing line and modify the copy accordingly. Alternatively, if you want to transfer less information for each asset, you can simply delete the unnecessary lines in the formatting blocks.

Macro can be used as a template
As you can see, only minor modifications to the above macro are required to deal with specific situations. In this context, it is an excellent template for transferring legacy data, as long as you have to migrate only small to medium-sized data volumes.

11.3.4 Assigning the Data to ERP Fields (Mapping)

Now that your data is available in the format expected by the SAP ERP system, you can assign the fields in your *Upload.xls* file to the corresponding fields in the SAP ERP system. Assign the ERP **Company Code** field to field **BUKRS** in your Excel file, for example. This procedure is called *mapping*.

To conduct the mapping, choose menu path **Financial Accounting ·
Asset Accounting · Asset Data Transfer · Legacy Data Transfer using
Microsoft Excel** or enter transaction code AS100 (see Figure 11.10).

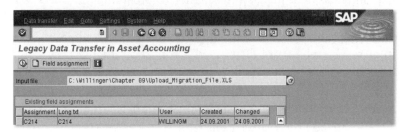

Figure 11.10 Initial Screen — Legacy Data Transfer with Microsoft Excel

In this initial screen, which starts the legacy data transfer using the
Excel procedure, you first have to specify the path of the *Upload.xls*
file. You can then choose whether you want to use an existing mapping or define a new one. One alternative is to select the corresponding mapping and click on the **Start Mapping** button. The second
alternative requires you to click on the **Create Mapping** button and
then enter a name for the mapping and an explanatory long text.

Upload.xls

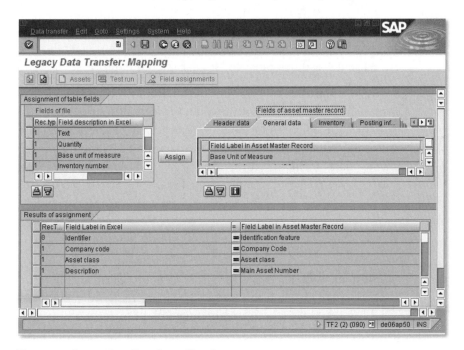

Figure 11.11 Legacy Data Transfer — Mapping

335

Performing Mapping

In this table, the system lists only the field texts that are defined in the header section of your *Upload.xls* file in the **Fields of file** table (see Figure 11.11). They are sorted by record type 0, 1, 2, 3, and 4. The potential fields of the asset master records in the SAP ERP system are distributed among different tabs. The potential ERP fields for record types 0 and 1 are located in the **Header data** tab. The fields from record type 2 are distributed across several tabs. They range from **time-dependent data** to **leasing**. The same applies to the fields of record type 3, which are located in the tabs **Depreciation Areas**, **Accumulated Values**, and **Posted Values**. All fields from record type 4 are located on the **Transactions** tab.

SAP ERP plausibility checks

To define the specific mapping, select one row from the **Fields of file** table and **Fields of the asset master record** tab, and then click on the **Assign** button. Note that the system doesn't check whether this mapping makes sense. It merely verifies that each field from the *Upload.xls* file is assigned to exactly one ERP field. As mentioned previously, you have to assign the identifier, the company code, the asset class, and the capitalization date, along with any defined required entry fields.

Saving the mapping and checking the date format

The system asks whether you want to save the mapping prior to the data transfer. You can also save the mapping after the data transfer, however, with the **Saved Assignments** button. Consequently, you can reuse defined mappings for similar migration processes.

Before you start the data transfer to the SAP ERP system, you must ensure that the date format in your *Upload.xls* file agrees with the date format configured in the SAP ERP system. To check or change this setting, choose **Settings • Date Format**. SAP ERP supports the following date formats: North American format (MM/DD/YY or MM/DD/YYYY), European format (DD.MM.YY or DD.MM.YYYY), ISO format (YYYY-MM-DD), and SAP format (YYYYMMDD).

11.3.5 Uploading the Data to SAP ERP and Log File

You upload the assets to SAP ERP in the same transaction where you defined the mapping previously. You can choose between a *test run* and an *update run* of the asset migration program.

Test run

If you perform the migration as a test run (with the **Test run** pushbutton), the system lists completion confirmations without creating the assets in the database. Accordingly, the test run is equivalent to a simulation of the data migration, creating a comprehensive log for every fixed asset (see Figure 11.12).

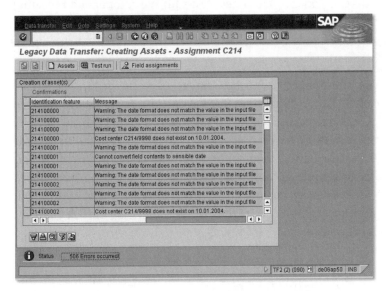

Figure 11.12 Log from Simulation of the Legacy Data Transfer

You can double-click on an entry in the log to display detailed information for the selected asset (see Figure 11.13).

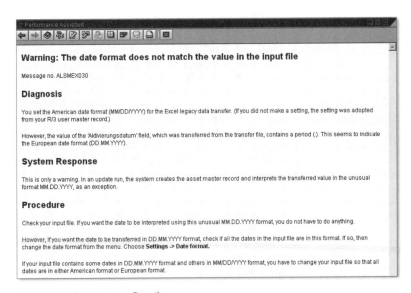

Figure 11.13 Error Log — Details

Cause of errors
The most frequent cause of errors is a discrepancy between asset values in the *Upload.xls* file and the SAP ERP Customizing of the corresponding asset class. Once you have changed the Customizing accordingly, you can start a new test run. We recommend repeating this iterative process until the test run ends free of errors. You can then start the update run by clicking on the **Assets** button (see Figure 11.12).

Update run
During the update run, the system uses the values from the *Upload.xls* file to create new fixed assets; the fields in SAP ERP are assigned values according to the defined mapping. To display the master records for successfully created assets, click on the **Details for Confirmation** button. A log of incorrect assets that could not be created is also displayed here. You can also download the error file to Microsoft Excel by clicking on the **Export Errors to File** button. You can now analyze and correct the errors, eliminating the last obstacles to a final upload.

11.4 Preparing to Go Live

Now that you have successfully transferred the assets into SAP ERP, several concluding activities are always required, regardless of which data transfer method you used.

11.4.1 Setting Reconciliation Accounts

Balance sheet asset accounts
Once you implement Asset Accounting, you can no longer post directly to the balance sheet asset accounts defined in the general ledger. Because the general ledger (G/L) is integrated with the Asset Accounting subledger, however, the balance sheet accounts are updated automatically whenever a transaction takes place for an asset. Therefore, the subledger is the leading system, while the general ledger is the receiving system.

As an alternative to setting reconciliation accounts manually in Financial Accounting, SAP ERP provides a report that you can use to define G/L accounts for reconciliation accounts in Asset Accounting. In the process, the report selects the G/L accounts that are defined as balance sheet accounts under account determination in Asset Accounting. To do so, choose menu path **Financial Accounting** •

Asset Accounting • Preparing for Production Startup • Production Startup • Set Reconciliation Accounts.

If you accidentally defined an incorrect account in account determination for Asset Accounting, or you have to make subsequent adjustment postings to Asset Accounting, you can use the following menu path to reset the reconciliation accounts: **Financial Accounting • Asset Accounting • Preparing for Production Startup • Production Startup • Reset Reconciliation Accounts**.

Resetting the reconciliation accounts and data consistency

In this case, however, please note that consistency is no longer guaranteed between the subledger and the general ledger, because the balance sheet accounts can once again be posted to directly, without subledger integration.

11.4.2 Transferring Balances

As mentioned above, this means the legacy data transfer does not support automatic integration between the general ledger and the subledger, as is normally the case for subledger postings. You therefore have to reconcile the balances manually with the involved G/L accounts in an additional step. You can omit this step if Financial Accounting was already active in your SAP ERP system prior to implementing Asset Accounting. In this case, the balance sheet accounts for the fixed assets and the corresponding depreciation accounts will already be up to date. Accordingly, you only have to define the balance sheet accounts for the fixed assets as reconciliation accounts (see Section 11.4.1).

Reconciliation between general ledger and subledger

If you have to transfer the balances, you will have to synchronize the balance sheet values from Asset Accounting with both the balance sheet asset accounts and the corresponding depreciation accounts in the general ledger. To do so, use menu path **System • Services • Reporting** to call Report RABEST01, which generates an asset list with a reporting date of January 1 of the current fiscal year. It is identical to the corresponding asset list from December 31 of the previous year, which means no depreciation from the current year is included. You now have to compare the asset list with the corresponding account balances from Financial Accounting, dated December 31 of the previous year.

Transferring the balances

Because transferring the balances requires postings to reconciliation accounts, which is not supported in the Financial Accounting application menu, you must enter this posting in Customizing for Asset Accounting. To do so, choose menu path **Financial Accounting • Asset Accounting • Preparing for Production Startup • Production Startup • Transfer Balances**.

The offsetting postings are generally made to an account that is set up especially for the data transfer (see Section 2.2.5).

11.4.3 Activating the Company Code

This is the last activity involved in the legacy data transfer. As previously mentioned, legacy data transfer is possible only when the company code is set to test or transfer status. Because the many change options available in test status make it unsuitable for long-term use in a production client, and the transfer status does not allow any postings to Asset Accounting aside from the asset migration, you have to set the company code to **Productive** status after the migration. Consequently, values can be changed only through new postings.

This chapter deals with several issues that are not directly related to the core subject of this book, but which can help to expand your overall understanding of the data migration area.

12   Outlook and Related Areas

12.1   Data Transfer Workbench

The *Data Transfer Workbench* (or *DX Workbench*) is a standard tool in your SAP ERP system. The corresponding transaction code is SXDA.

The DX Workbench helps you manage and organize your data migration projects. It provides tools for analyzing the corresponding SAP structures and gives you an integrated view of the standard SAP data transfer programs. It also allows you to register your own data transfer programs and auxiliary programs and use them as needed.

Managing data migration projects

From a functional perspective, there are overlaps between the DX Workbench and the LSM Workbench. The combined use of both tools can be extremely helpful in practice. One recommended procedure is described later on in this chapter. But first, let's get a detailed view of how the DX Workbench works.

12.1.1   Features

The Data Transfer Workbench supports the following organizational units: *project*, *subproject*, *run definition*, and *task* (see Figure 12.1). A project contains one or more subprojects. Each subproject is assigned exactly one business object and one data import technique; for example, customer master (business object) and batch input (data import technique). Each subproject also contains one or more run definitions, and each run definition consists of one or more tasks. Examples of typical tasks include:

Project, subproject, run definition, task

▶ Exporting legacy data

▶ Cleaning up legacy data

▶ Converting data (using the LSM Workbench, for example)

▶ Checking converted data

▶ Importing data into the SAP ERP system

Data Transfer
Workbench
framework

Nevertheless, you cannot expect that the DX Workbench will automatically supply suitable programs for every possible task. Instead, this tool is really a *framework* into which you can integrate your own programs.

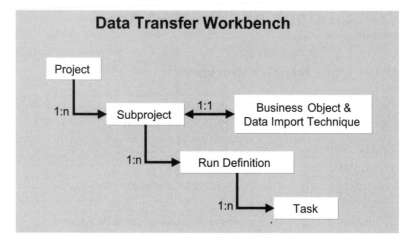

Figure 12.1 Organizational Units in the Data Transfer Workbench

Run

Once you have created a run definition, you can run it in dialog or in the background as often as you want. Each *run* is logged in the Data Transfer Workbench.

The following postprocessing options are available for runs that were not completed successfully:

▶ The run can be continued or cancelled.

▶ A specific task that has not been fully completed can be set to "completed."

▶ The run can be deleted.

Generating
test data

A particularly useful function in the Data Transfer Workbench is the ability to generate test data automatically. You can generate a file, even with sample data in some cases, that the data import programs (e.g., standard batch input programs such as RFBIDE00) can process.

This type of file can help you recognize the mapping of fields to data transfer structures (such as BKNA1).

Please note, however, that this function requires specific programs that are not available for all business objects. These business objects include G/L account master records (business object ID BUS3006), material master records (BUS1001006), sales documents (BUS2032), condition records (BUS3005), routings (BUS1012), and inspection plans (BUS1023).

The Data Transfer Workbench also has functions for editing files. For example, you can split a large file into several smaller ones. Conversely, you can also merge several small files to create one larger file.

Splitting and merging files

12.1.2 Particular Strength: Data Import via BAPI

The particular strength of the Data Transfer Workbench becomes evident when the BAPI technique is used to import the migration data. As you learned in Chapter 7, the LSM Workbench uses IDoc inbound processing to import legacy data using the BAPI import technique. While this technique is very safe and easy to use, its benefits are offset by its long runtimes and low throughput. Furthermore, it involves creating IDocs in the SAP ERP system, which require an archiving run to delete them. This is compounded by the fact that only successfully processed IDocs are archived.

The Data Transfer Workbench expects the import data in IDoc format, just like the LSM Workbench. The difference here is that the data is not passed on to inbound processing, as it is in the LSM Workbench. Instead, it is transferred directly to the BAPI. Consequently, throughput is much higher.

Greater throughput than the LSM Workbench

Due to this approach, separate error handling functions had to be developed for the Data Transfer Workbench:

Separate error handling

▶ You first define a specific *package size*. The package size defines the number of transactions that are passed on to the BAPI in one *LUW* (Logical Unit of Work). You have to select the package size carefully. The larger the packages, the smaller the load on the database, which, in turn, increases throughput. If an error occurs within a package, however, none of the transactions contained in that package will be updated.

▶ You now must decide where to store the transactions that couldn't be imported. There are two alternatives.

  ▶ The transactions can be saved in a separate error file.

  ▶ The transactions can be saved as IDocs and then processed using the standard inbound processing functions.

The interaction between the Data Transfer Workbench and the LSM Workbench is described in the next section.

12.1.3 Combination with the LSM Workbench

Starting the LSM Workbench
When you create a run definition in the Data Transfer Workbench, you can start the LSM Workbench to process the task "Map the Data" (convert the data to the SAP format).

To do so, you must define the corresponding project, subproject, and object from the LSM Workbench in the DX Workbench.

When you start a run in the DX Workbench, the data import program runs first, followed by the data conversion program from the LSM Workbench.

Recommendation
If you use the DX Workbench and the LSM Workbench together, the DX Workbench is always the "leading" workbench. This means the DX Workbench calls the functions of the LSM Workbench. Depending on which import technique you select, we recommend the following procedure for combined usage:

▶ **Batch input or direct input import technique**
In this case, the "value added" by the DX Workbench consists of the generation of test data described above. All other functions are covered by the LSM Workbench.

▶ **BAPI or IDoc import technique**
Due to the particular strength of the DX Workbench in importing data via BAPI, we recommend using the DX Workbench for the data import in this case. Use the LSM Workbench for all the other steps.

These recommendations are summarized in Table 12.1 below.

	Batch Input, Direct Input	BAPI, IDoc
DX Workbench	Generating test data	Importing data
LSM Workbench	Loading, converting, importing data	Loading and converting data

Table 12.1 Procedure for Combination of DX Workbench and LSM Workbench

12.2 Data Migration Between SAP ERP Systems or within an SAP ERP System

There are times when an SAP ERP system has already been success- **When do you have** fully installed and is used for production, but where the IT depart- **to extract data?** ment and user departments are still confronted with data migration requirements. Typical situations include changes resulting from business reengineering or the consolidation of two SAP ERP systems due to a takeover or merger. Regardless of your underlying motive, all of these scenarios have one thing in common: You have to extract and reallocate data within one or more production systems. If the system in question is an SAP ERP system, you can extract the data easily, provided that you know in which SAP ERP table the necessary data is stored. To help you find the right table, Appendix A lists the ERP tables that are used most frequently in data migration projects; however, this list is by no means complete.

If you want to extract *profit center master data*, for example, and you **Extracting profit** know the structure of the relevant table, CEPC, you could proceed as **centers** follows. When you choose menu path **Tools • ABAP Workbench • Overview • Data Browser** or Transaction SE16, and enter the name of ERP table CEPC, the corresponding fields and their contents appear, as shown in Figure 12.2.

You can configure the view shown here via **Settings • List Format •** **Field selection** **Choose Fields...** to display only those fields that are relevant to the data transfer. You can simply hide the unneeded fields, as shown in Figure 12.3.

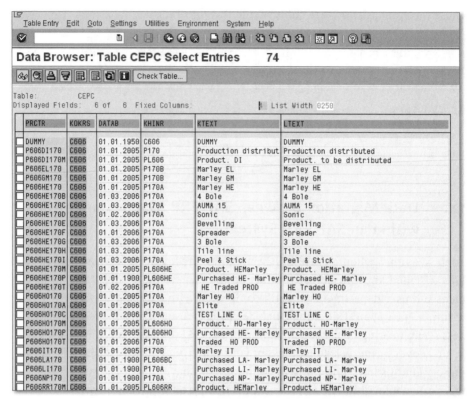

Figure 12.2 Profit Center Master Data, Displayed in the Data Browser (Transaction SE16)

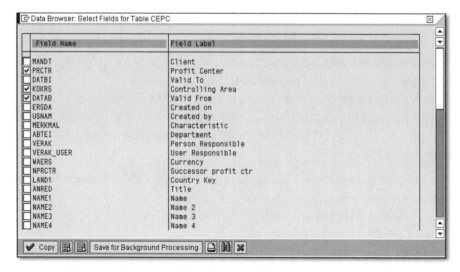

Figure 12.3 Data Browser — Selecting Fields

346

Once you have selected the fields that you want to display, you can choose **Edit • Download...** to make the dataset available in a spreadsheet program such as Microsoft Excel. See the dialog box in Figure 12.4.

Download

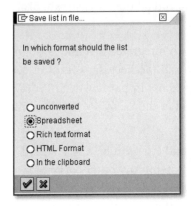

Figure 12.4 Data Browser — Download

All you have to do now is enter the path where you want to save the extracted dataset. Note that you always have to assign a format to the file name, which determines the program you will use to open the file later. If you want to process the file with Microsoft Excel, for example, choose file extension *.xls*, as shown in Figure 12.5.

Path and
file format

Figure 12.5 Data Browser — Download — File Format

Once you have postprocessed it, you can use this file as the foundation for data migration using the procedures introduced in Chapters 4 through 7.

12.3 Data Migration in SAP CRM

SAP Customer Relationship Management (SAP CRM) describes the management of customer relationships in its entirety. In many cases, the SAP CRM solution is used in combination with an SAP ERP sys-

Customer
Relationship
Management

tem. The latter is often called the "ERP backend system," indicating that the SAP CRM system, with all its "channels" (Internet applications, mobile applications, call centers), is focused on the customers, while the SAP ERP system is aimed at the "back office" and handles the execution, that is, order processing and all the downstream processes.

If you operate an SAP CRM system with integrated SAP ERP system, the SAP CRM system already contains all the necessary features for exchanging data between the two systems. In particular, SAP CRM has special functions for the initial load of the SAP CRM system with data from the SAP ERP system.

CRM independent of ERP since Release 3.0 of SAP R/3 or SAP ERP respectively
SAP CRM systems with a Release 3.0 and later can be operated independently of an SAP R/3 or SAP ERP system. Any other backend system can be used in place of the SAP R/3 or SAP ERP system, or you can do without a backend system altogether. In either case, you have a "standard" migration task, which involves transferring the data required in the SAP CRM system (such as customer data, product data, orders, conditions, and prices) from the non-SAP system.

External interfaces
To achieve this, the SAP CRM system provides *external interfaces*, which have IDoc format for "external" systems, which brings us back to the LSM Workbench. You can use the LSM Workbench with or without the Data Transfer Workbench (see Section 12.1.3) to transfer the data from a non-SAP system to an SAP CRM system. The process flow — illustrated schematically in Figure 12.6 — is as follows:

▸ You first transform your data from the non-SAP system to the suitable SAP IDoc format, as usual.

▸ You then submit the converted data to IDoc inbound processing, which takes care of all the additional steps. The data is converted to *BDoc format*[1] and passed on to the CRM Middleware[2] for distribution to all the involved components.

As a result, you use the familiar IDoc import technique with the LSM Workbench.

---

1 BDoc stands for business document. This format is used exclusively in the SAP CRM system.
2 CRM Middleware is a component of the SAP CRM system, and controls the distribution of data between the individual components.

To select one of these external interfaces from the SAP CRM system in the LSM Workbench, select import method **IDoc (Intermediate Document)** and an IDoc type whose name starts with "CRMXIF" in the data migration step **Maintain Object Attributes**. SAP CRM 5.0, for example, provides IDoc types for business partners, products, pricing conditions, orders, and invoices. For more information, please refer to the relevant information provided by SAP.

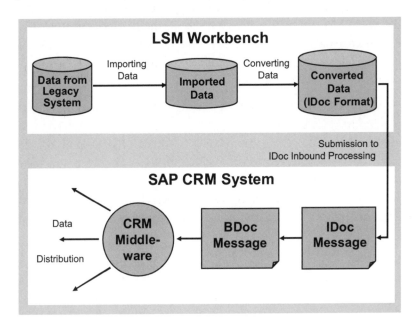

Figure 12.6 LSM Workbench and SAP CRM

Appendix

A   SAP ERP Tables for Selected Master and
     Transaction Data 353

B   Glossary 357

C   The Authors 365

A   SAP ERP Tables for Selected Master and Transaction Data

A.1   Financial Accounting

- **General ledger accounts**
  - SKA1: G/L accounts – chart of account
  - SKB1: G/L accounts – company code-specific data
  - GLT0: G/L accounts – transaction figures
- **Customers**
  - KNA1: Customers – general data
  - KNB1: Customers – company code-specific data
  - KNC1: Customers – transaction figures
- **Vendors**
  - LFA1: Vendors – general data
  - LFB1: Vendors – company code-specific data
  - LFC1: Vendors – transaction figures
- **Secondary index for document data**
  - BSIS: Secondary index for G/L accounts
  - BSAS: Secondary index for G/L accounts – cleared items
  - BSID: Secondary index for customers
  - BSAD: Secondary index for customers – cleared items
  - BSIK: Secondary index for vendors
  - BSAK: Secondary index for vendors – cleared items
- **Document header**
  - BKPF: Document header for accounting
- **Document line items/line items**
  - BSEG: Document segment for accounting
  - BSEC: Document segment for one-time data

- ► **Tax data**
  - ▹ BSET: Document segment for tax data

A.2   Controlling

- ► **Cost centers**
  - ▹ CSKS: Cost center master record
  - ▹ CSKT: Cost center texts
  - ▹ CSSK: Cost center/cost element
  - ▹ CSSL: Cost center/activity type
- ► **Internal orders**
  - ▹ AUFK: Order master data
- ► **CO production orders**
  - ▹ AFKO: Order header
  - ▹ AFPO: Order item
- ► **Settlement rules**
  - ▹ COBR: Settlement rules
- ► **Profit centers**
  - ▹ CEPC: Master data table for profit centers
  - ▹ CEPCT: Profit center master data texts
  - ▹ CEPC_BUKRS: Company code assignment of profit centers

A.3   Logistics

- ► **Material master**
  - ▹ MARA: General material data
  - ▹ MARC: Plant data for material
  - ▹ MARD: Storage location data for material
  - ▹ MARM: Units of measure for material
  - ▹ MARV: Material control record
  - ▹ MAKT: Material short texts
  - ▹ MVKE: Sales data for material

- **Bill of materials (BOM)**
  - STKO: BOM header
  - STPO: BOM item
  - STPU: BOM subitem
- **Sales document**
  - VBAK: Sales document – header data
  - VBAP: Sales document – item data
  - VBEP: Sales document – delivery scheduling data
  - VBKD: Sales document – business data
  - VBPK: Sales document – product proposal header
  - VBPV: Sales document – product proposal
  - VBUV: Sales document – incompleteness log
- **Work center**
  - CRHD: Work center – header data
  - CRCO: Work center – cost center assignment
  - CRCA: Work center – capacity assignment
  - CRTX: Work center – short name
- **Routing**
  - PLKO: Task list – header data
  - PLPO: Task list – operation/activity
  - PLFH: Task list – production resource/tool

B   Glossary

ABAP   Advanced Business Application Programming. A fourth-generation programming language developed by SAP for application development.

ABAP Dictionary   The ABAP Dictionary describes the logical structure of application development objects, as well as their representation in the structures of the underlying relational database.

All the components of the runtime environment, such as application programs and database interfaces, retrieve their information for these objects directly from the ABAP Dictionary, which is fully integrated in the ABAP Workbench.

Account   Structure that records value transactions within a company code. The account contains transaction figures, which include the changes to the values in a summarized form per posting period.

Account determination   Automatic procedure for locating the accounts for postings transactions in Financial Accounting without requiring user intervention.

Account group   Combination of characteristics to control the creation of master records in Financial Accounting. The account group determines the data that is relevant for the master record, and determines a number range from which numbers are selected for the master records. Each master record must be assigned an account group.

Account type   Key that specifies the accounting area to which an account belongs, such as asset accounts, customer accounts, or vendor accounts. In addition to the account number, the account type is required to identify an account, because the same account number can be used for each account type.

Acquisition and Production Costs (APC)   Upper limit for valuation of an asset in the balance sheet.

Asset Accounting   Subsidiary ledger accounting module in Financial Accounting. All business activities for fixed assets are recorded in Asset Accounting.

Asset class   Main criterion for classifying fixed assets according to legal and management requirements. For each asset class, control parameters and default values can be defined for depreciation calculation and other master data. Each master asset record must be assigned to one asset class.

Asset subnumber   A characteristic, that in combination with the main asset number, identifies an asset in the SAP system. The asset subnumber enables you to represent a complex fixed asset. The fixed asset is identified by the main asset number. The individual components or subsequent acquisitions can be represented by subnumbers. You must define separate master data for each subnumber.

Balance Amount resulting from the difference between the debit and credit side of an account or document. If the credit side is larger, it is called a *credit balance*; if the debit side is larger, it is called a *debit balance*.

Balance sheet account Account on which the debit and credit entries resulting from business transactions are recorded. The balance of a balance sheet account is carried forward at fiscal-year end and is always identified in the balance sheet.

Balance sheet asset account General ledger account in Financial Accounting on which asset transactions are recorded. It is the account to which acquisition and production costs are posted, as opposed to the accumulated depreciation account. Both of these accounts are asset accounts, however.

BAPI Business Application Programming Interface. A standardized programming interface that facilitates external access to business processes and data in the SAP ERP system. You define BAPIs in the *Business Object Repository* (BOR) as methods of SAP business objects. BAPIs offer an object-oriented view of business components in the SAP ERP system. They are implemented and stored as RFC-enabled function modules in the Function Builder of the ABAP Workbench.

Batch input Interface that enables you to transfer large volumes of data to an SAP system. You can use batch input for both the initial migration of legacy data and the periodic import of external data.

Batch input session Sequence of transactions supplied with user data by a program. These transactions are stored in a stack. You can process a batch input session at a later stage. No database updates are performed until the session has been processed. Using this technique, you can transfer large amounts of data to the SAP system in a short time.

Business data object
→ *Data object*

Business object → *Data object*

CATT Computer Aided Test Tool. Predecessor of → *eCATT*

Chart of accounts List of all G/L accounts that are jointly used by one or several company codes. For each G/L account, the chart of accounts contains the account number, the account name, and technical information that controls the function of the G/L account and the creation of the G/L account in the company code.

Client In commercial, organizational, and technical terms, a self-contained unit in an SAP ERP system with separate master records and its own set of tables.

Company code Smallest organizational unit for which a complete, self-contained set of accounts can be drawn up for purposes of external reporting.

Constant Value that is defined during the initialization of program fields and which cannot be changed at runtime. In ABAP, constants are declared using the CONSTANTS statement.

Conversion → *Data conversion*

Cost center Organizational unit within a controlling area that represents a defined location of cost incurrence. The definition can be based on functional requirements, allocation criteria, physical location, or responsibility for costs.

Customer account Structure that records value movements in a company code that affect receivables or payables against a customer.

Customizing Settings that a system administrator has to configure during system implementation. The procedure aims to adjust the company-neutral and industry-specific delivered functions to your company's business requirements. Customizing is required prior to commissioning the system. You use the Implementation Guide (IMG) to customize the SAP ERP system.

Data conversion Involves modifying the structure or values of data according to defined rules.

Data migration The transfer of business data (master and transaction data) from any external system to an SAP ERP system.

Data migration object Describes a data object and other attributes that are relevant for data migration: The structure of the data object in the legacy system and the SAP ERP system, along with the mapping that connects the two structures.

Data object Business data unit, such as customer master, material master, and financial document.

Data transfer → *Data migration*

Data Transfer Workbench Tool for managing and organizing data transfer projects. Can be used in combination with the LSM Workbench.

Data transformation → *Data conversion*

Depreciation Reduction of the asset book value due to a decline in economic usefulness or because of legal requirements for taxes. Ordinary depreciation provides for the planned distribution of the acquisition and production costs over the useful life of the asset. Unplanned depreciation is justified by a foreseeable, lasting reduction in the value of the asset due to unplanned circumstances.

Depreciation area A depreciation area (for example, a financial statement, balance sheets for tax purposes, or management accounting values) represents the valuation of the fixed assets for a particular purpose. Along with "real" depreciation areas, you can define derived depreciation areas. The values for these derived areas are calculated from those of two or more real areas.

Depreciation posting run Depreciation is posted in Financial Accounting by starting the depreciation posting run. This program creates a batch input session that contains all the posting information for Financial Accounting. The corresponding posting documents are created as the session is processed.

Direct input Data migration technique in which the data for migration is checked directly — avoiding the dialog transaction — and written to the database of the SAP ERP system.

Document Proof of a business transaction. A distinction is made between original documents, such as incoming invoices, bank statements or copies of outgoing invoices, and data processing (DP) documents. The latter include accounting documents, sample documents, and recurring entry documents. Whereas accounting documents are a representation of the original documents in the system, sample and recurring entry documents are simply templates to simplify the entry of accounting transactions.

Document header Object that contains information that applies to the entire document, such as the document date and document number.

Document type Key used to differentiate the various business transactions to be posted. The document type controls how the document is stored and defines the account types that will be posted to.

Domain Object that describes the technical attributes of a data element, such as the data type and length. The definition of a domain can also define a value range containing the valid values for fields that refer to that domain. You can group fields that have similar technical or business purposes under a single domain. All fields based on a domain are updated automatically when you change the domain. This ensures that the fields are consistent.

DX Workbench → *Data Transfer Workbench*

Dynpro Dynamic Program. A dynpro consists of a screen template and the underlying structure logic. The main components of a dynpro are attributes (such as screen number, next screen), layout (arrangement of texts, fields, and other elements), field attributes (definition of the attributes of the individual fields), and the flow logic (calls of relevant ABAP modules).

eCATT Extended Computer Aided Test Tool (eCATT) A tool in the SAP ERP system for testing business processes.

Elementary data type ABAP data type. ABAP supports eight predefined elementary data types: C (character strings), D (dates), F (floating point numbers), I (integers), N (numeric strings), P (packed numbers), T (times), and X (hexadecimal). Data types D, F, I, and T are predefined in all aspects, while data types C, N, P, and X can be defined additionally.

Field mapping The assignment of source fields to target fields and the corresponding conversion rules.

Fiscal year Period of usually 12 months, for which the company produces financial statements and takes inventory.

Frontend The workplace computer — usually a PC.

Function module Function for general use. Function modules are external subroutines written in ABAP that are developed in the Function Builder. They are managed in a central function library, and can therefore be called from any ABAP program. This helps to avoid redundant code and makes the programming process more effective. In contrast to Form routines, function modules have the same standard interface.

G/L account Structure that records value movements in a company code and represents the G/L account items in a chart of accounts. A G/L account has transaction figures that record changes to the account during a posting period.

General ledger A presentation based on which the balance sheet and profit and loss statement are created. The general ledger records values at company-code level.

Group asset Combination of a number of assets for the purpose of a common, summarized calculation of depreciation. A group asset is represented in the SAP system by a separate master record.

IDoc Intermediate Document. SAP format in which business messages are exchanged. The term *IDoc* (or *IDoc message*) specifies the specific message, while *IDoc type* refers to the structure.

Internal table Data structure that exists only at program runtime. The internal table is one of two structured data types in ABAP. It consists of any number of identically structured table rows with or without a header line. The header line is similar to a structure and serves as the work area of the internal table. The data type of the lines can be either elementary or structured.

Legacy data Business data that is to be transferred from the legacy system to the SAP ERP system.

Legacy system Business IT system that is to be replaced partially or completely within the course of an SAP ERP implementation project. As part of the replacement process, data will be migrated from this system to the SAP ERP system.

Legacy System Migration Workbench Tool based on the SAP ERP technology that supports single and periodic data transfers from legacy systems to SAP ERP systems.

Line item Individual line of a document.

Loop Sequence of program statements executed repeatedly. A loop is executed either a fixed number of times or until a certain condition becomes true or false.

LSM Workbench → *Legacy System Migration Workbench*

LSMW → *Legacy System Migration Workbench*

Mapping The assignment of fields between a legacy IT system and a successor system. This step is required to transfer field contents from the legacy system to the successor system during the data migration process.

Masterdata The information that remains the same over a long period of time. Master data contains information that is needed often and in the same form. Example: The master data of a cost center contains the name of the cost center, the person responsible for the cost center, the corresponding hierarchy area, and other information.

Migration Used synonymously with *data migration*.

Migration Workbench Tool developed by SAP especially for migrating data between SAP ERP systems. Currently only available in combination with SAP consulting services.

Non-SAP system → *Legacy system*

Object → *Data migration object*

Optional entry field Input field in which data entry is optional. In contrast to required entry fields, processing continues if you don't enter data in optional entry fields.

P&L account All business transactions that result in a change of stockholders' equity and thus of the overall company result, are posted to P/L accounts, which are a component of the profit and loss statement. Typical examples include sales revenues, personnel expenses, and costs of materials.

Parameters Data required to execute a function module or subroutine (import parameters) or returned by the method or subroutine after it is called (export parameters). The interface of the method call is determined when the parameters are defined.

Posting key Two-digit numeric key that determines the way line items are posted. This key determines several factors, including the account type, the type of posting (debit or credit), and the layout of entry screens

Primary window Main window of an application. Primary windows are the windows where the main action of an application is performed. Within each session, there is always one primary window on the screen. Primary windows can call secondary windows, or be replaced by another primary window.

Reconciliation account G/L account to which transactions in the subsidiary ledgers (such as in the customer, vendor, or assets areas) are updated automatically. Typically, several subledger accounts post to a common reconciliation account. This ensures that the developments in the subledger accounts are accurately reflected in the general ledger (that is, in line with balance sheet conventions).

Replacement value The current valuation of an asset, which is different from the acquisition and production costs. The replacement value of an asset can result, for example, due to price changes because of inflation or price changes because of technical advancements.

Required entry field Input field in which data entry is mandatory. Required fields are generally indicated by a question mark. Such screens cannot be processed successfully unless you enter data in all required entry fields. In contrast to required entry fields, processing continues if you don't enter data in optional entry fields.

SAP application server Part of the SAP client/server architecture. Describes the computer where the application logic of the SAP ERP system is running.

SAP Basis Release Release of the SAP Basis component of the SAP ERP system.

SAP ERP system SAP's enterprise resource planning system.

Sequential file File with sequential organization. The records in a sequential file are saved consecutively without a keyword.

Standard SAP ERP interface Interface to the SAP ERP system that has the type batch input, direct input, BAPI, or IDoc.

Status bar Element of the graphical user interface (GUI). The status bar contains an output field in which the SAP system displays mes-

sages issued by the primary window. Other fields in the status bar provide information on the system status. The status bar extends along the entire width of the lower edge of the primary window.

Subledger Ledger whose purpose is to represent business transactions with customers and vendors. Subledgers in asset accounting are ledgers that represent the development of asset values.

Subledger accounting Accounting at the subsidiary ledger level, such as customer, vendor, or asset. Subledgers provide more details on the postings made to the reconciliation accounts in the general ledger.

Subroutine Module of a program that can be called by multiple programs. You use subroutines to avoid having to write frequently used program components more than once. Data can be passed explicitly from and to subroutines.

Table-like file File in which all the records have the same structure.

Test configuration Framework that consists of a test script and test data.

Test script Unit of the SAP system that can be validated. Test scripts often map a specific business process or process chain.

Text file File with text information whose records are separated by end-of-record indicators.

Transaction Describes an application. To reach the initial screen of an application, you can navigate through the menu hierarchy or enter a four-character transaction code in the command field. Using the transaction saves you from having to navigate through the various menus, leading you directly to the initial screen.

Transaction code   Sequence of alphanumeric characters that identifies a transaction in the SAP ERP system. To call a transaction, you enter the transaction code in the command field and click on **Enter**.

Transaction data   Transaction-specific data that is temporary and assigned to certain master data. Individual posting documents are referred to as transaction data. For example, transaction data relating to sales development can be assigned to a vendor's master data. The total sales of a vendor consist of the data of the individual business transactions, namely, the transaction data.

Transaction figures   Sum of all postings to an account, separated by posting period and credit/debit.

Translation   Manipulating the values of field contents, based on a table that specifies which old values are to be replaced with which new values.

Transport request   Document for copying corrections between different system types. A transport request records released corrections. When the request is released, the transport is performed. For example, you can transport corrections from a development system to a consolidation system.

Variable   Placeholder used to store and address data under a particular name in a particular format. You can distinguish variables by their name, type, length, and structure.

C   The Authors

Michael Willinger was born in 1971 in Heidelberg, Germany. He studied business administration at the University of Mannheim from 1990 to 1996, focusing on bank management, financing, auditing, fiduciary structures, and statistics. Since he first encountered SAP R/3 during his graduate studies in business data processing, it has had a major impact on his career. From 1998 to 2001, Michael worked as an SAP consultant (focusing on Financial Accounting) at Bilfinger & Berger AG, a construction firm, before he moved to Tarkett, an internationally active manufacturer of flooring. At Tartkett, he was the project manager for the global implementation of the SAP Financial Accounting and Controlling modules. Currently, Michael works at SAP SI in the area of *System Landscape Optimization*, where he focuses on migration projects that go beyond the standard SAP ERP system and which have been described briefly in Chapter 8.

Johann Gradl was born in 1961. He studied mathematics and computer science at the Technische Universität München (Munich Polytechnic University) from 1980 to 1986. After taking a hiatus, during which he performed his civil service duty, he completed his doctorate in mathematics from 1988 to 1990. In 1993, Johann joined SAP. Initially, he worked in the R/2 Services department, and then turned his attention to the area of data migration. He was a driving force behind the development of the Legacy System Migration Workbench (LSMW), which is described in this book. He subsequently performed various tasks in SAP Customer Relationship Management (SAP CRM) development as Vice President for Installed Base Development, Middleware, and Test Automation. After moving to the Support area, he was responsible for the maintenance of the SAP CRM product. He is currently involved in strategic projects at SAP Service and Support.

Index

A

ABAP 67, 71, 357
ABAP Dictionary 52, 187, 357
Absolute amount 292
Accelerated Data Migration → SAP ADM
Account 65, 357
Account balances 339
Account determination 338, 357
Account group 357
Account type 31, 35, 357
Administration 174
APC 319
Application server 169
Asset
  class 324, 325, 326, 336, 338, 357
  classification 315
  list 339
  master record 315
  number 324
  section 324
  subnumber 316, 357
  values 28
Asset Accounting 315, 325, 338, 339,
  357
Authorization
  concept 175
  profile 175

B

Background processing 307
Balance 23, 358
Balance sheet account 28, 338, 339, 358
Balance sheet accounts 24
Balance sheet asset account 338, 358
Balance sheet item 27
BAPI 47, 167, 287, 288, 308, 309, 310,
  316, 343, 344, 358
Base insurable value 321
Batch input 16, 46, 63, 167, 286, 303,
  316, 344, 358
  background processing 81
  batch input session 308, 311
  include bdcrecx1 71

interface 316
overview 81
PERFORM close_group 71
PERFORM open_group 70
recording 58, 63, 64, 66, 308, 311
session 52, 58, 71, 76, 77, 81
Batch input interface 303
Batch input processing 51
Batch input session 71, 303, 358
  blocked 57
  blocking and releasing 58
  deleting 58
  display errors only 55, 81
  error 57
  in background 57
  in process 57
  in the background 55
  new 57
  nodata indicator 80
  process in foreground 55, 81
  processed 57
  processing automatically 57
  retain 80
  small log 80
Batch-Input
  batch input session 70
  PERFORM bdc_dynpro 70
  PERFORM bdc_field 70
  PERFORM bdc_transaction 71
BDCDATA 52
BDoc format 348
Bottom line 27
Browser 100
Business data object 41, 358
Business object 41, 341, 358
Business processes 38
Business reengineering 22, 33, 34, 36

C

Call transaction 71, 72, 82, 304
Capitalization date 325, 336
CATT 99, 358
Change request 247
Character field 75

Chart of accounts   25, 358
Client   66, 358
Client table   102, 148
Column formatting   132
Company code   324, 325, 326, 334, 336, 340, 358
  production status   340
  test status   340
  transfer status   340
Computer Aided Test Tool (CATT)   99, 358
Concatenation   200
Constant   331, 359
Conversion   44, 311, 359
Conversion rule   49, 190, 308
Convert Text to Columns Wizard   290
Converting   167
Cost center   324, 359
Credit posting   35
CRM Middleware   348
Currency formats   290
Customer account   65, 359
Customer master   60
Customer namespace   106, 149
Customer Relationship Management   348
Customizing   338, 359

D

Data
  conversion   43, 169, 308, 359
  converting   43
  exporting   42
  extracting   42
  importing   46
  Loading   46
  migration   359
  quality   307, 309
  reading   43
  security   37, 304, 310
  transfer   41, 359
  transformation   43, 281, 359
  transforming   43
  type   75
  unloading   42
  volume   309
Data Browser   298, 345
Data element   255

Data format   132
Data migration object   42, 171, 172, 359
Data object   41, 168, 255, 286, 308, 359
Data Transfer Workbench   169, 359
  error handling   343
  project   341
  run   342
  run definition   341
  subproject   341
  task   341
Database   65, 66, 337
  database tables   46
Database server   303
Date format   286, 336
  European format   336
  ISO format   336
  North American format   336
  SAP format   336
Date values   286
DDMMYY   44
Debit posting   35
Decimal point   288
Decision matrix   313
Default value   123
Delete function   266
Depreciation   315, 359
  accumulated   319
  depreciation posting run   321, 357, 360
  extraordinary   321
  scheduled   321
Depreciation area   321, 324, 359
  independent   321
Development class   68
Development cockpit   268
Dialog processing   65, 303
Direct input   46, 167, 308, 310, 315, 344, 360
Direct input session   225
Display variant   252
Document   360
  document header   64, 65, 360
  document line items   353
  document type   31, 360
Domain   185, 255, 360
Dormant data   23
DX Workbench   169, 310, 341, 360
Dynpro   66, 70, 360

E

eCATT   48, 99, 102, 148, 167, 306, 310, 360
Editor   328
Elementary data types   360
ERP backend system   348
Error file   344
Error log   337
Error messages   260
Exception   75
Extended Computer Aided Test Tool (eCATT)   48, 99, 102, 148, 167, 306, 310, 360

F

FB01   150
Field   256
Field mapping   43, 190, 361
File   42, 209
   amount fields   218
   character set   210
   code page   210
   date values   218
   end-of-record indictor   209
   file format   124, 311
   fixed record length   209
   read authorization   213
   separator   209
   sequential   209
   table   209
   text file   209
   wildcards   215
   write authorization   213
Financial Accounting   35
Financial documents   61
Fiscal year   319, 361
Fixed asset card file   315
Fixed values   121, 138
Flag file   244
Form routine   71, 73
Frontend   42, 211, 361
FSS0   143
Function module   71, 74, 75, 361

G

G/L account   65, 339, 361

G/L account master   61
General ledger   27, 338, 339, 361
General ledger account   28, 31
General ledger accounting   28
Group asset   315, 361
GUI control technology   100

H

Handshake   244
Header data   336
Header section   324, 326
Historical data   266

I

Identifier   325, 331, 336
IDoc   47, 167, 249, 287, 288, 308, 309, 343, 344, 361
   creating an IDoc overview   225
   format   343
   IDoc inbound processing   249, 251
   IDoc type   47
   inbound processing   343
   starting the IDoc creation   225
   starting the IDoc processing   225
   work item   226
Import technique   179
Inbound processing   47
Income statement accounts   24
Integer   331
Intermediate Document (IDoc)   47, 167, 249, 287, 288, 308, 309, 343, 344, 361
Internal number assignment   297
Internal table   74, 361
Investment support   316
Invoice   65
ISO codes   44
Iteration   39

J

Join   283

L

Leading zeros   293
Legacy data   41, 361
Legacy system   41, 167, 361

Legacy System Migration Workbench
361
Line item 23, 28, 361
Loading 46
Local object 107, 154
Lock date 80
Log 105, 138
Logical file name 215
Logical path 215
Logical Unit of Work 343
Long texts 237
Loop 76, 331, 361
LSM Workbench 45, 344
LSMW 43, 45, 167, 288, 289, 304, 307,
  309, 310, 362
  action log 178
  ALE-EDI Customizing 226
  assigning files 216
  attributes 179
  authorization concept 175
  authorization profiles 175
  conversion program 245
  conversion rules 168, 236, 240
  converting data 221, 243
  default setting 197
  display variant 197, 241
  equal rank 182
  exporting projects 247
  field length 184
  field mapping 236, 240
  field type 184
  fixed value 199, 202, 203
  fixed values 202
  flag file 244
  global data definitions 253
  global functions 254
  global variable 253
  identifying field value 184
  IDoc inbound processing 249
  import 167
  import technique 179, 235, 239
  importing data 224, 243
  importing projects 248
  labels 241
  main program 243
  main steps 175
  my objects 180
  object 172, 239
  object attributes 178, 239, 243

object overview 177, 226
object type 179, 235, 239
OK flag 205
owner 180
periodic data transfer 181
personal menu 176
processing times 241, 253
profile 175
project 171, 307
project documentation 173
read program 245
reading 167
reading data 217, 243
recording function 167
recordings 228
required target structures 188
reusable rules 255
selection parameters 217
source field 182, 190, 239
source structure 181, 216, 282
source strucure 239
specifying files 211
structure relations 235, 240
subordinate 182
subproject 172, 307
system-dependent file names 181
target field 190
target structure 282
technical fields 197
translation 200, 202, 203
translations 202
user-defined routine 201, 202
version 174
LUW 343

M

Macro 327, 331, 334
Mail merge processing 16, 84, 305, 309
Maintaining tables with eCATT
  Customizing tables 146
Mapping 34, 35, 43, 334, 335, 362
Master data 14, 23, 362
Material BOMs 62
Material documents 63
Message type 180
Microsoft Access 284
Microsoft Excel 72
Migration 41, 362

Migration account 27
Migration Workbench 264, 362
Modification
  field contents 282
MOVE 199
MWB 264
MWBSP 268

N

NetWeaver 101
Nodata character 198
Non-SAP GUI 100, 101, 102
Non-SAP system 362
Number formats 288

O

Object 42, 362
Opening balance sheet 28
Opening balance sheet account 28
Optional entry field 36, 362

P

P&L account 29, 362
Package size 343
Parameter 71, 73, 122, 138, 139, 141
Parameterization 310
Parameters 362
Partner 180
Partner agreement 180
Performance 82
Periodic data transfer 243
Port
  file port 250
  tRFC port 250
Posting document 23
Posting key 31, 35, 65, 292, 362
Prefix 200
Primary window 362
Process cockpit 268
Processing external variants 130, 133
Production status 318
Profit center 345
Purchase requisitions 62

R

R/2-R/3 Migration Workbench 167
RABEST01 339
RCSBI010 62
RCSBI020 62
RCSBI030 62
RCSBI040 62
Reconciliation account 28, 338, 339, 362
Reconciliation of balances 339
Record type 181, 325
  record type 0 331
  record type 1 332
  record type 2 332
  record type 3 332
  record type 4 326
Recording 48, 58, 106, 167, 305, 309
Recording overview 67
Regional options 289
Replacement value 321, 363
Required entry field 34, 35, 64, 325, 363
Retained earnings account 29
RFBIBL00 61
RFBIDE00 60
RFBIKR00 61
RFBISA00 61, 228
RM06BBI0 62
RM07MMBL 63
Runtime error 75
Runtimes 179

S

SAP ADM 263
  availability 263
  checklist 280
  data import 275
  development cockpit 268
  migration customizing 271
  Migration Workbench 264
  MWB 264
  overview 264
  process cockpit 268
  runtime objects 275
  scope 270
  throughput 264
SAP Application Server 42, 212, 363
SAP Basis Release 169, 363

SAP Change and Transport Manage-
ment 247
SAP change request 247
SAP CRM System 348
SAP ERP 6.0 169
SAP GUI 99, 162
SAP home directory 214
SAP Service Marketplace 169
SAP transport system 247
SAPMF05A 70
Screen 66
Secondary index 353
Select query 284
Sequential file 26, 42, 363
Simulation 337
Simulation run 266
SM30 145
Source structure 181
Source system 243
Standard batch input 308
Standard batch input program 48, 58,
59, 303, 309
Standard interface 46, 169
Standard SAP ERP interface 363
Status bar 65, 363
Subledger 28, 339, 363
Subledger accounting 28, 363
Subroutine 70, 363
Suffix 200

T

Table CEPC 345
Table field 66
Table maintenance 145
Table maintenance with eCATT 145
    customer-specific tables 145
Table-like file 42, 363
Target structure 188
Template 327, 330, 334
Test 105
    configuration 105
Test case 306
    changing 155
    fixed values 156, 158
    Function Editor 155
    log 163
    processing mode 164
    recording 149

transaction code 150
transaction recorder 150
Test data 136, 342
Test run 336
Test script 105, 106, 107, 113, 136, 139,
141, 145, 146, 317, 363
    attributes 108
    changing 122
    error behavior 115
    error messages 120
    executing 113, 115, 116, 117, 118,
119, 120, 121, 138, 142
    fixed values 123
    loading the file 134
    log 120
    modifying 139
    parameterization 121, 144
    recording 138, 145
    start mode 114
    variant 133
Testing
    test configuration 134, 145
    test data 125, 141, 307
    test status 318
Text file 36, 42, 129, 141, 142, 363
Text Import Wizard 131
Text key 238
Thousand separator 288
Throughput 306, 343
Tralation 295
Transaction 66, 70, 363
    AL11 214
    AS91 317
    code 63, 364
    data 14, 23, 38, 324, 364
    FB01 70, 72
    figures 364
    FS01 229
    recorder 58, 63, 65, 105, 109, 143,
228
    SE16 298
    SM35 63, 81
    SXDA 169, 341
Transfer status 318
Transformation 35, 43
Translation 44, 45, 364
Transport request 68, 107, 146, 154,
364
Transport system 247

U

Update run   336
Upload   46, 327
User profile   286

V

Variable   76, 331, 332, 364
Variant   331

Vendor master   61
Visual Basic module   327

W

Work item   226

Y

YYYYMMDD   44

Understand the principles of administration and development

Gain insights on KM, collaboration, unification, application management, and the transport system

462 pp., 2008, 69,95 Euro / US$ 69.95
ISBN 978-1-59229-145-8

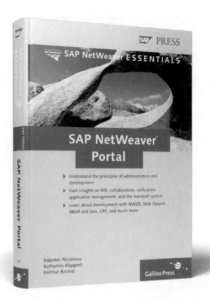

SAP NetWeaver Portal

www.sap-press.com

Valentin Nicolescu, Katharina Klappert,
Helmut Krcmar

SAP NetWeaver Portal

This book introduces IT managers, portal administrators and consultants to the structure and application areas of SAP NetWeaver Portal (Release 7.0). A main focus is to describe key portal functions and the underlying architecture – all from the technical viewpoint. Topics covered include role management, authentication mechanisms, knowledge and content management, developing and administrating applications, application and system integration, as well as many more. Readers gain a solid technical grounding in all the relevant aspects of the SAP NetWeaver Portal, and the skills needed to effectively implement them in practice.

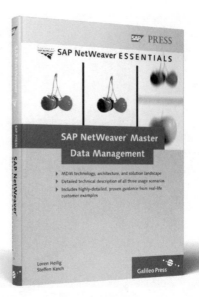

SAP NetWeaver
Master Data Management

www.sap-press.com

Loren Heilig, Steffen Karch, Oliver Böttcher,
Christiane Hofmann, Roland Pfennig

SAP NetWeaver Master Data Management

This book provides system architects, administrators, and IT managers with a description of the structure and usage scenarios of SAP NetWeaver MDM. It uses three comprehensive real-life examples to give you practical insights into the consolidation, harmonization, and central management of master data. Plus, more than 120 pages are dedicated to an MDM compendium, complete with detailed information on individual components, data extraction, options for integration with SAP NetWeaver XI, SAP NetWeaver BI, and the SAP Portal (including user management), as well as on workflows and the Java API.

Expert insights on local SAP
scheduling facilities such as
CCMS, BI and Mass Activities

Techniques to maximize the full
capabilities of SAP central job
scheduling by Redwood

312 pp., 2006, 69,95 Euro / US$ 69.95
ISBN 1-59229-093-0

Job Scheduling for SAP

www.sap-press.com

K. Verruijt, A. Roebers, A. de Heus

Job Scheduling for SAP

With this book, you'll learn the ins and outs of job
scheduling with "SAP Central Job Scheduling by
Redwood" and "Redwood Cronacle." Uncover critical
details on the architecture, plus exclusive technical
insights that cannot be found elsewhere. The authors
cover both decentralized and centralized SAP job
scheduling and provide you with practical advice to
drastically bolster standard installation and configuration guides. Special attention is paid to both
individual CCMS and SAP BI jobs as well as to
integration methods for these enterprise-level job
chains. Best Practices from real-world case studies
ensure that this book leaves no stone unturned.

Revised new edition, completely up-to-date for SAP ERP 6.0

New functions and technologies: Archive Routing, Transaction TAANA, XML-based archiving, and many more

405 pp., 2. edition 2007, 69,95 Euro / US$ 69,95
ISBN 978-1-59229-116-8

Archiving Your SAP Data

www.sap-press.com

Helmut Stefani

Archiving Your SAP Data

This much anticipated, completely revised edition of our bestseller is up-to-date for SAP ERP 6.0, and provides you with valuable knowledge to master data archiving with SAP. Fully updated, this new edition includes two all-new chapters on XML-based data archiving and archiving in SAP ERP HCM and contains detailed descriptions of all the new functions and technologies such as Archive Routing and the TAANA transaction. Readers uncover all the underlying technologies and quickly familiarize themselves with all activities of data archiving—archivability checks, the archiving process, storage of archive files, and display of archived data. The book focuses on the requirements of system and database administrators as well as project collaborators who are responsible for implementing data archiving in an SAP customer project.

Covers the core principles and key methods needed to obtain reliable sizing results

Teaches how to use SAP's Quick Sizer efficiently to validate your data basis

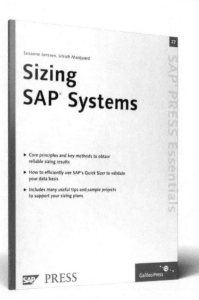

109 pp., 2007, 68,– Euro / US$ 85,00
ISBN 978-1-59229-156-4

Sizing SAP Systems

www.sap-hefte.de

Susanne Janssen, Ulrich Marquard

Sizing SAP Systems

SAP PRESS Essentials 27

This technical guide provides system administrators, technical project managers, and consultants with comprehensive answers to all of the most pressing questions related to sizing: How can I set up a sizing project? How do I obtain the necessary data? How can I validate a sizing process? How do I interpret the results of my sizing project? Volumes of step-by-step descriptions related to SAP's Quick Sizer and other tools, sample calculations, and best practices for project planning make this exclusive guide an indispensable companion for your sizing projects.

Interested in reading more?

Please visit our Web site for all
new book releases from SAP PRESS.

www.sap-press.com